The Montessori Method

I place at the beginning of this volume, her fatherland, the dear name of Alice Hallgarten of New York, who by her marriage to Baron Leopold Franchetti became by choice our compatriot.

Ever a firm believer in the principles underlying the Case dei Bambini, she, with her husband, forwarded the publication of this book in Italy, and, throughout the last years of her short life, greatly desired the English translation which should introduce to the land of her birth, the United States, the work so near her heart.

To her memory I dedicate this book, whose pages, like an ever-living flower, perpetuate the recollection of her beneficence.

The Montessori Method

Scientific Pedagogy as Applied to Child Education

Maria Montessori

Translated from the Italian by
Anne E. George

with an Introduction by
Professor Henry W. Holmes
Harvard University

AAKAR

THE MONTESSORI METHOD
Maria Montessori

First Published 2015

ISBN 978-93-5002-325-9 (Hb)

Published by
AAKAR BOOKS
28 E Pocket IV, Mayur Vihar Phase I, Delhi 110 091
Phone : 011 2279 5505 Telefax : 011 2279 5641
aakarbooks@gmail.com; www.aakarbooks.com

Printed at
Sapra Brothers, Delhi 110 095

Contents

Preface

In February, 1911, Professor Henry W. Holmes, of the Division of Education of Harvard University, did me the honour to suggest that an English translation be made of my Italian volume, *"Il Metodo della Pedagogia Scientifica applicato all' educazione infantile nelle Case dei Bambini."* This suggestion represented one of the greatest events in the history of my educational work. To-day, that to which I then looked forward as an unusual privilege has become an accomplished fact.

The Italian edition of *"Il Metodo della Pedagogia Scientifica"* had no preface, because the book itself I consider nothing more than the preface to a more comprehensive work, the aim and extent of which it only indicates. For the educational method for children of from three to six years set forth here is but the earnest of a work that, developing the same principle and method, shall cover in a like manner the successive stages of education. Moreover, the method which obtains in the *Case dei Bambini* offers, it seems to me, an experimental field for the study of man, and promises, perhaps, the development of a science that shall disclose other secrets of nature.

In the period that has elapsed between the publication of the Italian and American editions, I have had, with my pupils, the opportunity to simplify and render more exact certain practical details of the method, and to gather additional observations concerning discipline. The results attest the vitality of the method and the necessity for an extended scientific collaboration in the near future, and are embodied in two new chapters written for the American edition. I know that my method has been widely spoken of in America, thanks to Mr.

S.S. McClure, who has presented it through the pages of his well-known magazine. Indeed, many Americans have already come to Rome for the purpose of observing personally the practical application of the method in my little schools. If, encouraged by this movement, I may express a hope for the future, it is that my work in Rome shall become the centre of an efficient and helpful collaboration.

To the Harvard professors who have made my work known in America and to *McClure's Magazine*, a mere acknowledgment of what I owe them is a barren response; but it is my hope that the method itself, in its effect upon the children of America, may prove an adequate expression of my gratitude.

Rome, 1912 **Maria Montessori**

Introduction

An audience already thoroughly interested awaits this translation of a remarkable book. For years no educational document has been so eagerly expected by so large a public, and not many have better merited general anticipation. That this widespread interest exists is due to the enthusiastic and ingenious articles in *McClure's Magazine* for May and December, 1911, and January, 1912; but before the first of these articles appeared a number of English and American teachers had given careful study to Dr. Montessori's work, and had found it novel and important. The astonishing welcome accorded to the first popular expositions of the Montessori system may mean much or little for its future in England and America; it is rather the earlier approval of a few trained teachers and professional students that commends it to the educational workers who must ultimately decide upon its value, interpret its technicalities to the country at large, and adapt it to English and American conditions. To them as well as to the general public this brief critical Introduction is addressed.

It is wholly within the bounds of safe judgment to call Dr. Montessori's work remarkable, novel, and important. It is remarkable, if for no other reason, because it represents the constructive effort of a woman. We have no other example of an educational system—original at least in its systematic wholeness and in its practical application—worked out and inaugurated by the feminine mind and hand. It is remarkable, also, because it springs from a combination of womanly sympathy and intuition, broad social outlook, scientific training, intensive and long-continued study of educational problems, and, to crown all, varied and unusual experience as a teacher and educational leader. No other woman who has dealt with Dr. Montessori's problem—the education of young children—has brought to it personal resources so richly diverse as hers. These resources, furthermore, she has devoted to her work with an enthusiasm, an absolute abandon, like that of Pestalozzi and Froebel, and she presents her convictions with an apostolic ardour which commands attention. A system which embodies such a capital of human effort could not be unimportant. Then, too, certain aspects of the system are in themselves striking and significant: it adapts to the education of normal children methods and apparatus originally used for deficients; it is based on a radical conception of liberty for the pupil; it entails a highly formal training of separate sensory, motor, and mental capacities; and it leads to rapid, easy, and substantial mastery of the elements of reading, writing, and arithmetic. All this will be apparent to the most casual reader of this book.

None of these things, to be sure, is absolutely new in the educational world. All have been proposed in theory; some have been put more or less completely into practice. It is not unjust, for instance, to point out that much of the material used by Dr. Walter E. Fernald, Superintendent of the Massachusetts Institution for the Feeble-Minded at Waverley, is almost identical with the Montessori material, and that Dr. Fernald has long maintained that it could be used to good effect in the education of normal children. (It may interest American readers to know that Séguin, on whose work that of Dr. Montessori is based, was once head of the school at Waverley.) So, too, formal training in various psycho-physical processes has been much urged of late by a good many workers in experimental pedagogy, especially by Meumann. But before Montessori, no one had produced a system in which the elements named above were combined. She conceived it, elaborated it in practice, and established it in schools. It is indeed the final result, as Dr. Montessori proudly asserts, of years of experimental effort both on her own part and on the part of her great predecessors; but the crystallisation of these experiments in a programme of education for normal children is due to Dr. Montessori alone. The incidental features which she has frankly taken over from other modern educators she has chosen because they fit into the fundamental form of her own scheme, and she has unified them all in her general conception of method. The system is not original in the sense in which Froebel's system was original; but as a system it is the novel product of a single woman's creative genius.

As such, no student of elementary education ought to ignore it. The system doubtless fails to solve all the problems in the education of young children; possibly some of the solutions it proposes are partly or completely mistaken; some are probably unavailable in English and American schools; but a system of education does not have to attain perfection in order to merit study, investigation, and experimental use. Dr. Montessori is too large-minded to claim infallibility, and too thoroughly scientific in her attitude to object to careful scrutiny of her scheme and the thorough testing of its results. She expressly states that it is not yet complete. Practically, it is highly probable that the system ultimately adopted in our schools will combine elements of the Montessori programme with elements of the kindergarten programme, both "liberal" and "conservative." In its actual procedure school work must always be thus eclectic. An all-or-nothing policy for a single system inevitably courts defeat; for the public is not interested in systems as systems, and refuses in the end to believe that any one system contains every good thing. Nor can we doubt that this attitude is essentially sound. If we continue, despite the pragmatists, to believe in absolute principles, we may yet remain skeptical about the logic of their reduction to practice—at least in any fixed programme of education. We are not yet justified, at any rate, in adopting one programme to the exclusion of every other simply because it is based on the most intelligible or the most inspiring philosophy. The pragmatic test must also be applied, and rigorously. We must try out several combinations, watch and record the results, compare them, and proceed cautiously to new experiments. This procedure is desirable for every stage and grade of education, but especially for the earliest stage, because there it has been least attempted and is most difficult. Certainly a system so radical, so clearly defined, and so well developed as that of Dr. Montessori offers for the thoroughgoing comparative study of methods in early education new material of exceptional importance. Without accepting every detail of the system, without even accepting unqualifiedly its fundamental principles, one may welcome it, thus, as of great and immediate value. If early education is worth studying at all, the educator who devotes his attention to it will find it necessary to define the differences in principle between the Montessori programme and other programmes, and to carry out careful tests of the results obtainable from the various systems and their feasible combinations.

One such combination this Introduction will suggest, and it will discuss also the possible uses of the Montessori apparatus in the home; but it may be helpful first to present the outstanding characteristics of the Montessori system as compared with the modern kindergarten in its two main forms.

Certain similarities in principle are soon apparent. Dr. Montessori's views of childhood are in some respects identical with those of Froebel, although in general decidedly more radical. Both defend the child's right to be active, to explore his environment and develop his own inner resources through every form of investigation and creative effort. Education is to guide activity, not repress it. Environment cannot create human power, but only give it scope and material, direct it, or at most but call it forth; and the teacher's task is first to nourish and assist, to watch, encourage, guide, induce, rather than to interfere, prescribe, or restrict. To most American teachers and to all kindergartners this principle has long been familiar; they will but welcome now a new and eloquent statement of it from a modern viewpoint. In the practical interpretation of the principle, however, there is decided divergence between the Montessori school and the kindergarten. The Montessori "directress" does not teach children in groups, with the practical requirement, no matter how well "mediated," that each member of the group shall join in the exercise. The Montessori pupil does about as he pleases, so long as he does not do any harm.

Montessori and Froebel stand in agreement also on the need for training of the senses; but Montessori's scheme for this training is at once more elaborate and more direct than Froebel's. She has devised out of Séguin's apparatus a comprehensive and scientific scheme for formal gymnastic of the senses; Froebel originated a series of objects designed for a much broader and more creative use by the children, but by no means so closely adapted to the training of sensory discrimination. The Montessori material carries out the fundamental principle of Pestalozzi, which he tried in vain to embody in a successful system of his own: it "develops piece by piece the pupil's mental capacities" by training separately, through repeated exercises, his several senses and his ability to distinguish, compare, and handle typical objects. In the kindergarten system, and particularly in the "liberal" modifications of it, sense training is incidental to constructive and imaginative activity in which the children are pursuing larger ends than the mere arrangement of forms or colours. Even in the most formal work in kindergarten design the children are "making a picture," and are encouraged to tell what it looks like—"a star," "a kite," "a flower."

As to physical education, the two systems agree in much the same way: both affirm the need for free bodily activity, for rhythmic exercises, and for the development of muscular control; but whereas the kindergarten seeks much of all this through group games with an imaginative or social content, the Montessori scheme places the emphasis on special exercises designed to give formal training in separate physical functions.

In another general aspect, however, the agreement between the two systems, strong in principle, leaves the Montessori system less formal rather than more formal in practice. The principle in this case consists of the affirmation of the child's need for social training. In the conservative kindergarten this training is sought once more, largely in group games. These are usually imaginative, and sometimes decidedly symbolic:

that is, the children play at being farmers, millers, shoemakers, mothers and fathers, birds, animals, knights, or soldiers; they sing songs, go through certain semi-dramatic activities—such as "opening the pigeon house," "mowing the grass," "showing the good child to the knights," and the like; and each takes his part in the representation of some typical social situation. The social training involved in these games is formal only in the sense that the children are not engaged, as the Montessori children often are, in a real social enterprise, such as that of serving dinner, cleaning the room, caring for animals, building a toy house, or making a garden. It cannot be too strongly emphasized that even the most conservative kindergarten does not, on principle, exclude "real" enterprises of this latter sort; but in a three-hour session it does rather little with them. Liberal kindergartens do more, particularly in Europe, where the session is often longer. Nor does the Montessori system wholly exclude imaginative group games. But Dr. Montessori, despite an evidently profound interest not only in social training, but also in æsthetic, idealistic, and even religious development, speaks of "games and foolish stories" in a casual and derogatory way, which shows that she is as yet unfamiliar with the American kindergartner's remarkable skill and power in the use of these resources. (Of course the American kindergartner does not use "foolish" stories; but stories she does use, and to good effect.) The Montessori programme involves much direct social experience, both in the general life of the school and in the manual work done by the pupils; the kindergarten extends the range of the child's social consciousness through the imagination. The groupings of the Montessori children are largely free and unregulated; the groupings of kindergarten children are more often formal and prescribed.

On one point the Montessori system agrees with the conservative kindergarten, but not with the liberal: it prepares directly for the mastery of the school arts. There can be no doubt that Dr. Montessori has devised a peculiarly successful scheme for teaching children to write, an effective method for the introduction of reading, and good material for early number work. Both types of kindergarten increase, to be sure, the child's general capacity for expression: kindergarten activity adds to his stock of ideas, awakens and guides his imagination, increases his vocabulary, and trains him in the effective use of it. Children in a good kindergarten hear stories and tell them, recount their own experiences, sing songs, and recite verses, all in a company of friendly but fairly critical listeners, which does even more to stimulate and guide expression than does the circle at home. But even the conservative kindergarten does not teach children to write and to read. It does teach them a good deal about number; and it may fairly be questioned whether it does not do more fundamental work in this field than the Montessori system itself. The Froebelian gifts offer exceptional opportunity for concrete illustration of the conceptions of *whole* and *part*, through the creation of wholes from parts, and the breaking up of wholes into parts. This aspect of number is at least as important as the series aspect, which children get in counting and for which the Montessori "Long Stair" provides such good material. The Froebelian material may be used very readily for counting, however, and the Montessori material gives some slight opportunity for uniting and dividing. So far as preparation for arithmetic is concerned, a combination of the two bodies of material is both feasible and desirable. The liberal kindergarten, meanwhile, abandoning the use of the gifts and occupations for mathematical purposes, makes no attempt to prepare its pupils directly for the school arts.

Compared with the kindergarten, then, the Montessori system presents these main points of interest: it carries out far more radically the principle of unrestricted liberty; its materials are intended for the direct and formal training of the senses; it includes apparatus designed to aid in the purely physical development of the children; its social training is carried out mainly by means of present and actual social activities; and it affords direct preparation for the school arts. The kindergarten, on the other hand, involves a certain amount of group-teaching, in which children are held—not necessarily by the enforcement of authority, yet by authority, confessedly, when other means fail—to definite activities; its materials are intended primarily for creative use by the children and offer opportunity for mathematical analysis and the teaching of design; and its procedure is rich in resources for the imagination. One thing should be made entirely clear and emphatic: in none of these characteristics are the two systems rigidly antagonistic. Much kindergarten activity is free, and the principle of prescription is not wholly given over by the "Houses of Childhood"—witness their *Rules and Regulations*; the kindergarten involves direct sense training, and the Montessori system admits some of the Froebel blocks for building and design; there are many purely muscular activities in the kindergarten, and some of the usual kindergarten games are used by Montessori; the kindergarten conducts some gardening, care of animals, construction-work, and domestic business, and the Montessori system admits a few imaginative social plays; both systems (but not the liberal form of the kindergarten) work directly toward the school arts. Since the difference between the two programmes is one of arrangement, emphasis, and degree, there is no fundamental reason why a combination especially adapted to English and American schools cannot be worked out.

The broad contrast between a Montessori school and a kindergarten appears on actual observation to be this: whereas the Montessori children spend almost all their time handling *things*, largely according to their individual inclination and under individual guidance, kindergarten children are generally engaged in group work and games with an imaginative background and appeal. A possible principle of adjustment between the two systems might be stated thus: work with objects designed for formal sensory, motor, and intellectual training should be done individually or in purely voluntary groups; imaginative and social activity should be carried on in regulated groups. This principle is suggested only as a possible basis for education during the kindergarten age; for as children grow older they must be taught in classes, and they naturally learn how to carry out imaginative and social enterprises in free groups, and the former often alone. Nor should it be supposed that the principle is suggested as a rule to which there can be no exception. It is suggested simply as a general working hypothesis, the value of which must be tested in experience. Although it has long been observed by kindergartners themselves that group-work with the Froebelian materials, especially such work as involves geometrical analysis and formal design, soon tires the children, it has been held that the kindergartner could safeguard her pupils from loss of interest or real fatigue by watching carefully for the first signs of weariness and stopping the work promptly on their appearance. For small groups of the older children, who can do work of this sort with ease and enjoyment, no doubt the inevitable restraint of group teaching is a negligible factor, the fatiguing effects of which any good kindergartner can forestall. But for younger children a régime of complete freedom would seem to promise better results—at least so far as work with objects is concerned. In games, on the other hand, group teaching means very little restraint and the whole process is less tiring any way. To differentiate in method between these two kinds of activity may be the best way to keep them both in an effective educational programme.

To speak of an effective educational programme leads at once, however, to an important aspect of the Montessori system, quite aside from its relation to the kindergarten, with which this Introduction must now deal. This is the social aspect, which finds its explanation in Dr. Montessori's own story of her first school. In any discussion of the availability of the Montessori system in English and American schools—particularly in American public schools and English "Board" schools—two general conditions under which Dr. Montessori did her early work in Rome should be borne in mind. She had her pupils almost all day long, practically controlling their lives in their waking hours; and her pupils came for the most part from families of the laboring class. We cannot expect to achieve the results Dr. Montessori has achieved if we have our pupils under our guidance only two or three hours in the morning, nor can we expect exactly similar results from children whose heredity and experience make them at once more sensitive, more active, and less amenable to suggestion than hers. If we are to make practical application of the Montessori scheme we must not neglect to consider the modifications of it which differing social conditions may render necessary.

The conditions under which Dr. Montessori started her original school in Rome do not, indeed, lack counterpart in large cities the world over. When one reads her eloquent "Inaugural Address" it is impossible not to wish that a "School within the Home" might stand as a centre of hopeful child life in the midst of every close-built city block. Better, of course, if there were no hive-like city tenements at all, and if every family could give to its own children on its own premises enough of "happy play in grassy places." Better if every mother and father were in certain ways an expert in child psychology and hygiene. But while so many unfortunate thousands still live in the hateful cliff-dwellings of our modern cities, we must welcome Dr. Montessori's large conception of the social function of her "Houses of Childhood" as a new gospel for the schools which serve the city poor. No matter what didactic apparatus such schools may use, they should learn of Dr. Montessori the need of longer hours, complete care of the children, closer co-operation with the home, and larger aims. In such schools, too, it is probable that the two fundamental features of Dr. Montessori's work—her principle of liberty and her scheme for sense training—will find their completest and most fruitful application.

It is just these fundamental features, however, which will be most bitterly attacked whenever the social status of the original *Casa dei Bambini* is forgotten. Anthropometric measurements, baths, training in personal self-care, the serving of meals, gardening, and the care of animals we may hear sweepingly recommended for all schools, even for those with a three-hour session and a socially favored class of pupils; but the need for individual liberty and for the training of the senses will be denied even in the work of schools where the conditions correspond closely to those at San Lorenzo. Of course no practical educator will actually propose bathtubs for all schools, and no doubt there will be plenty of wise conservatism about transferring to a given school any function now well discharged by the homes that support it. The problems raised by the proposal to apply in all schools the Montessori conception of discipline and the Montessori sense-training are really more difficult to solve. Is individual liberty a universal educational principle, or a principle which must be modified in the case of a school with no such social status as that of the original "House of Childhood"? Do all children need sense training, or only those of unfavorable inheritance and home environment? No serious discussion of the Montessori system can avoid these questions. What is said in answer to them here is written in the hope that subsequent discussion may be somewhat influenced to keep in view the really deciding factor in each case—the actual situation in the school.

There is occasion enough in these questions, to be sure, for philosophical and scientific argument. The first question involves an ethical issue, the second a psychological issue, and both may be followed through to purely metaphysical issues. Dr. Montessori believes in liberty for the pupil because she thinks of life "as a superb goddess, ever advancing to new conquests." Submission, loyalty, self-sacrifice seem to her, apparently, only incidental necessities of life, not essential elements of its eternal form. There is obvious opportunity here for profound difference of philosophic theory and belief. She seems to hold, too, that sense perception forms the sole basis for the mental and hence for the moral life; that "sense training will prepare the ordered foundation upon which the child may build up a clear and strong mentality," including, apparently, his moral ideals; and that the cultivation of purpose and of the imaginative and creative capacities of children is far less important than the development of the power to learn from the environment by means of the senses. These views seem to agree rather closely with those of Herbart and to some extent with those of Locke. Certainly they offer material for both psychological and ethical debate. Possibly, however, Dr.

Montessori would not accept the views here ascribed to her on the evidence of this book; and in any case these are matters for the philosopher and the psychologist. A pedagogical issue is never wholly an issue of high principle.

Can it reasonably be maintained, then, that an actual situation like that in the first "House of Childhood" at Rome is the only situation in which the Montessori principle of liberty can justifiably find full application? Evidently the Roman school is a true Republic of Childhood, in which nothing need take precedence of the child's claim to pursue an active purpose of his own. Social restraints are here reduced to a minimum; the children must, to be sure, subordinate individual caprice to the demands of the common good, they are not allowed to quarrel or to interfere with each other, and they have duties to perform at stated times; but each child is a citizen in a community governed wholly in the interests of the equally privileged members thereof, his liberty is rarely interfered with, he is free to carry out his own purposes, and he has as much influence in the affairs of the commonwealth as the average member of an adult democracy. This situation is never duplicated in the home, for a child is not only a member of the family, whose interests are to be considered with the rest, but literally a subordinate member, whose interests must often be frankly set aside for those of an adult member or for those of the household itself. Children must come to dinner at dinner time, even if continued digging in the sand would be more to their liking or better for their general development of muscle, mind, or will. It is possible, of course, to refine on the theory of the child's membership in the family community and of the right of elders to command, but practically it remains true that the common conditions of family life prohibit any such freedom as is exercised in a Montessori school. In the same way a school of large enrollment that elects to cover in a given time so much work that individual initiative cannot be trusted to compass it, is forced to teach certain things at nine o'clock and others at ten, and to teach in groups; and the individual whose life is thus cabined and confined must get what he can. For a given school the obvious question is, Considering the work to be done in the time allowed, can we give up the safeguards of a fixed programme and group teaching? The deeper question lies here: Is the work to be done in itself so important that it is worth while to have the children go through it under compulsion or on interest induced by the teacher? Or to put it another way: May not the work be so much less important than the child's freedom that we had better trust to native curiosity and cleverly devised materials anyway and run the risk of his losing part of the work, or even the whole of it?

For schools beyond the primary grade there will be no doubt as to the answer to this question. There are many ways in which school work may safely be kept from being the deadening and depressing process it so often is, but the giving up of all fixed and limited schedules and the prescriptions of class teaching is not one of them. Even if complete liberty of individual action were possible in schools of higher grade, it is not certain that it would be desirable: for we must learn to take up many of our purposes in life under social imperative. But with young children the question becomes more difficult. What work do we wish to make sure that each child does? If our schools can keep but half a day, is there time enough for every child to cover this work without group teaching at stated times? Is the prescription and restraint involved in such group teaching really enough to do the children any harm or to make our teaching less effective? Can we not give up prescription altogether for parts of the work and minimise it for others? The general question of individual liberty is thus reduced to a series of practical problems of adjustment. It is no longer a question of total liberty or no liberty at all, but a question of the practical mediation of these extremes. When we consider, furthermore, that the teacher's skill and the attractiveness of her personality, the alluring power of the didactic apparatus and the ease with which it enables children to learn, to say nothing of a cheerful and pleasant room and the absence of set desks and seats, may all work together to prevent scheduled teaching in groups from becoming in the least an occasion for restraint, it is plain that in any given school there may be ample justification for abating the rigour of Dr. Montessori's principle of freedom. Every school must work out its own solution of the problem in the face of its particular conditions.

The adoption of sense-training would seem to be much less a matter for variable decision. Some children may need less than others, but for all children between the ages of three and five the Montessori material will prove fascinating as well as profitable. A good deal of modern educational theory has been based on the belief that children are interested only in what has social value, social content, or "real use"; yet a day with any normal child will give ample evidence of the delight that children take in purely formal exercises. The sheer fascination of tucking cards under the edge of a rug will keep a baby happy until any ordinary supply of cards is exhausted; and the wholly sensory appeal of throwing stones into the water gives satisfaction enough to absorb for a long time the attention of older children—to say nothing of grown-ups. The Montessori apparatus satisfies sense hunger when it is keen for new material, and it has besides a puzzle-interest which children eagerly respond to. Dr. Montessori subordinates the value of the concrete mental content her material supplies to its value in rendering the senses more acute; yet it is by no means certain that this content—purely formal as it is—does not also give the material much of its importance. Indeed, the refinement of sensory discrimination may not in itself be particularly valuable. What Professor G.M. Whipple says on this point in his *Manual of Menial and Physical Tests* has much weight:

> The use of sensory tests in correlation work is particularly interesting. In general, some writers are convinced that keen discrimination is a prerequisite to keen intelligence, while others are equally convinced that intelligence is essentially conditioned by "higher" processes, and only remotely by sensory capacity—barring, of course, such diminution of capacity as to interfere seriously with the experiencing of sensations, as in partial deafness or partial loss of vision. While it is scarcely the place here to discuss the evolutionary significance of discriminative sensitivity, it may

> be pointed out that the normal capacity is many times in excess of the actual demands of life, and that it is consequently difficult to understand why nature has been so prolific and generous; to understand, in other words, what is the sanction for the seemingly hypertrophied discriminative capacity of the human sense organs. The usual "teleological explanations" of our sensory life fail to account for this discrepancy. Again, the very fact of the existence of this surplus capacity seems to negative at the outset the notion that sensory capacity can be a conditioning factor in intelligence—with the qualification already noted.

It is quite possible that the real pedagogical value of the Montessori apparatus is due to the fact that it keeps children happily engaged in the exercise of their senses and their fingers when they crave such exercise most and to the further fact that it teaches them without the least strain a good deal about forms and materials. These values are not likely to be much affected by differing school conditions.

In the use of the material for sense-training, English and American teachers may find profit in two general warnings. First, it should not be supposed that sense training alone will accomplish all that Dr. Montessori accomplishes through the whole range of her school activities. To fill up most of a morning with sense-training is to give it (except perhaps in the case of the youngest pupils) undue importance. It is not even certain that the general use of the senses will be much affected by it, to say nothing of the loss of opportunity for larger physical and social activity. Second, the isolation of the senses should be used with some care. To shut off sight is to take one step toward sleep, and the requirement that a child concentrate his attention, in this situation, on the sense perceptions he gets by other means than vision must not be maintained too long. No small strain is involved in mental action without the usual means of information and control.

The proposal, mentioned above, of a feasible combination of the Montessori system and the kindergarten may now be set forth. If it is put very briefly and without defense or prophecy, it is because it is made without dogmatism, simply in the hope that it will prove suggestive to some open-minded teacher who is willing to try out any scheme that promises well for her pupils. The conditions supposed are those of the ordinary American public-school kindergarten, with a two-year programme beginning with children three and a half or four years old, a kindergarten with not too many pupils, with a competent kindergartner and assistant kindergartner, and with some help from training-school students.

The first proposal is for the use of the Montessori material during the better part of the first year instead of the regular Froebelian material. To the use of the Montessori devices—including the gymnastic apparatus—some of the time now devoted to pictures and stories should also be applied. It is not suggested that no Froebelian material should be used, but that the two systems be woven into each other, with a gradual transition from the free, individual use of the Montessori objects to the same sort of use of the large sizes of the Froebel gifts, especially the second, third, and fourth. When the children seem to be ready for it, a certain amount of more formal work with the gifts should be begun. In the second year the Froebelian gift work should predominate, without absolute exclusion of the Montessori exercises. In the latter part of the second year the Montessori exercises preparatory to writing should be introduced. Throughout the second year the full time for stories and picture work should be given to them, and in both years the morning circle and the games should be carried on as usual. The luncheon period should of course remain the same. One part of Dr. Montessori's programme the kindergartner and her assistant should use every effort to incorporate in their work—the valuable training in self-help and independent action afforded in the care of the materials and equipment by the children themselves. This need not be confined to the Montessori apparatus. Children who have been trained to take out, use, and put away the Montessori objects until they are ready for the far richer variety of material in the Froebelian system, should be able to care for it also. Of course if there are children who can return in the afternoon, it would be very interesting to attempt the gardening, which both Froebel and Montessori recommend, and the Montessori vase-work.

For the possible scorn of those to whom all compromise is distasteful, the author of this Introduction seeks but one compensation—that any kindergartner who may happen to adopt his suggestion will let him study the results.

As to the use of the Montessori system in the home, one or two remarks must suffice. In the first place, parents should not expect that the mere presence of the material in the nursery will be enough to work an educational miracle. A Montessori directress does no common "teaching," but she is called upon for very skillful and very tiring effort. She must watch, assist, inspire, suggest, guide, explain, correct, inhibit. She is supposed, in addition, to contribute by her work to the upbuilding of a new science of pedagogy; but her educational efforts—and education is not an investigative and experimental effort, but a practical and constructive one—are enough to exhaust all her time, strength, and ingenuity. It will do no harm—except perhaps to the material itself—to have the Montessori material at hand in the home, but it must be used under proper guidance if it is to be educationally effective. And besides, it must not be forgotten that the material is by no means the most important feature of the Montessori programme. The best use of the Montessori system in the home will come through the reading of this book. If parents shall learn from Dr. Montessori something of the value of child life, of its need for activity, of its characteristic modes of expression, and of its possibilities, and shall apply this knowledge wisely, the work of the great Italian educator will be successful enough.

This Introduction cannot close without some discussion, however limited, of the important problems suggested by the Montessori method of teaching children to write and to read. We have in American schools admirable methods for the teaching of reading; by the Aldine method, for instance, children of fair ability read without difficulty ten or more readers in the first school year, and advance rapidly toward independent power. Our instruction in writing, however, has never been particularly noteworthy. We have been trying recently to teach children to write a flowing hand by the "arm movement," without much formation of separate letters by the fingers, and our results seem to prove that the effort with children before the age of ten is not worth while. Sensible school officers are content to let children in the first four grades write largely by drawing the letters, and there has been, a fairly general conviction that writing is not in any case especially important before the age of eight or nine. In view of Dr. Montessori's success in teaching children of four and five to write with ease and skill, must we not revise our estimate of the value of writing and our procedure in teaching it? What changes may we profitably introduce in our teaching of reading?

Here again our theory and our practice have suffered from the headstrong advocacy of general principles. Because by clumsy methods children used to be kept at the task of learning the school arts to the undoubted detriment of their minds and bodies, certain writers have advocated the total exclusion of reading and writing from the early grades. Many parents refuse to send their children to school until they are eight, preferring to let them "run wild." This attitude is well justified by school conditions in some places; but where the schools are good, it ignores not only the obvious advantages of school life quite aside from instruction in written language, but also the almost complete absence of strain afforded by modern methods. Now that the Montessori system adds a new and promising method to our resources, it is the more unreasonable: for as a fact normal children are eager to read and write at six, and have plenty of use for these accomplishments.

This does not mean, however, that reading and writing are so important for young children that they should be unduly emphasised. If we can teach them without strain, let us do so, and the more effectively the better; but let us remember, as Dr. Montessori does, that reading and writing should form but a subordinate part of the experience of a child and should minister in general to his other needs. With the best of methods the value of reading and writing before six is questionable. Our conscious life is bookish enough as it is, and it would seem on general grounds a safer policy to defer written language until the age of normal interest in it, and even then not to devote to it more time than an easy and gradual mastery demands.

Of the technical advantages of the Montessori scheme for writing there can be little doubt. The child gains ready control over his pencil through exercises which have their own simple but absorbing interest; and if he does not learn to write with an "arm movement," we may be quite content with his ability to draw a legible and handsome script. Then he learns the letters—their forms, their names, and how to make them—through exercises which have the very important technical characteristic of involving a *thorough sensory analysis* of the material to be mastered. Meumann has taught us of late the great value in all memory work of complete impression through prolonged and intensive analytical study. In the teaching of spelling, for instance, it is comparatively useless to devise schemes for remembering unless the original impressions are made strong and elaborate; and it is only by careful, varied, and detailed sense impression that such material as the alphabet can be thus impressed. So effective is the Montessori scheme for impressing the letters—especially because of its novel use of the sense of touch—that the children learn how to make the whole alphabet before the abstract and formal character of the material leads to any diminution of interest or enthusiasm. Their initial curiosity over the characters they see their elders use is enough to carry them through.

In Italian the next step is easy. The letters once learned, it is a simple matter to combine them into words, for Italian spelling is so nearly phonetic that it presents very little difficulty to any one who knows how to pronounce. It is at just this point that the teaching of English reading by the Montessori method will find its greatest obstacle. Indeed, it is the unphonetic character of English spelling that has largely influenced us to give up the alphabet method of teaching children to read. Other reasons, to be sure, have also induced us to teach by the word and the sentence method; but this one has been and will continue to be the deciding factor. We have found it more effective to teach children whole words, sentences, or rhymes by sight, adding to sense impressions the interest aroused by a wide range of associations, and then analysing the words thus acquired into their phonetic elements to give the children independent power in the acquisition of new words. Our marked success with this method makes it by no means certain that it is "in the characteristic process of natural development" for children to build up written words from their elements—sounds and syllables. It would seem, on the contrary, as James concluded, that the mind works quite as naturally in the opposite direction—grasping wholes first, especially such as have a practical interest, and then working down to their formal elements. In the teaching of spelling, of course, the wholes (words) are already known at sight—that is, the pupil recognises them easily in reading—and the process aims at impressing upon the child's mind the exact order of their constituent elements. It is because reading and spelling are in English such completely separate processes that we can teach a child to read admirably without making him a "good speller" and are forced to bring him to the latter glorious state by new endeavours. We gain by this separation both in reading and in spelling, as experience and comparative tests—popular superstition to the contrary notwithstanding—have conclusively proved. The mastery of the alphabet by the Montessori method will be of great assistance in teaching our children to write, but of only incidental assistance in teaching them to read and to spell.

Once more, then, this Introduction attempts to suggest a compromise. In the school arts the programme used to such good effect in the Italian schools and the programme which has been so well worked out in English and American schools may be profitably combined. We can learn much about writing and reading from Dr. Montessori—especially from the freedom her children have in the process of learning to write and in the use of their newly acquired power, as well as from her device for teaching them to read connected prose. We can use her materials for sense training and lead as she does to easy mastery of the alphabetic symbols. Our own schemes for teaching reading we can retain, and doubtless the phonetic analysis they involve we shall find easier and more effective because of our adoption of the Montessori scheme for teaching the letters. The exact adjustment of the two methods is of course a task for teachers in practice and for educational leaders.

To all educators this book should prove most interesting. Not many of them will expect that the Montessori method will regenerate humanity. Not many will wish to see it—or any method—produce a generation of prodigies such as those who have been heralded recently in America. Not many will approve the very early acquisition by children of the arts of reading and writing. But all who are fair-minded will admit the genius that shines from the pages which follow, and the remarkable suggestiveness of Dr. Montessori's labors. It is the task of the professional student of education to-day to submit all systems to careful comparative study, and since Dr. Montessori's inventive power has sought its tests in practical experience rather than in comparative investigation, this duller task remains to be done. But however he may scrutinise the results of her work, the educator who reads of it here will honour in the Dottoressa Maria Montessori the enthusiasm, the patience, and the constructive insight of the scientist and the friend of humanity.

Henry W. Holmes
Harvard University

1

A Critical Consideration of the New Pedagogy in its Relation to Modern Science

It is not my intention to present a treatise on Scientific Pedagogy. The modest design of these incomplete notes is to give the results of an experiment that apparently opens the way for putting into practice those new principles of science which in these last years are tending to revolutionise the work of education.

Much has been said in the past decade concerning the tendency of pedagogy, following in the footsteps of medicine, to pass beyond the purely speculative stage and base its conclusions on the positive results of experimentation. Physiological or experimental psychology which, from Weber and Fechner to Wundt, has become organised into a new science, seems destined to furnish to the new pedagogy that fundamental preparation which the old-time metaphysical psychology furnished to philosophical pedagogy. Morphological anthropology applied to the physical study of children, is also a strong element in the growth of the new pedagogy.

But in spite of all these tendencies, Scientific Pedagogy has never yet been definitely constructed nor defined. It is something vague of which we speak, but which does not, in reality, exist. We might say that it has been, up to the present time, the mere intuition or suggestion of a science which, by the aid of the positive and experimental sciences that have renewed the thought of the nineteenth century, must emerge from the mist and clouds that have surrounded it. For man, who has formed a new world through scientific progress, must himself be prepared and developed through a new pedagogy. But I will not attempt to speak of this more fully here.

Several years ago, a well-known physician established in Italy a *School of Scientific Pedagogy*, the object of which was to prepare teachers to follow the new movement which had begun to be felt in the pedagogical world. This school had, for two or three years, a great success, so great, indeed, that teachers from all over Italy flocked to it, and it was endowed by the City of Milan with a splendid equipment of scientific material. Indeed, its beginnings were most propitious, and liberal help was afforded it in the hope that it might be possible to establish, through the experiments carried on there, "the science of forming man."

The enthusiasm which welcomed this school was, in a large measure, due to the warm support given it by the distinguished anthropologist, Giuseppe Sergi, who for more than thirty years had earnestly laboured to spread among the teachers of Italy the principles of a new civilisation based upon education. "To-day in the social world," said Sergi, "an imperative need makes itself felt—the reconstruction of educational methods; and he who fights for this cause, fights for human regeneration." In his pedagogical writings collected in a volume under the title of *Educazione ed Istruzione* (Pensieri),[1] he gives a résumé of the lectures in which he encouraged this new movement, and says that he believes the way to this desired regeneration lies in a methodical study of the one to be educated, carried on under the guidance of pedagogical anthropology and of experimental psychology.

"For several years I have done battle for an idea concerning the instruction and education of man, which appeared the more just and useful the more deeply I thought upon it. My idea was that in order to establish natural, rational methods, it was essential that we make numerous, exact, and rational observations of man as an individual, principally during infancy, which is the age at which the foundations of education and culture must be laid.

"To measure the head, the height, etc., does not indeed mean that we are establishing a system of pedagogy, but it indicates the road which we may follow to arrive at such a system, since if we are to educate an individual, we must have a definite and direct knowledge of him."

The authority of Sergi was enough to convince many that, given such a knowledge of the individual, the art of educating him would develop naturally. This, as often happens, led to a confusion of ideas among his followers, arising now from a too literal interpretation, now from an exaggeration, of the master's ideas. The chief trouble lay in confusing the experimental study of the pupil, with his education. And since the one was the road leading to the other, which should have grown from it naturally and rationally, they straightway gave the name of Scientific Pedagogy to what was in truth pedagogical anthropology. These new converts carried as their banner, the "Biographical Chart," believing that once this ensign was firmly planted upon the battle-field of the school, the victory would be won.

The so-called School of Scientific Pedagogy, therefore, instructed the teachers in the taking of anthropometric measurements, in the use of esthesiometric instruments, in the gathering of Psychological Data—and the army of new scientific teachers was formed.

It should be said that in this movement Italy showed herself to be abreast of the times. In France, in England, and especially in America, experiments have been made in the elementary schools, based upon a study of anthropology and psychological pedagogy, in the hope of finding in anthropometry and psychometry, the regeneration of the school. In these attempts it has rarely been the *teachers* who have carried on the research; the experiments have been, in most cases, in the hands of physicians who have taken more interest in their especial science than in education. They have usually sought to get from their experiments some contribution to psychology, or anthropology, rather than to attempt to organise their work and their results toward the formation of the long-sought Scientific Pedagogy. To sum up the situation briefly, anthropology and psychology have never devoted themselves to the question of educating children in the schools, nor have the scientifically trained teachers ever measured up to the standards of genuine scientists.

The truth is that the practical progress of the school demands a genuine *fusion* of these modern tendencies, in practice and thought; such a fusion as shall bring scientists directly into the important field of the school and at the same time raise teachers from the inferior intellectual level to which they are limited to-day. Toward this eminently practical ideal the University School of Pedagogy, founded in Italy by Credaro, is definitely working. It is the intention of this school to raise Pedagogy from the inferior position it has occupied as a secondary branch of philosophy, to the dignity of a definite science, which shall, as does Medicine, cover a broad and varied field of comparative study.

And among the branches affiliated with it will most certainly be found Pedagogical Hygiene, Pedagogical Anthropology, and Experimental Psychology.

Truly, Italy, the country of Lombroso, of De-Giovanni, and of Sergi, may claim the honour of being pre-eminent in the organisation of such a movement. In fact, these three scientists may be called the founders of the new tendency in Anthropology: the first leading the way in criminal anthropology, the second in medical anthropology, and the third in pedagogical anthropology. For the good fortune of science, all three of them have been the recognised leaders of their special lines of thought, and have been so prominent in the scientific world that they have not only made courageous and valuable disciples, but have also prepared the minds of the masses to receive the scientific regeneration which they have encouraged. (For reference, see my treatise "Pedagogical Anthropology.")[2]

Surely all this is something of which our country may be justly proud.

To-day, however, those things which occupy us in the field of education are the interests of humanity at large, and of civilisation, and before such great forces we can recognise only one country—the entire world. And in a cause of such great importance, all those who have given any contribution, even though it be only an attempt not crowned with success, are worthy of the respect of humanity throughout the civilised world. So, in Italy, the schools of Scientific Pedagogy and the Anthropological Laboratories, which have sprung up in the various cities through the efforts of elementary teachers and scholarly inspectors, and which have been abandoned almost before they became definitely organised, have nevertheless a great value by reason of the faith which inspired them, and because of the doors they have opened to thinking people.

It is needless to say that such attempts were premature and sprang from too slight a comprehension of new sciences still in the process of development. Every great cause is born from repeated failures and from imperfect achievements. When St. Francis of Assisi saw his Lord in a vision, and received from the Divine lips the command—"Francis, rebuild my Church!"—he believed that the Master spoke of the little church within which he knelt at that moment. And he immediately set about the task, carrying upon his shoulders the stones with which he meant to rebuild the fallen walls. It was not until later that he became aware of the fact that his mission was to renew the Catholic Church through the spirit of poverty. But the St. Francis who so ingenuously carried the stones, and the great reformer who so miraculously led the people to a triumph of the spirit, are one and the same person in different stages of development. So we, who work toward one great end, are members of one and the same body; and those who come after us will reach the goal only because there were those who believed and laboured before them. And, like St. Francis, we have believed that by carrying the hard and barren stones of the experimental laboratory to the old and crumbling walls of the school, we might rebuild it. We have looked upon the aids offered by the materialistic and mechanical sciences with the same hopefulness with which St. Francis looked upon the squares of granite, which he must carry upon his shoulders.

Thus we have been drawn into a false and narrow way, from which we must free ourselves, if we are to establish true and living methods for the training of future generations.

To prepare teachers in the method of the experimental sciences is not an easy matter. When we shall have instructed them in anthropometry and psychometry in the most minute manner possible, we shall have only created machines, whose usefulness will be most doubtful. Indeed, if it is after this fashion that we are to initiate our teachers into experiment, we shall remain forever in the field of theory. The teachers of the old school, prepared according to the principles of metaphysical philosophy, understood the ideas of certain men regarded as authorities, and moved the muscles of speech in talking of them, and the muscles of the eye in reading their theories. Our scientific teachers, instead, are familiar with certain instruments and know how to move the muscles of the hand and arm in order to use these instruments; besides this, they have an intellectual preparation which consists of a series of typical tests, which they have, in a barren and mechanical way, learned how to apply.

The difference is not substantial, for profound differences cannot exist in exterior technique alone, but lie rather within the inner man. Not with all our initiation into scientific experiment have we prepared *new masters*, for, after all, we have left them standing without the door of real experimental science; we have not admitted them to the noblest and most profound phase of such study,—to that experience which makes real scientists.

And, indeed, what is a scientist? Not, certainly, he who knows how to manipulate all the instruments in the physical laboratory, or who in the laboratory of the chemist handles the various reactives with deftness and security, or who in biology knows how to make ready the specimens for the microscope. Indeed, it is often the case that an assistant has a greater dexterity in experimental technique than the master scientist himself. We give the name scientist to the type of man who has felt experiment to be a means guiding him to search out the deep truth of life, to lift a veil from its fascinating secrets, and who, in this pursuit, has felt arising within him a love for the mysteries of nature, so passionate as to annihilate the thought of himself. The scientist is not the clever manipulator of instruments, he is the worshipper of nature and he bears the external symbols of his passion as does the follower of some religious order. To this body of real scientists belong those who, forgetting, like the Trappists of the Middle Ages, the world about them, live only in the laboratory, careless often in matters of food and dress because they no longer think of themselves; those who, through years of unwearied use of the microscope, become blind; those who in their scientific ardour inoculate themselves with tuberculosis germs; those who handle the excrement of cholera patients in their eagerness to learn the vehicle through which the diseases are transmitted; and those who, knowing that a certain chemical preparation may be an explosive, still persist in testing their theories at the risk of their lives. This is the spirit of the men of science, to whom nature freely reveals her secrets, crowning their labours with the glory of discovery.

There exists, then, the "spirit" of the scientist, a thing far above his mere "mechanical skill," and the scientist is at the height of his achievement when the spirit has triumphed over the mechanism. When he has reached this point, science will receive from him not only new revelations of nature, but philosophic syntheses of pure thought.

It is my belief that the thing which we should cultivate in our teachers is more the *spirit* than the mechanical skill of the scientist; that is, the *direction* of the *preparation* should be toward the spirit rather than toward the mechanism. For example, when we considered the scientific preparation of teachers to be simply the acquiring of the technique of science, we did not attempt to make these elementary teachers perfect anthropologists, expert experimental psychologists, or masters of infant hygiene; we wished only to *direct them* toward the field of experimental science, teaching them to manage the various instruments with a certain degree of skill. So now, we wish to *direct* the teacher, trying to awaken in him, in connection with his own particular field, the school, that scientific *spirit* which opens the door for him to broader and bigger possibilities. In other words, we wish to awaken in the mind and heart of the educator an *interest in natural phenomena* to such an extent that, loving nature, he shall understand the anxious and expectant attitude of one who has prepared an experiment and who awaits a revelation from it.[3]

The instruments are like the alphabet, and we must know how to manage them if we are to read nature; but as the book, which contains the revelation of the greatest thoughts of an author, uses in the alphabet the means of composing the external symbols or words, so nature, through the mechanism of the experiment, gives us an infinite series of revelations, unfolding for us her secrets.

Now one who has learned to spell mechanically all the words in his spelling-book, would be able to read in the same mechanical way the words in one of Shakespeare's plays, provided the print were sufficiently clear. He who is initiated solely into the making of the bare experiment, is like one who spells out the literal sense of the words in the spelling-book; it is on such a level that we leave the teachers if we limit their preparation to technique alone.

We must, instead, make of them worshippers and interpreters of the spirit of nature. They must be like him who, having learned to spell, finds himself, one day, able to read behind the written symbols the *thought* of Shakespeare, or Goethe, or Dante. As may be seen, the difference is great, and the road long. Our first error was, however, a natural one. The child who has mastered the spelling-book gives the impression of knowing how to read. Indeed, he does read the signs over the shop doors, the names of newspapers, and every word that comes under his eyes. It would be very natural if, entering a library, this child should be deluded into thinking that he knew how to read the sense of all the books he saw there. But attempting to do this, he would soon feel that "to know how to read mechanically" is nothing, and that he needs to go back to school. So it is with the teachers whom we have thought to prepare for scientific pedagogy by teaching them anthropometry and psychometry.

But let us put aside the difficulty of preparing scientific masters in the accepted sense of the word. We will not even attempt to outline a programme of such preparation, since this would lead us into a discussion which has no place here. Let us suppose, instead, that we have already prepared teachers through long and patient exercises for the*observation* of *nature*, and that we have led them, for example, to the point attained by those students of natural sciences who rise at night and go into the woods and fields that they may surprise the awakening and the early activities of some family of insects in which they are interested. Here we have the scientist who, though he may be sleepy and tired with walking, is full of watchfulness, who is not aware that he is muddy or dusty, that the mist wets him, or the sun burns him; but is intent only upon not revealing in the least degree his presence, in order that the insects may, hour after hour, carry on peacefully those natural functions which he wishes to observe. Let us suppose these teachers to have reached the standpoint of the scientist who, half blind, still watches through his microscope the spontaneous movements of some particular infusory animalcule. These creatures seem to this scientific watcher, in their manner of avoiding each other and in their way of selecting their food, to possess a dim intelligence. He then disturbs this sluggish life by an electric stimulus, observing how some group themselves about the positive pole, and others about the negative. Experimenting further, with a luminous stimulus, he notices how some run toward the light, while others fly from it. He investigates these and like phenomena; having always in mind this question: whether the fleeing from or running to the stimulus be of the same character as the avoidance of one another or the selection of food—that is, whether such differences are the result of choice and are due to that dim consciousness, rather than to physical attraction or repulsion similar to that of the magnet. And let us suppose that this scientist, finding it to be four o'clock in the afternoon, and that he has not yet lunched, is conscious, with a feeling of pleasure, of the fact that he has been at work in his laboratory instead of in his own home, where they would have called him hours ago, interrupting his interesting observation, in order that he might eat.

Let us imagine, I say, that the teacher has arrived, independently of his scientific training, at such an attitude of interest in the observation of natural phenomena. Very well, but such a preparation is not enough. The master, indeed, is destined in his particular mission not to the observation of insects or of bacteria, but of man. He is not to make a study of man in the manifestations of his daily physical habits as one studies some family of insects, following their movements from the hour of their morning awakening. The master is to study man in the awakening of his intellectual life.

The interest in humanity to which we wish to educate the teacher must be characterised by the intimate relationship between the observer and the individual to be observed; a relationship which does not exist between the student of zoology or botany and that form of nature which he studies. Man cannot love the insect or the chemical reaction which he studies, without sacrificing a part of himself. This self-sacrifice seems to one who looks at it from the standpoint of the world, a veritable renunciation of life itself, almost a martyrdom.

But the love of man for man is a far more tender thing, and so simple that it is universal. To love in this way is not the privilege of any especially prepared intellectual class, but lies within the reach of all men.

To give an idea of this second form of preparation, that of the spirit, let us try to enter into the minds and hearts of those first followers of Christ Jesus as they heard Him speak of a Kingdom not of this world, greater far than any earthly kingdom, no matter how royally conceived. In their simplicity they asked of Him, "Master, tell us who shall be greatest in the Kingdom of Heaven!" To which Christ, caressing the head of a little child who, with reverent, wondering eyes, looked into His face, replied, "Whosoever shall become as one of these little ones, he shall be greatest in the Kingdom of Heaven." Now let us picture among those to whom these words were spoken, an ardent, worshipping soul, who takes them into his heart. With a mixture of respect and love, of sacred curiosity and of a desire to achieve this spiritual greatness, he sets himself to observe every manifestation of this little child. Even such an observer placed in a classroom filled with little children will not be the new educator whom we wish to form. But let us seek to implant in the soul the self-sacrificing spirit of the scientist with the reverent love of the disciple of Christ, and we shall have prepared the *spirit* of the teacher. From the child itself he will learn how to perfect himself as an educator.

Let us consider the attitude of the teacher in the light of another example. Picture to yourself one of our botanists or zoologists experienced in the technique of observation and experimentation; one who has travelled in order to study "certain fungi" in their native environment. This scientist has made his observations in open country and, then, by the aid of his microscope and of all his laboratory appliances, has carried on the later research work in the most minute way possible. He is, in fact, a scientist who understands what it is to study nature, and who is conversant with all the means which modern experimental science offers for this study.

Now let us imagine such a man appointed, by reason of the original work he has done, to a chair of science in some university, with the task before him of doing further original research work with hymenoptera. Let us suppose that, arrived at his post, he is shown a glass-covered case containing a number of beautiful butterflies, mounted by means of pins, their outspread wings motionless. The student will say that this is some child's play, not material for scientific study, that these specimens in the box are more fitly a part of the game which the little boys play, chasing butterflies and catching them in a net. With such material as this the experimental scientist can do nothing.

The situation would be very much the same if we should place a teacher who, according to our conception of the term, is scientifically prepared, in one of the public schools where the children are repressed in the spontaneous expression of their personality till they are almost like dead beings. In such a school the children, like butterflies mounted on pins, are fastened each to his place, the desk, spreading the useless wings of barren and meaningless knowledge which they have acquired.

It is not enough, then, to prepare in our Masters the scientific spirit. We must also make ready the *school* for their observation. The school must permit the *free, natural manifestations* of the *child* if in the school scientific pedagogy is to be born. This is the essential reform.

No one may affirm that such a principle already exists in pedagogy and in the school. It is true that some pedagogues, led by Rousseau, have given voice to impracticable principles and vague aspirations for the liberty of the child, but the true concept of liberty is practically unknown to educators. They often have the same concept of liberty which animates a people in the hour of rebellion from slavery, or perhaps, the conception of *social liberty*, which although it is a more elevated idea is still invariably restricted. *Social liberty* signifies always one more round of Jacob's ladder. In other words it signifies a partial liberation, the liberation of a country, of a class, or of thought.

That concept of liberty which must inspire pedagogy is, instead, universal. The biological sciences of the nineteenth century have shown it to us when they have offered us the means for studying life. If, therefore, the old-time pedagogy foresaw or vaguely expressed the principle of studying the pupil before educating him, and of leaving him free in his spontaneous manifestations, such an intuition, indefinite and barely expressed, was made possible of practical attainment only after the contribution of the experimental sciences during the last century. This is not a case for sophistry or discussion, it is enough that we state our point. He who would say that the principle of liberty informs the pedagogy of to-day, would make us smile as at a child who, before the box of mounted butterflies, should insist that they were alive and could fly. The principle of slavery still pervades pedagogy, and, therefore, the same principle pervades the school. I need only give one proof—the stationary desks and chairs. Here we have, for example, a striking evidence of the errors of the early materialistic scientific pedagogy which, with mistaken zeal and energy, carried the barren stones of science to the rebuilding of the crumbling walls of the school. The schools were at first furnished with the long, narrow benches upon which the children were crowded together. Then came science and perfected the bench. In this work much attention was paid to the recent contributions of anthropology. The age of the child and the length of his limbs were considered in placing the seat at the right height. The distance between the seat and the desk was calculated with infinite care, in order that the child's back should not become deformed, and, finally, the seats were separated and the width so closely calculated that the child could barely seat himself upon it, while to stretch himself by making any lateral movements was impossible. This was done in order that he might be separated from his neighbour. These desks are constructed in such a way as to render the child visible in all his immobility. One of the ends sought through this separation is the prevention of immoral acts in the schoolroom. What shall we say of such prudence in a state of society where it would be considered scandalous to give voice to principles of sex morality in education, for fear we might thus contaminate innocence? And, yet, here we have science lending itself to this hypocrisy, fabricating machines! Not only this; obliging science goes farther still, perfecting the benches in such a way as to permit to the greatest possible extent the immobility of the child, or, if you wish, to repress every movement of the child.

It is all so arranged that, when the child is well-fitted into his place, the desk and chair themselves force him to assume the position considered to be hygienically comfortable. The seat, the foot-rest, the desks are arranged in such a way that the child can never stand at his work. He is allotted only sufficient space for sitting in an erect position. It is in such ways that schoolroom desks and benches have advanced toward perfection. Every cult of the so-called scientific pedagogy has designed a model scientific desk. Not a few nations have become proud of their "national desk,"—and in the struggle of competition these various machines have been patented.

Undoubtedly there is much that is scientific underlying the construction of these benches. Anthropology has been drawn upon in the measuring of the body and the diagnosis of the age; physiology, in the study of muscular movements; psychology, in regard to perversion of instincts; and, above all, hygiene, in the effort to prevent curvature of the spine. These desks were indeed scientific, following in their construction the anthropological study of the child. We have here, as I have said, an example of the literal application of science to the schools.

I believe that before very long we shall all be struck with great surprise by this attitude. It will seem incomprehensible that the fundamental error of the desk should not have been revealed earlier through the attention given to the study of infant hygiene, anthropology, and sociology, and through the general progress of thought. The marvel is greater when we consider that during the past years there has been stirring in almost every nation a movement toward the protection of the child.

I believe that it will not be many years before the public, scarcely believing the descriptions of these scientific benches, will come to touch with wondering bands the amazing seats that were constructed for the purpose of preventing among our school children curvature of the spine!

The development of these scientific benches means that the pupils were subjected to a régime, which, even though they were born strong and straight, made it possible for them to become humpbacked! The vertebral column, biologically the most primitive, fundamental, and oldest part of the skeleton, the most fixed portion, of our body, since the skeleton is the most solid portion of the organism—the vertebral column, which resisted and was strong through the desperate struggles of primitive man when he fought against the desert-lion, when he conquered the mammoth, when he quarried the solid rock and shaped the iron to his uses, bends, and cannot resist, under the yoke of the school.

It is incomprehensible that so-called *science* should have

worked to perfect an instrument of slavery in the school without being enlightened by one ray from the movement of social liberation, growing and developing throughout the world. For the age of scientific benches was also the age of the redemption of the working classes from the yoke of unjust labor.

The tendency toward social liberty is most evident, and manifests itself on every hand. The leaders of the people make it their slogan, the labouring masses repeat the cry, scientific and socialistic publications voice the same movement, our journals are full of it. The underfed workman does not ask for a tonic, but for better economic conditions which shall prevent malnutrition. The miner who, through the stooping position maintained during many hours of the day, is subject to inguinal rupture, does not ask for an abdominal support, but demands shorter hours and bettor working conditions, in order that he may be able to lead a healthy life like other men.

And when, during this same social epoch, we find that the children in our schoolrooms are working amid unhygienic conditions, so poorly adapted to normal development that even the skeleton becomes deformed, our response to this terrible revelation is an orthopedic bench. It is much as if we offered to the miner the abdominal brace, or arsenic to the underfed workman.

Some time ago a woman, believing me to be in sympathy with all scientific innovations concerning the school, showed me with evident satisfaction *a corset or brace for pupils*. She had invented this and felt that it would complete the work of the bench.

Surgery has still other means for the treatment of spinal curvature. I might mention orthopedic instruments, braces, and a method of periodically suspending the child, by the head or shoulders, in such a fashion that the weight of the body stretches and thus straightens the vertebral column. In the school, the orthopedic instrument in the shape of the desk is in great favour to-day; someone proposes the brace—one step farther and it will be suggested that we give the scholars a systematic course in the suspension method!

All this is the logical consequence of a material application of the methods of science to the decadent school. Evidently the rational method of combating spinal curvature in the pupils, is to change the form of their work—so that they shall no longer be obliged to remain for so many hours a day in a harmful position. It is a conquest of liberty which the school needs, not the mechanism of a bench.

Even were the stationary seat helpful to the child's body, it would still be a dangerous and unhygienic feature of the environment, through the difficulty of cleaning the room perfectly when the furniture cannot be moved. The foot-rests, which cannot be removed, accumulate the dirt carried in daily from the street by the many little feet. To-day there is a general transformation in the matter of house furnishings. They are made lighter and simpler so that they may be easily moved, dusted, and even washed. But the school seems blind to the transformation of the social environment.

It behooves us to think of what may happen to the *spirit* of the child who is condemned to grow in conditions so artificial that his very bones may become deformed. When we speak of the redemption of the workingman, it is always understood that beneath the most apparent form of suffering, such as poverty of the blood, or ruptures, there exists that other wound from which the soul of the man who is subjected to any form of slavery must suffer. It is at this deeper wrong that we aim when we say that the workman must be redeemed through liberty. We know only too well that when a man's very blood has been consumed or his intestines wasted away through his work, his soul must have lain oppressed in darkness, rendered insensible, or, it may be, killed within him. The *moral* degradation of the slave is, above all things, the weight that opposes the progress of humanity—humanity striving to rise and held back by this great burden. The cry of redemption speaks far more clearly for the souls of men than for their bodies.

What shall we say then, when the question before us is that of *educating children*?

We know only too well the sorry spectacle of the teacher who, in the ordinary schoolroom, must pour certain cut and dried facts into the heads of the scholars. In order to succeed in this barren task, she finds it necessary to discipline her pupils into immobility and to force their attention. Prizes and punishments are every-ready and efficient aids to the master who must force into a given attitude of mind and body those who are condemned to be his listeners.

It is true that to-day it is deemed expedient to abolish official whippings and habitual blows, just as the awarding of prizes has become less ceremonious. These partial reforms are another prop approved of by science, and offered to the support of the decadent school. Such prizes and punishments are, if I may be allowed the expression, the *bench* of the soul, the instrument of slavery for the spirit. Here, however, these are not applied to lessen deformities, but to provoke them. The prize and the punishment are incentives toward unnatural or forced effort, and, therefore we certainly cannot speak of the natural development of the child in connection with them. The jockey offers a piece of sugar to his horse before jumping into the saddle, the coachman beats his horse that he may respond to the signs given by the reins; and, yet, neither of these runs so superbly as the free horse of the plains.

And here, in the case of education, shall man place the yoke upon man?

True, we say that social man is natural man yoked to society. But if we give a comprehensive glance to the moral progress of society, we shall see that little by little, the yoke is being made easier, in other words, we shall see that nature, or life, moves gradually toward triumph. The yoke of the slave yields to that of the servant, and the yoke of the servant to that of the workman.

All forms of slavery tend little by little to weaken and disappear, even the sexual slavery of woman. The history of civilisation is a history of conquest and of liberation. We should ask in what stage of civilisation we find ourselves and if, in truth, the good of prizes and of punishments be necessary to our advancement. If we have indeed gone beyond this point, then to apply such a form of education would be to draw the new generation back to a lower level, not to lead them into their true heritage of progress.

Something very like this condition of the school exists in society, in the relation between the government and the great numbers of the men employed in its administrative departments. These clerks work day after day for the general national good, yet they do not feel or see the advantage of their work in any immediate reward. That is, they do not realise that the state carries on its great business through their daily tasks, and that the whole nation is benefited by their work. For them the immediate good is promotion, as passing to a higher class is for the child in school. The man who loses sight of the really big aim of his work is like a child who has been placed in a class below his real standing: like a slave, he is cheated of something which is his right. His dignity as a man is reduced to the limits of the dignity of a machine which must be oiled if it is to be kept going, because it does not have within itself the impulse of life. All those petty things such as the desire for decorations or medals, are but artificial stimuli, lightening for the moment the dark, barren path in which he treads.

In the same way we give prizes to school children. And the fear of not achieving promotion, withholds the clerk from running away, and binds him to his monotonous work, even as the fear of not passing into the next class drives the pupil to his book. The reproof of the superior is in every way similar to the scolding of the teacher. The correction of badly executed clerical work is equivalent to the bad mark placed by the teacher upon the scholar's poor composition. The parallel is almost perfect.

But if the administrative departments are not carried on in a way which would seem suitable to a nation's greatness; if corruption too easily finds a place; it is the result of having extinguished the true greatness of man in the mind of the employee, and of having restricted his vision to those petty, immediate facts, which he has come to look upon as prizes and punishments. The country stands, because the rectitude of the greater number of its employees is such that they resist the corruption of the prizes and punishments, and follow an irresistible current of honesty. Even as life in the social environment triumphs against every cause of poverty and death, and proceeds to new conquests, so the instinct of liberty conquers all obstacles, going from victory to victory.

It is this personal and yet universal force of life, a force often latent within the soul, that sends the world forward.

But he who accomplishes a truly human work, he who does something really great and victorious, is never spurred to his task by those trifling attractions called by the name of "prizes," nor by the fear of those petty ills which we call "punishments." If in a war a great army of giants should fight with no inspiration beyond the desire to win promotion, epaulets, or medals, or through fear of being shot, if these men were to oppose a handful of pygmies who were inflamed by love of country, the victory would go to the latter. When real heroism has died within an army, prizes and punishments cannot do more than finish the work of deterioration, bringing in corruption and cowardice.

All human victories, all human progress, stand upon the inner force.

Thus a young student may become a great doctor if he is spurred to his study by an interest which makes medicine his real vocation. But if he works in the hope of an inheritance, or of making a desirable marriage, or if indeed he is inspired by any material advantage, he will never become a true master or a great doctor, and the world will never make one step forward because of his work. He to whom such stimuli are necessary, had far better never become a physician. Everyone has a special tendency, a special vocation, modest, perhaps, but certainly useful. The system of prizes may turn an individual aside from this vocation, may make him choose a false road, for him a vain one, and forced to follow it, the natural activity of a human being may be warped, lessened, even annihilated.

We repeat always that the world *progresses* and that we must urge men forward to obtain progress. But progress comes from the *new things that are born,* and these, not being foreseen, are not rewarded with prizes: rather, they often carry the leader to martyrdom. God forbid that poems should ever be born of the desire to be crowned in the Capitol! Such a vision need only come into the heart of the poet and the muse will vanish. The poem must spring from the soul of the poet, when he thinks neither of himself nor of the prize. And if he does win the laurel, he will feel the vanity of such a prize. The true reward lies in the revelation through the poem of his own triumphant inner force.

There does exist, however, an external prize for man; when, for example, the orator sees the faces of his listeners change with the emotions he has awakened, he experiences something so great that it can only be likened to the intense joy with which one discovers that he is loved. Our joy is to touch, and conquer souls, and this is the one prize which can bring us a true compensation.

Sometimes there is given to us a moment when we fancy ourselves to be among the great ones of the world. These are moments of happiness given to man that he may continue his existence in peace. It may be through love attained or because of the gift of a son, through a glorious discovery or the publication of a book; in some such moment we feel that there exists no man who is above us. If, in such a moment, someone vested with authority comes forward to offer us a medal or a prize, he is the important destroyer of our real reward—"And who are you?" our vanished illusion shall cry, "Who are you that recalls me to the fact that I am not the first among men? Who stands so far above me that he may give me a prize?" The prize of such a man in such a moment can only be Divine.

As for punishments, the soul of the normal man grows perfect through expanding, and punishment as commonly understood is always a form of *repression*. It may bring results with those inferior natures who grow in evil, but these are very few, and social progress is not affected by them. The penal code threatens us with punishment if we are dishonest within the limits indicated by the laws. But we are not honest through fear of the laws; if we do not rob, if we do not kill, it is because we love peace, because the natural trend of our lives leads us forward, leading us ever farther and more definitely away from the peril of low and evil acts.

Without going into the ethical or metaphysical aspects of the question, we may safely affirm that the delinquent before he transgresses the law, has, *if he knows of the existence of a punishment*, felt the threatening weight of the criminal code upon him. He has defined it, or he has been lured into the crime, deluding himself with the idea that he would be able to avoid the punishment of the law. But there has occurred within his mind, a *struggle between the crime and the punishment*. Whether it be efficacious in hindering crime or not, this penal code is undoubtedly made for a very limited class of individuals; namely, criminals. The enormous majority of citizens are honest without any regard whatever to the threats of the law.

The real punishment of normal man is the loss of the consciousness of that individual power and greatness which are the sources of his inner life. Such a punishment often falls upon men in the fullness of success. A man whom we would consider crowned by happiness and fortune may be suffering from this form of punishment. Far too often man does not see the real punishment which threatens him.

And it is just here that education may help.

To-day we hold the pupils in school, restricted by those instruments so degrading to body and spirit, the desk—and material prizes and punishments. Our aim in all this is to reduce them to the discipline of immobility and silence,—to lead them,—where? Far too often toward no definite end.

Often the education of children consists in pouring into their intelligence the intellectual contents of school programmes. And often these programmes have been compiled in the official department of education, and their use is imposed by law upon the teacher and the child.

Ah, before such dense and wilful disregard of the life which is growing within these children, we should hide our heads in shame and cover our guilty faces with our hands!

Sergi says truly: "To-day an urgent need imposes itself upon society: the reconstruction of methods in education and instruction, and he who fights for this cause, fights for human regeneration."

NOTES

1. Trevisini, 1892.
2. Montessori: "L'Antropologia Pedagogica." Vallardi.
3. See in my treatise on Pedagogical Anthropology the chapter on "The Method Used in Experimental Sciences."

2

History of Methods

If we are to develop a system of scientific pedagogy, we must, then, proceed along lines very different from those which have been followed up to the present time. The transformation of the school must be contemporaneous with the preparation of the teacher. For if we make of the teacher an observer, familiar with the experimental methods, then we must make it possible for her to observe and to experiment in the school. The fundamental principle of scientific pedagogy must be, indeed, the *liberty of the pupil;*—such liberty as shall permit a development of individual, spontaneous manifestations of the child's nature. If a new and scientific pedagogy is to arise from the *study of the individual,* such study must occupy itself with the observation of *free* children. In vain should we await a practical renewing of pedagogical methods from methodical examinations of pupils made under the guidance offered to-day by pedagogy, anthropology, and experimental psychology.

Every branch of experimental science has grown out of the application of a method peculiar to itself. Bacteriology owes its scientific content to the method of isolation and culture of microbes. Criminal, medical, and pedagogical anthropology owe their progress to the application of anthropological methods to individuals of various classes, such as criminals, the insane, the sick of the clinics, scholars. So experimental psychology needs as its starting point an exact definition of the technique to be used in making the experiment.

To put it broadly, it is important to define *the method, the technique,* and from its application to *await* the definite result, which must be gathered entirely from actual experience. One of the characteristics of experimental sciences is to proceed to the making of an experiment *without preconceptions of any sort* as to the final result of the experiment itself. For example, should we wish to make scientific observations concerning the development of the head as related to varying degrees of intelligence, one of the conditions of such an experiment would be to ignore, in the taking of the measurements, which were the most intelligent and which the most backward among the scholars examined. And this because the preconceived idea that the most intelligent should have the head more fully developed will inevitably alter the results of the research.

He who experiments must, while doing so, divest himself of every preconception. It is clear then that if we wish to make use of a method of experimental psychology, the first thing necessary is to renounce all former creeds and to proceed by means of the *method* in the search for truth.

We must not start, for example, from any dogmatic ideas which we may happen to have held upon the subject of child psychology. Instead, we must proceed by a method which shall tend to make possible to the child complete liberty. This we must do if we are to draw from the observation of his spontaneous manifestations conclusions which shall lead to the establishment of a truly scientific child psychology. It may be that such a method holds for us great surprises, unexpected possibilities.

Child psychology and pedagogy must establish their content by successive conquests arrived at through the method of experimentation.

Our problem then, is this: to establish the *method peculiar* to experimental pedagogy. It cannot be that used in other experimental sciences. It is true that scientific pedagogy is rounded out by hygiene, anthropology, and psychology, and adopts in part the technical method characteristic of all three, although limiting itself to a special study of the individual to be educated. But in pedagogy this study of the individual, though it must accompany the very different work of *education,* is a limited and secondary part of the science as a whole.

This present study deals in part with the *method* used in experimental pedagogy, and is the result of my experiences during two years in the "Children's Houses." I offer only a beginning of the method, which I have applied to children between the ages of three and six. But I believe that these tentative experiments, because of the surprising results which they have given, will be the means of inspiring a continuation of the work thus undertaken.

Indeed, although our educational system, which experience has demonstrated to be excellent, is not yet entirely completed, it nevertheless constitutes a system well enough established to be practical in all institutions where young children are cared for, and in the first elementary classes.

Perhaps I am not exact when I say that the present work springs from two years of experience. I do not believe that these later attempts of mine could alone have rendered possible all that I set forth in this book. The origin of the educational system in use in the "Children's Houses" is much more remote, and if this experience with normal children seems indeed rather brief, it should be remembered that it sprang from preceding pedagogical experiences with abnormal children, and that considered in this way, it represents a long and thoughtful endeavour.

About fifteen years ago, being assistant doctor at the Psychiatric Clinic of the University of Rome, I had occasion to frequent the insane asylums to study the sick and to select subjects for the clinics. In this way I became interested in the idiot children who were at that time housed in the general insane asylums. In those days thyroid organotherapy was in full development, and this drew the attention of physicians to deficient children. I myself, having completed my regular hospital services, had already turned my attention to the study of children's diseases.

It was thus that, being interested in the idiot children, I became conversant with the special method of education devised for these unhappy little ones by Edward Séguin, and was led to study thoroughly the idea, then beginning to be prevalent among the physicians, of the efficacy of "pedagogical treatment" for various morbid forms of disease such as deafness, paralysis, idiocy, rickets, etc. The fact that pedagogy must join with medicine in the treatment of disease was the practical outcome of the thought of the time. And because of this tendency the method of treating disease by gymnastics became widely popular. I, however, differed from my colleagues in that I felt that mental deficiency presented chiefly a pedagogical, rather than mainly a medical, problem. Much was said in the medical congresses of the medico-pedagogic method for the treatment and education of the feeble minded, and I expressed my differing opinion in an address on *Moral Education* at the Pedagogical Congress of Turin in 1898. I believe that I touched a chord already vibrant, because the idea, making its way among the physicians and elementary teachers, spread in a flash as presenting a question of lively interest to the school.

In fact I was called upon by my master, Guido Baccelli, the great Minister of Education, to deliver to the teachers of Rome a course of lectures on the education of feeble-minded children. This course soon developed into the State Orthophrenic School, which I directed for more than two years.

In this school we had an all-day class of children composed of those who in the elementary schools were considered hopelessly deficient. Later on, through the help of a philanthropic organisation, there was founded a Medical Pedagogic Institute where, besides the children from the public schools, we brought together all of the idiot children from the insane asylums in Rome.

I spent these two years with the help of my colleagues in preparing the teachers of Rome for a special method of observation and education of feeble-minded children. Not only did I train teachers, but what was much more important, after I had been in London and Paris for the purpose of studying in a practical way the education of deficients, I gave myself over completely to the actual teaching of the children, directing at the same time the work of the other teachers in our institute.

I was more than an elementary teacher, for I was present,

or directly taught the children, from eight in the morning to seven in the evening without interruption. These two years of practice are my first and indeed my true degree in pedagogy. From the very beginning of my work with deficient children (1898 to 1900) I felt that the methods which I used had in them nothing peculiarly limited to the instruction of idiots. I believed that they contained educational principles *more rational* than those in use, so much more so, indeed, that through their means an inferior mentality would be able to grow and develop. This feeling, so deep as to be in the nature of an intuition, became my controlling idea after I had left the school for deficients, and, little by little, I became convinced that similar methods applied to normal children would develop or set free their personality in a marvellous and surprising way.

It was then that I began a genuine and thorough study of what is known as remedial pedagogy, and, then, wishing to undertake the study of normal pedagogy and of the principles upon which it is based, I registered as a student of philosophy at the University. A great faith animated me, and although I did not know that I should ever be able to test the truth of my idea, I gave up every other occupation to deepen and broaden its conception. It was almost as if I prepared myself for an unknown mission.

The methods for the education of deficients had their origin at the time of the French Revolution in the work of a physician whose achievements occupy a prominent place in the history of medicine, as he was the founder of that branch of medical science which to-day is known as Otiatria (diseases of the ear).

He was the first to attempt a methodical education of the sense of hearing. He made these experiments in the institute for deaf mutes founded in Paris by Pereire, and actually succeeded in making the semi-deaf hear clearly. Later on, having in charge for eight years the idiot boy known as "the wild boy of Aveyron," he extended to the treatment of all the senses those educational methods which had already given such excellent results in the treatment of the sense of hearing. A student of Pinel, Itard, was the first educator to practise *the observation* of the pupil in the way in which the sick are observed in the hospitals, especially those suffering from diseases of the nervous system.

The pedagogic writings of Itard are most interesting and minute descriptions of educational efforts and experiences, and anyone reading them to-day must admit that they were practically the first attempts at experimental psychology. But the merit of having completed a genuine educational system for deficient children was due to Edward Séguin, first a teacher and then a physician. He took the experiences of Itard as his starting point, applying these methods, modifying and completing them during a period of ten years' experience with children taken from the insane asylums and placed in, a little school in Rue Pigalle in Paris. This method was described for the first time in a volume of more than six hundred pages, published in Paris in 1846, with the title: "Traitement Moral, Hygiène et Education des Idiots." Later Séguin emigrated to the United States of America where he founded many institutions for deficients, and where, after another twenty years of experience, he published the second edition of his method, under a very different title: *Idiocy and its Treatment by the Physiological Method*. This volume was published in New York in 1886, and in it Séguin had carefully defined his method of education, calling it the *physiological method*. He no longer referred in the title to a method for the "education of idiots" as if the method were special to them, but spoke now of idiocy treated by a physiological method. If we consider that pedagogy always had psychology as its base, and that Wundt defines a "physiological psychology," the coincidence of these ideas must strike us, and lead us to suspect in the physiological method some connection with physiological psychology.

While I was assistant at the Psychiatric Clinic, I had read Edward Séguin's French book, with great interest. But the English book which was published in New York twenty years later, although it was quoted in the works about special education by Bourneville, was not to be found in any library. I made a vain quest for it, going from house to house of nearly all the English physicians, who were known to be specially interested in deficient children, or who were superintendents of special schools. The fact that this book was unknown in England, although it had been published in the English language, made me think that the Séguin system had never been understood. In fact, although Séguin was constantly quoted in all the publications dealing with institutions for deficients, the educational *applications* described, were quite different from the applications of Séguin's system.

Almost everywhere the methods applied to deficients are more or less the same as those in use for normal children. In Germany, especially, a friend who had gone there in order to help me in my researches, noticed that although special materials existed here and there in the pedagogical museums of the schools for deficients, these materials were rarely used. Indeed, the German educators hold the principle that it is well to adapt to the teaching of backward children, the same method used for normal ones; but these methods are much more objective in Germany than with us.

At the Bicêtre, where I spent some time, I saw that it was the didactic apparatus of Séguin far more than his *method* which was being used, although, the French text was in the hands of the educators. The teaching there was purely mechanical, each teacher following the rules according to the letter. I found, however, wherever I went, in London as well as in Paris, a desire for fresh counsel and for new experiences, since far too often Séguin's claim that with his methods the education of idiots was actually possible, had proved only a delusion.

After this study of the methods in use throughout Europe I concluded my experiments upon the deficients of Rome, and taught them throughout two years. I followed Séguin's book, and also derived much help from the remarkable experiments of Itard.

Guided by the work of these two men, I had manufactured a great variety of didactic material. These materials, which I have never seen complete in any institution, became in the hands of those who knew how to apply them, a most remarkable and efficient means, but unless rightly presented, they failed to attract the attention of the deficients.

I felt that I understood the discouragement of those working with feeble-minded children, and could see why they had, in so many cases, abandoned the method. The prejudice that the educator must place himself on a level with the one to be educated, sinks the teacher of deficients into a species of apathy. He accepts the fact that he is educating an inferior personality, and for that very reason he does not succeed. Even so those who teach little children too often have the idea that they are educating babies and seek to place themselves on the child's level by approaching him with games, and often with foolish stories. Instead of all this, we must know how to call to the *man* which lies dormant within the soul of the child. I felt this, intuitively, and believed that not the didactic material, but my voice which called to them, *awakened* the children, and encouraged them to use the didactic material, and through it, to educate themselves. I was guided in my work by the deep respect which I felt for their misfortune, and by the love which these unhappy children know how to awaken in those who are near them.

Séguin, too, expressed himself in the same way on this subject. Reading his patient attempts, I understand clearly that the first didactic material used by him was *spiritual*. Indeed, at the close of the French volume, the author, giving a résumé of his work, concludes by saying rather sadly, that all he has established will be lost or useless, if the *teachers* are not prepared for their work. He holds rather original views concerning the preparation of teachers of deficients. He would have them good to look upon, pleasant-voiced, careful in every detail of their personal appearance, doing everything possible to make themselves attractive. They must, he says, render themselves attractive in voice and manner, since it is their task to awaken souls which are frail and weary, and to lead them forth to lay hold upon the beauty and strength of life.

This belief that we must act upon the spirit, served as a sort of *secret key*, opening to me the long series of didactic experiments so wonderfully analysed by Edward Séguin,—experiments which, properly understood, are really most efficacious in the education of idiots. I myself obtained most surprising results through their application, but I must confess that, while my efforts showed themselves in the intellectual progress of my pupils, a peculiar form of exhaustion prostrated me. It was as if I gave to them some vital force from within me. Those things which we call encouragement, comfort, love, respect, are drawn from the soul of man, and the more freely we give of them, the more do we renew and reinvigorate the life about us.

Without such inspiration the most perfect *external stimulus* may pass unobserved. Thus the blind Saul, before the glory of the sun, exclaimed, "This?—It is the dense fog!"

Thus prepared, I was able to proceed to new experiments on my own account. This is not the place for a report of these experiments, and I will only note that at this time I attempted an original method for the teaching of reading and writing, a part of the education of the child which was most imperfectly treated in the works of both Itard and Séguin.

I succeeded in teaching a number of the idiots from the asylums both to read and to write so well that I was able to present them at a public school for an examination together with normal children. And they passed the examination successfully.

These results seemed almost miraculous to those who saw them. To me, however, the boys from the asylums had been able to compete with the normal children only because they had been taught in a different way. They had been helped in their psychic development, and the normal children had, instead, been suffocated, held back. I found myself thinking that if, some day, the special education which had developed these idiot children in such a marvellous fashion, could be applied to the development of normal children, the "miracle" of which my friends talked would no longer be possible. The abyss between the inferior mentality of the idiot and that of the normal brain can never be bridged if the normal child has reached his full development.

While everyone was admiring the progress of my idiots, I was searching for the reasons which could keep the happy healthy children of the common schools on so low a plane that they could be equalled in tests of intelligence by my unfortunate pupils!

One day, a directress in the Institute for Deficients, asked me to read one of the prophecies of Ezekiel which had made a profound impression upon her, as it seemed to prophesy the education of deficients.

"The hand of the Lord was upon me, and carried me out in the spirit of the Lord, and set me down in the midst of the valley which was full of bones.

"And caused me to pass by them round about: and, behold, there were very many in the open valley; and, lo, they were very dry.

"And he said unto me, Son of man, can these bones live? And I answered, O Lord God, thou knowest.

"Again he said unto me, Prophesy upon these bones, and say unto them, O ye dry hones, hear the word of the Lord.

"Thus saith the Lord God unto these bones; Behold, I will cause breath to enter into you, and ye shall live:

"And I will lay sinews upon you, and will bring up flesh upon you, and cover you with skin, and put breath in you, and ye shall live; and ye shall know that I am the Lord.

"So I prophesied as I was commanded: and as I prophesied, there was a noise, and behold a shaking, and the bones came together, bone to his bone.

"And when I beheld, lo, the sinews and the flesh came up upon them, and the skin covered them above: but there was no breath in them.

"Then said he unto me, Prophesy unto the wind, prophesy, son of man, and say to the wind, Thus saith the Lord God; Come from the four winds, O breath, and breathe upon these slain, that they may live.

"So I prophesied as He commanded me, and the breath came into them, and they lived, and stood up upon their feet, an exceeding great army.

"Then he said unto me, Son of man, these bones are the whole house of Israel: behold, they say, Our bones are dried, and our hope is lost: we are cut off for our parts."

In fact, the words—"I will cause breath to enter into you, and ye shall live," seem to me to refer to the direct individual work of the master who encourages, calls to, and helps his pupil, preparing him for education. And the remainder—"I will lay sinews upon you, and will bring up flesh upon you," recalled the fundamental phrase which sums up Séguin's whole method,—"to lead the child, as it were, by the hand, from the education of the muscular system, to that of the nervous system, and of the senses." It was thus that Séguin taught the idiots how to walk, how to maintain their equilibrium in the most difficult movements of the body—such as going up stairs, jumping, etc., and finally, to feel, beginning the education of the muscular sensations by touching, and reading the difference of temperature, and ending with the education of the particular senses.

But if the training goes no further than this, we have only led these children to adapt themselves to a low order of life (almost a vegetable existence). "Call to the Spirit," says the prophecy, and the spirit shall enter into them, and they shall have life. Séguin, indeed, led the idiot from the vegetative to the intellectual life, "from the education, of the senses to general notions, from general notions to abstract thought, from abstract thought to morality." But when this wonderful work is accomplished, and by means of a minute physiological analysis and of a gradual progression in method, the idiot has become a man, he is still an inferior in the midst of his fellow men, an individual who will never be able fully to adapt himself to the social environment: "Our bones are dried, and our hope is lost; we are cut off for our parts."

This gives us another reason why the tedious method of Séguin was so often abandoned; the tremendous difficulty of the means, did not justify the end. Everyone felt this, and many said, "There is still so much to be done for normal children!"

Having through actual experience justified my faith in Séguin's method, I withdrew from active work among deficients, and began a more thorough study of the works of Itard and Séguin. I felt the need of meditation. I did a thing which I had not done before, and which perhaps few students have been willing to do,—I translated into Italian and copied out with my own hand, the writings of these men, from beginning to end, making for myself books as the old Benedictines used to do before the diffusion of printing.

I chose to do this by hand, in order that I might have time to weigh the sense of each word, and to read, in truth, the *spirit* of the author. I had just finished copying the 600 pages of Séguin's French volume when I received from New York a copy of the English book published in 1866. This old volume had been found among the books discarded from the private library of a New York physician. I translated it with the help of an English friend. This volume did not add much in the way of new pedagogical experiments, but dealt with the philosophy of the experiences described in the first volume. The man who had studied abnormal children for thirty years expressed the idea that the physiological method, which has as its base the individual study of the pupil and which forms its educative methods upon the analysis of physiological and psychological phenomena, must come also to be applied to normal children. This step, he believed, would show the way to a complete human regeneration.

The voice of Séguin seemed to be like the voice of the forerunner crying in the wilderness, and my thoughts were filled with the immensity and importance of a work which should be able to reform the school and education.

At this time I was registered at the University as a student of philosophy, and followed the courses in experimental psychology, which had only recently been established in Italian universities, namely, at Turin, Rome and Naples. At the same time I made researches in Pedagogic Anthropology in the elementary schools, studying in this way the methods in organisation used for the education of normal children. This work led to the teaching of Pedagogic Anthropology in the University of Rome.

I had long wished to experiment with the methods for deficients in a first elementary class of normal children, but I had never thought of making use of the homes or institutions where very young children were cared for. It was pure chance that brought this new idea to my mind.

It was near the end of the year 1906, and I had just returned from Milan, where I had been one of a committee at the International Exhibition for the assignment of prizes in the subjects of Scientific Pedagogy and Experimental Psychology. A great opportunity came to me, for I was invited by Edoardo Talamo, the Director General of the Roman Association for Good Building, to undertake the organisation of infant schools in its model tenements. It was Signor Talamo's happy idea to gather together in a large room all the little ones between the ages of three and seven belonging to the families living in the tenement. The play and work of these children was to be carried on under the guidance of a teacher who should have her own apartment in the tenement house. It was intended that every house should have its school, and as the Association for Good Building already owned more than 400 tenements in Rome the work seemed to offer tremendous possibilities of development. The first school was to be established in January, 1907, in a large tenement house in the Quarter of San Lorenzo. In the same Quarter the Association already owned fifty-eight buildings, and according to Signor Talamo's plans we should soon be able to open sixteen of these "schools within the house."

This new kind of school was christened by Signora Olga Lodi, a mutual friend of Signor Talamo and myself, under the fortunate title of *Casa dei Bambini* or "The Children's House." Under this name the first of our schools was opened on the sixth of January, 1907, at 58 Via dei Masi. It was confided to the care of Candida Nuccitelli and was under my guidance and direction.

From the very first I perceived, in all its immensity, the social and pedagogical importance of such institutions, and while at that time my visions of a triumphant future seemed exaggerated, to-day many are beginning to understand that what I saw before was indeed the truth.

On the seventh of April of the same year, 1907, a second "Children's House" was opened in the Quarter of San Lorenzo; and on the eighteenth of October, 1908, another was inaugurated by the Humanitarian Society in Milan in the Quarter inhabited by workingmen. The workshops of this same society undertook the manufacture of the materials which we used.

On the fourth of November following, a third "Children's House" was opened in Rome, this time not in the people's Quarter, but in a modern building for the middle classes, situated in Via Famagosta, in that part of the city known as the Prati di Castello; and in January, 1909, Italian Switzerland began to transform its orphan asylums and children's homes in which the Froebel system had been used, into "Children's Houses" adopting our methods and materials.

The "Children's House" has a twofold importance: the social importance which it assumes through its peculiarity of being a school within the house, and its purely pedagogic importance gained through its methods for the education of very young children, of which I now made a trial.

As I have said, Signor Talamo's invitation gave me a wonderful opportunity for applying the methods used with deficients to normal children, not of the elementary school age, but of the age usual in infant asylums.

If a parallel between the deficient and the normal child is possible, this will be during the period of early infancy *when the child who has not the force to develop* and *he who is not yet developed* are in some ways alike.

The very young child has not yet acquired a secure co-ordination of muscular movements, and, therefore, walks imperfectly, and is not able to perform the ordinary acts of life, such as fastening and unfastening its garments. The sense organs, such as the power of accommodation of the eye, are not yet completely developed; the language is primordial and shows those defects common to the speech of the very young child. The difficulty of fixing the attention, the general instability, etc., are characteristics which the normal infant and the deficient child have in common. Preyer, also, in his psychological study of children has turned aside to illustrate the parallel between pathological linguistic defects, and those of normal children in the process of developing.

Methods which made growth possible to the mental personality of the idiot ought, therefore, to *aid the development of young children*, and should be so adapted as to constitute a hygienic education of the entire personality of a normal human being. Many defects which become permanent, such as speech defects, the child acquires through being neglected during the most important period of his age, the period between three and six, at which time he forms and establishes his principal functions.

Here lies the significance of my pedagogical experiment in the "Children's Houses." It represents the results of a series of trials made by me, in the education of young children, with methods already used with deficients. My work has not been in any way an application, pure and simple, of the methods of Séguin to young children, as anyone who will consult the works of the author will readily see. But it is none the less true that, underlying these two years of trial, there is a basis of experiment which goes back to the days of the French Revolution, and which represents the earnest work of the lives of Itard and Séguin.

As for me, thirty years after the publication of Séguin's second book, I took up again the ideas and, I may even say, the work of this great man, with the same freshness of spirit with which he received the inheritance of the work and ideas of his master Itard. For *ten years* I not only made practical experiments according to their methods, but through reverent meditation absorbed the works of these noble and consecrated men, who have left to humanity most vital proof of their obscure heroism.

Thus my ten years of work may in a sense be considered as a summing up of the forty years of work done by Itard and Séguin. Viewed in this light, fifty years of active work preceded and prepared for this apparently brief trial of only two years, and I feel that I am not wrong in saying that these experiments represent the successive work of three physicians, who from Itard to me show in a greater or less degree the first steps along the path of psychiatry.

As definite factors in the civilisation of the people, the "Children's Houses" deserve a separate volume. They have, in fact, solved so many of the social and pedagogic problems in ways which have seemed to be Utopian, that they are a part of that modern transformation of the home which must most surely be realised before many years have passed. In this way they touch directly the most important side of the social question—that which deals with the intimate or home life of the people.

It is enough here to reproduce the inaugural discourse delivered by me on the occasion of the opening of the second "Children's House" in Rome, and to present the rules and regulations which I arranged in accordance with the wishes of Signor Talamo.

It will be noticed that the club to which I refer, and the dispensary which is also an out-patients' institution for medical and surgical treatment (all such institutions being free to the inhabitants) have already been established. In the modern tenement—Casa Moderna in the Prati di Castello, opened November 4, 1908, through the philanthropy of Signor Talamo—they are also planning to annex a "communal kitchen."

3

Inaugural Address Delivered on the Occasion of the Opening of One of the "Children's Houses"

It may be that the life lived by the very poor is a thing which some of you here to-day have never actually looked upon in all its degradation. You may have only felt the misery of deep human poverty through the medium of some great book, or some gifted actor may have made your soul vibrato with its horror.

Let us suppose that in some such moment a voice should cry to you, "Go look upon these homes of misery and blackest poverty. For there have sprung up amid the terror and the suffering, cases of happiness, of cleanliness, of peace. The poor are to have an ideal house which shall be their own. In Quarters where poverty and vice ruled, a work of moral redemption is going on. The soul of the people is being set free from the torpor of vice, from the shadows of ignorance. The little children too have a 'House' of their own. The new generation goes forward to meet the new era, the time when misery shall no longer be deplored but destroyed. They go to meet the time when the dark dens of vice and wretchedness shall have become things of the past, and when no trace of them shall be found among the living." What a change of emotions we should experience! and how we should hasten here, as the wise men guided by a dream and a star hastened to Bethlehem!

I have spoken thus in order that you may understand the great significance, the real beauty, of this humble room, which seems like a bit of the house itself set apart by a mother's hand for the use and happiness of the children of the Quarter. This is the second "Children's House"[1] which has been established within the ill-favoured Quarter of San Lorenzo.

The Quarter of San Lorenzo is celebrated, for every newspaper in the city is filled with almost daily accounts of its wretched happenings. Yet there are many who are not familiar with the origin of this portion of our city.

It was never intended to build up here a tenement district for the people. And indeed San Lorenzo is not the *People's* Quarter, it is the Quarter of the *poor*. It is the Quarter where lives the underpaid, often unemployed workingman, a common type in a city which has no factory industries. It is the home of him who undergoes the period of surveillance to which he is condemned after his prison sentence is ended. They are all here, mingled, huddled together.

The district of San Lorenzo sprang into being between 1884 and 1888 at the time of the great building fever. No standards either social or hygienic guided these new constructions. The aim in building was simply to cover with walls square foot after square foot of ground. The more space covered, the greater the gain of the interested Banks and Companies. All this with a complete disregard of the disastrous future which they were preparing. It was natural that no one should concern himself with the stability of the building he was creating, since in no case would the property remain in the possession of him who built it.

When the storm burst, in the shape of the inevitable building panic of 1888 to 1890, these unfortunate houses remained for a long time untenanted. Then, little by little, the need of dwelling-places began to make itself felt, and these great houses began to fill. Now, those speculators who had been so unfortunate as to remain possessors of these buildings could not, and did not wish to, add fresh capital to that already lost, so the houses constructed in the first place in utter disregard of all laws of hygiene, and rendered still worse by having been used as temporary habitations, came to be occupied by the poorest class in the city.

The apartments not being prepared for the working class, were too large, consisting of five, six, or seven rooms. These were rented at a price which, while exceedingly low in relation to the size, was yet too high for any one family of very poor people. This led to the evil of subletting. The tenant who has taken a six room apartment at eight dollars a month sublets rooms at one dollar and a half or two dollars a month to those who can pay so much, and a corner of a room, or a corridor, to a poorer tenant, thus making an income of fifteen dollars or more, over and above the cost of his own rent.

This means that the problem of existence is in great part solved for him, and that in every case he adds to his income through usury. The one who holds the lease traffics in the misery of his fellow tenants, lending small sums at a rate which generally corresponds to twenty cents a week for the loan of two dollars, equivalent to an annual rate of 500 per cent.

Thus we have in the evil of subletting the most cruel form of usury: that which only the poor know how to practise upon the poor.

To this we must add the evils of crowded living, promiscuousness, immorality, crime. Every little while the newspapers uncover for us one of these *intérieurs*: a large family, growing boys and girls, sleep in one room; while one corner of the room is occupied by an outsider, a woman who receives the nightly visits of men. This is seen by the girls and the boys; evil passions are kindled that lead to the crime and bloodshed which unveil for a brief instant before our eyes, in some lurid paragraph, this little detail of the mass of misery.

Whoever enters, for the first time, one of these apartments is astonished and horrified. For this spectacle of genuine misery is not at all like the garish scene he has imagined. We enter here a world of shadows, and that which strikes us first is the darkness which, even though it be midday, makes it impossible to distinguish any of the details of the room.

When the eye has grown accustomed to the gloom, we perceive, within, the outlines of a bed upon which lies huddled a figure—someone ill and suffering. If we have come to bring money from some society for mutual aid, a candle must be lighted before the sum can be counted and the receipt signed. Oh, when we talk of social problems, how often we speak vaguely, drawing upon our fancy for details instead of preparing ourselves to judge intelligently through a personal investigation of facts and conditions.

We discuss earnestly the question of home study for school children, when for many of them home means a straw pallet thrown down in the corner of some dark hovel. We wish to establish circulating libraries that the poor may read at home. We plan to send among these people books which shall form their domestic literature—books through whose influence they shall come to higher standards of living. We hope through the printed page to educate these poor people in matters of hygiene, of morality, of culture, and in this we show ourselves profoundly ignorant of their most crying needs. For many of them have no light by which to read!

There lies before the social crusader of the present day a problem more profound than that of the intellectual elevation of the poor; the problem, indeed, of *life*.

In speaking of the children born in these places, even the conventional expressions must be changed, for they do not "first see the light of day"; they come into a world of gloom. They grow among the poisonous shadows which envelope over-crowded humanity. These children cannot be other than filthy in body, since the water supply in an apartment originally intended to be occupied by three or four persons, when distributed among twenty or thirty is scarcely enough for drinking purposes!

We Italians have elevated our word "casa" to the almost sacred significance of the English word "home," the enclosed temple of domestic affection, accessible only to dear ones.

Far removed from this conception is the condition of the many who have no "casa," but only ghastly walls within which the most intimate acts of life are exposed upon the pillory. Here, there can be no privacy, no modesty, no gentleness; here, there is often not even light, nor air, nor water! It seems a cruel mockery to introduce here our idea of the home as essential to the education of the masses, and as furnishing, along with the family, the only solid basis for the social structure. In doing this we would be not practical reformers but visionary poets.

Conditions such as I have described make it more decorous, more hygienic, for these people to take refuge in the street and to let their children live there. But how often these streets are the scene of bloodshed, of quarrel, of sights so vile as to be almost inconceivable. The papers tell us of women pursued and killed by drunken husbands! Of young girls with the fear of worse than death, stoned by low men. Again, we see untellable things—a wretched woman thrown, by the drunken men who have preyed upon her, forth into the gutter. There, when day has come, the children of the neighbourhood crowd about her like scavengers about their dead prey, shouting and laughing at the sight of this wreck of womanhood, kicking her bruised and filthy body as it lies in the mud of the gutter!

Such spectacles of extreme brutality are possible here at the very gate of a cosmopolitan city, the mother of civilisation and queen of the fine arts, because of a new fact which was unknown to past centuries, namely, *the isolation of the masses of the poor*.

In the Middle Ages, leprosy was isolated: the Catholics isolated the Hebrews in the Ghetto; but poverty was never considered a peril and an infamy so great that it must be isolated. The homes of the poor were scattered among those of the rich and the contrast between these was a commonplace in literature up to our own times. Indeed, when I was a child in school, teachers, for the purpose of moral education, frequently resorted to the illustration of the kind princess who sends help to the poor cottage next door, or of the good children from the great house who carry food to the sick woman in the neighbouring attic.

To-day all this would be as unreal and artificial as a fairy tale. The poor may no longer learn from their more fortunate neighbours lessons in courtesy and good breeding, they no longer have the hope of help from them in cases of extreme need. We have herded them together far from us, without the walls, leaving them to learn of each other, in the abandon of desperation, the cruel lessons of brutality and vice. Anyone in whom the social conscience is awake must see that we have thus created infected regions that threaten with deadly peril the city which, wishing to make all beautiful and shining according to an æsthetic and aristocratic ideal, has thrust without its walls whatever is ugly or diseased.

When I passed for the first time through these streets, it was as if I found myself in a city upon which some great disaster had fallen. It seemed to me that the shadow of some recent struggle still oppressed the unhappy people who, with something very like terror in their pale faces, passed me in these silent streets. The very silence seemed to signify the life of a community interrupted, broken. Not a carriage, not even the cheerful voice of the ever-present street vender, nor the sound of the hand-organ playing in the hope of a few pennies, not even these things, so characteristic of poor quarters, enter here to lighten this sad and heavy silence.

Observing these streets with their deep holes, the doorsteps broken and tumbling, we might almost suppose that this disaster had been in the nature of a great inundation which had carried the very earth away; but looking about us at the houses stripped of all decorations, the walls broken and scarred, we are inclined to think that it was perhaps an earthquake which has afflicted this quarter. Then, looking still more closely, we see that in all this thickly settled neighbourhood there is not a shop to be found. So poor is the community that it has not been possible to establish even one of those popular bazars where necessary articles are sold at so low a price as to put them within the reach of anyone. The only shops of any sort are the low wine shops which open their evil-smelling doors to the passer-by. As we look upon all this, it is borne upon us that the disaster which has placed its weight of suffering upon these people is not a convulsion of nature, but poverty—poverty with its inseparable companion, vice.

This unhappy and dangerous state of things, to which our attention is called at intervals by newspaper accounts of violent and immoral crime, stirs the hearts and consciences of many who come to undertake among these people some work of generous benevolence. One might almost say that every form of misery inspires a special remedy and that all have been tried here, from the attempt to introduce hygienic principles into each house, to the establishment of crêches, "Children's Houses," and dispensaries.

But what indeed is benevolence? Little more than an expression of sorrow; it is pity translated into action. The benefits of such a form of charity cannot be great, and through the absence of any continued income and the lack of organisation it is restricted to a small number of persons. The great and widespread peril of evil demands, on the other hand, a broad and comprehensive work directed toward the redemption of the entire community. Only such an organisation, as, working for the good of others, shall itself grow and prosper through the general prosperity which it has made possible, can make a place for itself in this quarter and accomplish a permanent good work.

It is to meet this dire necessity that the great and kindly work of the Roman Association of Good Building has been undertaken. The advanced and highly modern way in which this work is being carried on is due to Edoardo Talamo, Director General of the Association. His plans, so original, so comprehensive, yet so practical, are without counterpart in Italy or elsewhere.

This Association was incorporated three years ago in Rome, its plan being to acquire city tenements, remodel them, put them into a productive condition, and administer them as a good father of a family would.

The first property acquired comprised a large portion of the Quarter of San Lorenzo, where to-day the Association possesses fifty-eight houses, occupying a ground space of about 30,000 square metres, and containing, independent of the ground floor, 1,600 small apartments. Thousands of people will in this way receive the beneficent influence of the protective reforms of the Good Building Association. Following its beneficent programme, the Association set about transforming these old houses, according to the most modern standards, paying as much attention to questions related to hygiene and morals as to those relating to buildings. The constructional changes would make the property of real and lasting value, while the hygienic and moral transformation, would, through the improved condition of the inmates, make the rent from these apartments a more definite asset.

The Association of Good Building therefore decided upon a programme which would permit of a gradual attainment of their ideal. It is necessary to proceed slowly because it is not easy to empty a tenement house at a time when houses are scarce, and the humanitarian principles which govern the entire movement make it impossible to proceed more rapidly in this work of regeneration. So it is, that the Association has up to the present time transformed only three houses in the Quarter of San Lorenzo. The plan followed in this transformation is as follows:

A: To demolish in every building all portions of the structure not originally constructed with the idea of making homes, but, from a purely commercial standpoint, of making the rental roll larger. In other words, the new management tore down those parts of the building which encumbered the central court, thus doing away with dark, ill-ventilated apartments, and giving air and light to the remaining portion of the tenement. Broad airy courts take the place of the inadequate air and light shafts, rendering the remaining apartments more valuable and infinitely more desirable.

B: To increase the number of stairways, and to divide the room space in a more practical way. The large six or seven room suites are reduced to small apartments of one, two, or three rooms, and a kitchen.

The importance of such changes may be recognised from the economic point of view of the proprietor as well as from the standpoint of the moral and material welfare of the tenant. Increasing the number of stairways diminishes that abuse of walls and stairs inevitable where so many persons must pass up and down. The tenants more readily learn to respect the building and acquire habits of cleanliness and order. Not only this, but in reducing the chances of contact among the inhabitants of the house, especially late at night, a great advance has been made in the matter of moral hygiene.

The division of the house into small apartments has done much toward this moral regeneration. Each family is thus set apart, *homes* are made possible, while the menacing evil of subletting together with all its disastrous consequences of overcrowding and immorality is checked in the most radical way.

On one side this arrangement lessens the burden of the individual lease holders, and on the other increases the income of the proprietor, who now receives those earnings which were the unlawful gain of the system of subletting. When the proprietor who originally rented an apartment of six rooms for a monthly rental of eight dollars, makes such an apartment over into three small, sunny, and airy suites consisting of one room and a kitchen, it is evident that he increases his income.

The moral importance of this reform as it stands to-day is tremendous, for it has done away with those evil influences and low opportunities which arise from crowding and from promiscuous contact, and has brought to life among these people, for the first time, the gentle sentiment of feeling themselves free within their own homes, in the intimacy of the family.

But the project of the Association goes beyond even this. The house which it offers to its tenants is not only sunny and airy, but in perfect order and repair, almost shining, and as if perfumed with purity and freshness. These good things, however, carry with them a responsibility which the tenant must assume if he wishes to enjoy them. He must pay an actual tax of *care* and *good will*. The tenant who receives a clean house must keep it so, must respect the walls from the big general entrance to the interior of his own little apartment. He who keeps his house in good condition receives the recognition and consideration due such a tenant. Thus all the tenants unite in an ennobling warfare for practical hygiene, an end made possible by the simple task of *conserving* the already perfect conditions.

Here indeed is something new! So far only our great national buildings have had a continued *maintenance fund*. Here, in these houses offered to the people, the maintenance is confided to a hundred or so workingmen, that is, to all the occupants of the building. This care is almost perfect. The people keep the house in perfect condition, without a single spot. The building in which we find ourselves to-day has been for two years under the sole protection of the tenants, and the work of maintenance has been left entirely to them. Yet few of our houses can compare in cleanliness and freshness with this home of the poor.

The experiment has been tried and the result is remarkable. The people acquire together with the lore of home-making, that of cleanliness. They come, moreover, to wish to beautify their homes. The Association helps this by placing growing plants and trees in the courts and about the halls.

Out of this honest rivalry in matters so productive of good, grows a species of pride new to this quarter; this is the pride which the entire body of tenants takes in having the best-cared-for building and in having risen to a higher and more civilised plane of living. They not only live in a house, but they *know how to live*, they *know how to respect* the house in which they live.

This first impulse has led to other reforms. From the clean home will come personal cleanliness. Dirty furniture cannot be tolerated in a clean house, and those persons living in a permanently clean house will come to desire personal cleanliness.

One of the most important hygienic reforms of the Association is that of *the baths*. Each remodeled tenement has a place set apart for bathrooms, furnished with tubs or shower, and having hot and cold water. All the tenants in regular turn may use these baths, as, for example, in various tenements the occupants go according to turn, to wash their clothes in the fountain in the court. This is a great convenience which invites the people to be clean. These hot and cold baths *within the house* are a great improvement upon the general public baths. In this way we make possible to these people, at one and the same time, health and refinement, opening not only to the sun, but to progress, those dark habitations once the *vile caves* of misery.

But in striving to realise its ideal of a semi-gratuitous maintenance of its buildings, the Association met with a difficulty in regard to those children under school age, who must often be left alone during the entire day while their parents went out to work. These little ones, not being able to understand the educative motives which taught their parents to respect the house, became ignorant little vandals, defacing the walls and stairs. And here we have another reform the expense of which may be considered as indirectly assumed by the tenants as was the care of the building. This reform may be considered as the most brilliant transformation of a tax which progress and civilisation have as yet devised. The "Children's House" is earned by the parents through the care of the building. Its expenses are met by the sum that the Association would have otherwise been forced to spend upon repairs. A wonderful climax, this, of moral benefits received! Within the "Children's House," which belongs exclusively to those children under school age, working mothers may safely leave their little ones, and may proceed with a feeling of great relief and freedom to their own work. But this benefit, like that of the care of the house, is not conferred without a tax of care and of good will. The Regulations posted on the walls announce it thus:

"The mothers are obliged to send their children to the 'Children's House' clean, and to co-operate with the Directress in the educational work."

Two obligations: namely, the physical and moral care of their own children. If the child shows through its conversation that the educational work of the school is being undermined by the attitude taken in his home, he will be sent back to his parents, to teach them thus how to take advantage of their good opportunities. Those who give themselves over to low-living, to fighting, and to brutality, shall feel upon them the weight of those little lives, so needing care. They shall feel that they themselves have once more cast into the darkness of neglect those little creatures who are the dearest part of the family. In other words, the parents must learn to *deserve* the benefit of having within the house the great advantage of a school for their little ones.

"Good will," a willingness to meet the demands of the Association is enough, for the directress is ready and willing to teach them how. The regulations say that the mother must go at least once a week, to confer with the directress, giving an account of her child, and accepting any helpful advice which the directress may be able to give. The advice thus given will undoubtedly prove most illuminating in regard to the child's health and education, since to each of the "Children's Houses" is assigned a physician as well as a directress.

The directress is always at the disposition of the mothers, and her life, as a cultured and educated person, is a constant example to the inhabitants of the house, for she is obliged to live in the tenement and to be therefore a co-habitant with the families of all her little pupils. This is a fact of immense importance. Among these almost savage people, into these houses where at night no one dared go about unarmed, there has come not only to teach, *but to live the very life they live*, a gentlewoman of culture, an educator by profession, who dedicates her time and her life to helping those about her! A true missionary, a moral queen among the people, she may, if she be possessed of sufficient tact and heart, reap an unheard-of harvest of good from her social work.

This house is verily *new;* it would seem a dream impossible of realisation, but it has been tried. It is true that there have been before this attempts made by generous persons to go and live among the poor to civilise them. But such work is not practical, unless the house of the poor is hygienic, making it possible for people of better standards to live there. Nor can such work succeed in its purpose unless some common advantage or interest unites all of the tenants in an effort toward better things.

This tenement is new also because of the pedagogical organisation of the "Children's House." This is not simply a place where the children are kept, not just an *asylum*, but a true school for their education, and its methods are inspired by the rational principles of scientific pedagogy.

The physical development of the children is followed, each child being studied from the anthropological standpoint. Linguistic exercises, a systematic sense-training, and exercises which directly fit the child for the duties of practical life, form the basis of the work done. The teaching is decidedly objective, and presents an unusual richness of didactic material.

It is not possible to speak of all this in detail. I must, however, mention that there already exists in connection with the school a bathroom, where the children may be given hot or cold baths and where they may learn to take a partial bath, hands, face, neck, ears. Wherever possible the Association has provided a piece of ground in which the children may learn to cultivate the vegetables in common use.

It is important that I speak here of the pedagogical progress attained by the "Children's House" as an institution. Those who are conversant with the chief problems of the school know that to-day much attention is given to a great principle, one that is ideal and almost beyond realisation,—the union of the family and the school in the matter of educational aims. But the family is always something far away from the school, and is almost always regarded as rebelling against its ideals. It is a species of phantom upon which the school can never lay its hands. The home is closed not only to pedagogical progress, but often to social progress. We see here for the first time the possibility of realising the long-talked-of pedagogical ideal. We have put *the school within the house*; and this is not all. We have placed it within the house as the *property of the collectivity*, leaving under the eyes of the parents the whole life of the teacher in the accomplishment of her high mission.

This idea of the collective ownership of the school is new and very beautiful and profoundly educational.

The parents know that the "Children's House" is their

property, and is maintained by a portion of the rent they pay. The mothers may go at any hour of the day to watch, to admire, or to meditate upon the life there. It is in every way a continual stimulus to reflection, and a fount of evident blessing and help to their own children. We may say that the mothers *adore* the "Children's House," and the directress. How many delicate and thoughtful attentions these good mothers show the teacher of their little ones! They often leave sweets or flowers upon the sill of the schoolroom window, as a silent token, reverently, almost religiously, given.

And when after three years of such a novitiate, the mothers send their children to the common schools, they will be excellently prepared to co-operate in the work of education, and will have acquired a sentiment, rarely found even among the best classes; namely, the idea that they must *merit* through their own conduct and with their own virtue, the possession of an educated son.

Another advance made by the "Children's Houses" as an institution is related to scientific pedagogy. This branch of pedagogy, heretofore, being based upon the anthropological study of the pupil whom it is to educate, has touched only a few of the positive questions which tend to transform education. For a man is not only a biological but a social product, and the social environment of individuals in the process of education, is the home. Scientific pedagogy will seek in vain to better the new generation if it does not succeed in influencing also the environment within which this new generation grows! I believe, therefore, that in opening the house to the light of new truths, and to the progress of civilisation we have solved the problem of being able to modify directly, the *environment* of the new generation, and have thus made it possible to apply, in a practical way, the fundamental principles of scientific pedagogy.

The "Children's House" marks still another triumph; it is the first step toward the *socialisation of the house*. The inmates find under their own roof the convenience of being able to leave their little ones in a place, not only safe, but where they have every advantage.

And let it be remembered that *all* the mothers in the tenement may enjoy this privilege, going away to their work with easy minds. Until the present time only one class in society might have this advantage. Rich women were able to go about their various occupations and amusements, leaving their children in the hands of a nurse or a governess. To-day the women of the people who live in these remodeled houses, may say, like the great lady, "I have left my son with the governess and the nurse." More than this, they may add, like the princess of the blood, "And the house physician watches over them and directs their sane and sturdy growth." These women, like the most advanced class of English and American mothers, possess a "Biographical Chart," which, filled for the mother by the directress and the doctor, gives her the most practical knowledge of her child's growth and condition.

We are all familiar with the ordinary advantages of the communistic transformation of the general environment. For example, the collective use of railway carriages, of street lights, of the telephone, all these are great advantages. The enormous production of useful articles, brought about by industrial progress, makes possible to all, clean clothes, carpets, curtains, table-delicacies, better tableware, etc. The making of such benefits generally tends to level social caste. All this we have seen in its reality. But the communising of *persons* is new. That the collectivity shall benefit from the services of the servant, the nurse, the teacher—this is a modern ideal.

We have in the "Children's Houses" a demonstration of this ideal which is unique in Italy or elsewhere. Its significance is most profound, for it corresponds to a need of the times. We can no longer say that the convenience of leaving their children takes away from the mother a natural social duty of first importance; namely, that of caring for and educating her tender offspring. No, for to-day the social and economic evolution calls the working-woman to take her place among wage-earners, and takes away from her by force those duties which would be most dear to her! The mother must, in any event, leave her child, and often with the pain of knowing him to be abandoned. The advantages furnished by such institutions are not limited to the labouring classes, but extend also to the general middle-class, many of whom work with the brain. Teachers, professors, often obliged to give private lessons after school hours, frequently leave their children to the care, of some rough and ignorant maid-of-all-work. Indeed, the first announcement of the "Children's House" was followed by a deluge of letters from persons of the better class demanding that these helpful reforms be extended to their dwellings.

We are, then, communising a "maternal function," a feminine duty, within the house. We may see here in this practical act the solving of many of woman's problems which have seemed to many impossible of solution. What then will become of the home, one asks, if the woman goes away from it? The home will be transformed and will assume the functions of the woman.

I believe that in the future of society other forms of communistic life will come.

Take, for example, the infirmary; woman is the natural nurse for the dear ones of her household. But who does not know how often in these days she is obliged to tear herself unwillingly from the bedside of her sick to go to her work? Competition is great, and her absence from her post threatens the tenure of the position from which she draws the means of support. To be able to leave the sick one in a "house-infirmary," to which she may have access any free moments she may have, and where she is at liberty to watch during the night, would be an evident advantage to such a woman.

And how great would be the progress made in the matter of family hygiene, in all that relates to isolation and disinfection! Who does not know the difficulties of a poor family when one child is ill of some contagions disease, and should be isolated from the others? Often such a family may have no kindred or friends in the city to whom the other children may be sent.

Much more distant, but not impossible, is the communal kitchen, where the dinner ordered in the morning is sent at the proper time, by means of a dumb-waiter, to the family dining-room. Indeed, this has been successfully tried in America. Such a reform would be of the greatest advantage to those families of the middle-class who must confide their health and the pleasures of the table to the hands of an ignorant servant who ruins the food. At present, the only alternative in such cases is to go outside the home to some café where a cheap table d'hôte may be had.

Indeed, the transformation of the house must compensate for the loss in the family of the presence of the woman who has become a social wage-earner.

In this way the house will become a centre, drawing into itself all those good things which have hitherto been lacking: schools, public baths, hospitals, etc.

Thus the tendency will be to change the tenement houses, which have been places of vice and peril, into centres of education, of refinement, of comfort. This will be helped if, besides the schools for the children, there may grow up also *clubs* and reading-rooms for the inhabitants, especially for the men, who will find there a way to pass the evening pleasantly and decently. The tenement-club, as possible and as useful in all social classes as is the "Children's House," will do much toward closing the gambling-houses and saloons to the great moral advantage of the people. And I believe that the Association of Good Building will before long establish such clubs in its reformed tenements here in the Quarter of San Lorenzo; clubs where the tenants may find newspapers and books, and where they may hear simple and helpful lectures.

We are, then, very far from the dreaded dissolution of the home and of the family, through the fact that woman has been forced by changed social and economic conditions to give her time and strength to remunerative work. The home itself assumes the gentle feminine attributes of the domestic housewife. The day may come when the tenant, having given to the proprietor of the house a certain sum, shall receive in exchange whatever is necessary to the *comfort* of life; in other words, the administration shall become the *steward* of the family.

The house, thus considered, tends to assume in its evolution a significance more exalted than even the English word "home" expresses. It does not consist of walls alone, though these walls be the pure and shining guardians of that intimacy which is the sacred symbol of the family. The home shall become more than this. It lives! It has a soul. It may be said to embrace its inmates with the tender, consoling arms of woman. It is the giver of moral life, of blessings; it cares for, it educates and feeds the little ones. Within it, the tired workman shall find rest and newness of life. He shall find there the intimate life of the family, and its happiness.

The new woman, like the butterfly come forth from the chrysalis, shall be liberated from all those attributes which once made her desirable to man only as the source of the material blessings of existence. She shall be, like man, an individual, a free human being, a social worker; and, like man, she shall seek blessing and repose within the house, the house which has been reformed and communised.

She shall wish to be loved for herself and not as a giver of comfort and repose. She shall wish a love free from every form of servile labour. The goal of human love is not the egotistical end of assuring its own satisfaction—it is the sublime goal of multiplying the forces of the free spirit, making it almost Divine, and, within such beauty and light, perpetuating the species.

This ideal love is made incarnate by Frederick Nietzsche, in the woman of Zarathustra, who conscientiously wished her son to be better than she. "Why do you desire me?" she asks the man. "Perhaps because of the perils of a solitary life?

"In that case go far from me. I wish the man who has conquered himself, who has made his soul great. I wish the man who has conserved a clean and robust body. I wish the man who desires to unite with me, body and soul, to create a son! A son better, more perfect, stronger, than any created heretofore!"

To better the species consciously, cultivating his own health, his own virtue, this should be the goal of man's married life. It is a sublime concept of which, as yet, few think. And the socialised home of the future, living, provident, kindly; educator and comforter; is the true and worthy home of those human mates who wish to better the species, and to send the race forward triumphant into the eternity of life!

RULES AND REGULATIONS OF THE "CHILDREN'S HOUSES"

- The Roman Association of Good Building hereby establishes within its tenement house number, a "Children's House," in which may be gathered together all children under common school age, belonging to the families of the tenants.
- The chief aim of the "Children's House" is to offer, free of charge, to the children of those parents who are obliged to absent themselves for their work, the personal care which the parents are not able to give.
- In the "Children's House" attention is given to the education, the health, the physical and moral development of the children. This work is carried on in a way suited to the age of the children.
- There shall be connected with the "Children's House" a Directress, a Physician, and a Caretaker.
- The programme and hours of the "Children's House" shall be fixed by the Directress.
- There may be admitted to the "Children's House" all the children in the tenement between the ages of three and seven.
- The parents who wish to avail themselves of the advantages of the "Children's House" pay nothing. They must, however, assume these binding obligations:

  (a) To send their children to the "Children's House" at the appointed time, clean in body and clothing, and provided with a suitable apron.

  (b) To show the greatest respect and deference toward the Directress and toward all persons connected with the "Children's House," and to co-operate with the Directress herself in the education of the

Once a week, at least, the mothers may talk with the Directress, giving her information concerning the home life of the child, and receiving helpful advice from her.

There shall be expelled from the "Children's House":

(a) Those children who present themselves unwashed, or in soiled clothing.
(b) Those who show themselves to be incorrigible.
(c) Those whose parents fail in respect to the persons connected with the "Children's House," or who destroy through bad conduct the educational work of the institution.

NOTE

1. Dr. Montessori no longer directs the work in the Casa dei Bambini in the Quarter of San Lorenzo.

4

Pedagogical Methods used in the "Children's Houses"

As soon as I knew that I had at my disposal a class of little children, it was my wish to make of this school a field for scientific experimental pedagogy and child psychology. I started with a view in which Wundt concurs; namely, that child psychology does not exist. Indeed, experimental researches in regard to childhood, as, for example, those of Preyer and Baldwin, have been made upon not more than two or three subjects, children of the investigators. Moreover, the instruments of psychometry must be greatly modified and simplified before they can be used with children, who do not lend themselves passively as subjects for experimentation. Child psychology can be established only through the method of external observation. We must renounce all idea of making any record of internal states, which can be revealed only by the introspection of the subject himself. The instruments of psychometric research, as applied to pedagogy, have up to the present time been limited to the esthesiometric phase of the study.

My intention was to keep in touch with the researches of others, but to make myself independent of them, proceeding to my work without preconceptions of any kind. I retained as the only essential, the affirmation, or, rather, the definition of Wundt, that "all methods of experimental psychology may be reduced to one; namely, carefully recorded observation of the subject."

Treating of children, another factor must necessarily intervene: the study of the development. Here too, I retained the same general criterion, but without clinging to any dogma about the activity of the child according to age.

ANTHROPOLOGICAL CONSIDERATION

In regard to physical development, my first thought was given to the regulating of anthropometric observations, and to the selection of the most important observations to be made.

I designed an anthropometer provided with the metric scale, varying between .50 metre and 1.50 metres. A small stool, 30 centimetres high, could be placed upon the floor of the anthropometer for measurements taken in a sitting position. I now advise making the anthropometer with a platform on either side of the pole bearing the scale, so that on one side the total stature can be measured, and on the other the height of the body when seated. In the second case, the zero is indicated at 30 centimetres; that is, it corresponds to the seat of the stool, which is fixed. The indicators on the vertical post are independent one of the other and this makes it possible to measure two children at the same time. In this way the inconvenience and waste of time caused by having to move the seat about, is obviated, and also the trouble of having to calculate the difference in the metric scale.

Having thus facilitated the technique of the researches, I decided to take the measurements of the children's stature, seated and standing, every month, and in order to have these regulated as exactly as possible in their relation to development, and also to give greater regularity to the research work of the teacher, I made a rule that the measurements should be taken on the day on which the child completed each month of his age. For this purpose I designed a register arranged on the following plan:

Day of month	SEPTEMBER		OCTOBER		
	Stature		Stature		Etc.
	Standing	Sitting	Standing	Sitting	
1					
2					
3					
4					
Etc.					

The spaces opposite each number are used to register the name of the child born on that day of the month. Thus the teacher knows which scholars she must measure on the days which are marked on the calendar, and she fills in his measurements to correspond with the month in which he was born. In this way a most exact registration can be arrived at without having the teacher feel that she is overburdened, or fatigued.

With regard to the weight of the child, I have arranged that it shall be taken every week on a pair of scales which I have placed in the dressing-room where the children are given their bath. According to the day on which the child is born, Monday, Tuesday, Wednesday, etc., we have him weighed when he is ready to take a bath. Thus the children's baths (no small matter when we consider a class of fifty) are sub-divided into seven days, and from three to five children go to the bath every day. Certainly, theoretically, a daily bath would be desirable, but in order to manage this a large bath or a number of small ones would be necessary, so that a good many children could be bathed at once. Even a weekly bath entails many difficulties, and sometimes has to be given up. In any case, I have distributed the taking of the weight in the order stated with the intention of thus arranging for and making sure of periodical baths.[1]

The form here given shows the register which we use in recording the weight of the children. Every page of the register corresponds to a month.

It seems to me that the anthropological measurements, the

taking and recording of which I have just described, should be the only ones with which the schoolmistress need occupy herself; and, therefore, the only ones which should be taken actually within the school. It is my plan that other measurements should be taken by a physician, who either is, or is preparing to be, a specialist in infant anthropology. In the meantime, I take these special measurements myself.

	SEPTEMBER			
	1st week Lbs.	2nd week Lbs.	3rd week Lbs.	4th week Lbs.
Monday				
Tuesday				
Wednesday				
Etc.				

The examination made by the physician must necessarily be complex, and to facilitate and regulate the taking of these measurements I have designed and had printed biological charts, of which I here give an example.

Number .... *Date*...........................
Name and Surname.. *Age* ....
Name of Parents .... *Mother's Age* .... *Father's Age*.................
Professions ....
Details of Ilerditary Antecedents ....
....
....
....
Personel Antecedents ....
....
....
....

ANTHROPOLOGICAL NOTES

Standing Stature	Weight	Chess Mets.	Belled Stature	Index of Stature*	Penteral Index*	HEAD			
						Clr.	Dis. Front to Back	Dis. Across	Co-phalic Index

Physical Constitution ....
Condition of Muscles ....
Colour of Skin ....
Colour of Hair ....

NOTES

....
....
....
....

As will be seen, these charts are very simple. I made them so because I wished the doctor and the schoolmistress to be able to use them freely and independently.

By this method the anthropometrical records are arranged in an orderly way, while the simplicity of the mechanism, and the clearness of the charts, guarantee the making of such observations as I have considered fundamental. Referring to the physician's biographical chart, I advise that once a year the following measurements be taken: Circumference of the head; the two greater diameters of the head; the circumference of the chest; and the cephalic, ponderal, and stature indices. Further information concerning the selection of these measurements may be found in my treatise, "Antropologia Pedagogica." The physician is asked to take these measurements during the week, or at least within the month, in which the child completes a year of his age, and, if it is possible, on the birthday itself. In this way the task of the physician will also be made easier, because of its regularity. We have, at the most, fifty children in each of our schools, and the birthdays of these scattered over the 365 days of the year make it possible for the physician to take his measurements from time to time, so that the burden of his work is not heavy. It is the duty of the teacher to inform the doctor of the birthdays of the children.

The taking of these anthropometrical measurements has also an educational side to it, for the pupils, when they leave the "Children's House," know how to answer with clearness and certainty the following questions:

On what day of the week were you born?

On what day of the month?

When does your birthday come?

And with all this they will have acquired habits of order, and, above all, they will have formed the habit of observing themselves. Indeed, I may say here, that the children take a great pleasure in being measured; at the first glance of the teacher and at the word stature, the child begins instantly to take off his shoes, laughing and running to place himself upon the platform of the anthropometer; placing himself of his own accord in the normal position so perfectly that the teacher needs only to arrange the indicator and read the result.

Aside from the measurements which the physician takes with the ordinary instruments (calipers and metal yard measure), he makes observations upon the children's colouring, condition of their muscles, state of their lymphatic glands, the condition of the blood, etc. He notices any malformations; describes any pathological conditions with care (any tendency to rickets, infant paralysis, defective sight, etc.). This objective study of the child will guide the doctor when he finds it advisable to talk with the parents concerning its condition. Following this, when the doctor has found it desirable, he makes a thorough, sanitary inspection of the home of the child, prescribing necessary treatment and eventually doing away with such troubles as eczema, inflammation of the ear, feverish conditions, intestinal disturbances, etc. This careful following of the case in hand is greatly assisted by the existence of the *dispensary within the house*, which makes feasible direct treatment and continual observation.

I have found that the usual question asked patients who present themselves at the clinics, are not adapted for use in our schools, as the members of the families living in these tenements are for the greater part perfectly normal.

I therefore encourage the directress of the school togather from her conversations with the mothers information of a more practical sort. She informs herself as to the education of the parents, their habits, the wages earned, the money spent for household purposes, etc., and from all this she outlines a history of each family, much on the order of those used by Le-Play. This method is, of course, practical only where the directress lives among the families of her scholars.

In every case, however, the physician's advice to the mothers concerning the hygienic care of each particular child, as well as his directions concerning hygiene in general, will prove most helpful. The directress should act as the go-between in these matters, since she is in the confidence of the mothers, and since from her, such advice comes naturally.

ENVIRONMENT: SCHOOLROOM FURNISHINGS

The method of *observation* must undoubtedly include the *methodical observation* of the morphological growth of the pupils. But let me repeat that, while this element necessarily enters, it is not upon this particular kind of observation that the method is established.

The method of observation is established upon one fundamental base—*the liberty of the pupils in their spontaneous manifestations.*

With this in view, I first turned my attention to the question of environment, and this, of course, included the furnishing of the schoolroom. In considering an ample playground with space for a garden as an important part of this school environment, I am not suggesting anything new.

The novelty lies, perhaps, in my idea for the use of this open-air space, which is to be in direct communication with the schoolroom, so that the children may be free to go and come as they like, throughout the entire day. I shall speak of this more fully later on.

The principal modification in the matter of school furnishings is the abolition of desks, and benches or stationary chairs. I have had tables made with wide, solid, octagonal legs, spreading in such a way that the tables are at the same time solidly firm and very light, so light, indeed, that two four-year-old children can easily carry them about. These tables are rectangular and sufficiently large to accommodate two children on the long side, there being room for three if they sit rather close together. There are smaller tables at which one child may work alone.

I also designed and had manufactured little chairs. My first plan for these was to have them cane seated, but experience has shown the wear on these to be so great, that I now have chairs made entirely of wood. These are very light and of an attractive shape. In addition to these, I have in each schoolroom a number of comfortable little armchairs, some of wood and some of wicker.

Another piece of our school furniture consists of a little washstand, so low that it can be used by even a three-year-old child. This is painted with a white waterproof enamel and, besides the broad, upper and lower shelves which hold the little white enameled basins and pitchers, there are small side shelves for the soap-dishes, nail-brushes, towels, etc. There is also a receptacle into which the basins may be emptied. Wherever possible, a small cupboard provides each child with a space where he may keep his own soap, nail-brush, tooth-brush, etc.

In each of our schoolrooms we have provided a series of

long low cupboards, especially designed for the reception of the didactic materials. The doors of these cupboards open easily, and the care of the materials is confided to the children. The tops of these cases furnish room for potted plants, small aquariums, or for the various toys with which the children are allowed to play freely. We have ample blackboard space, and these boards are so hung as to be easily used by the smallest child. Each blackboard is provided with a small case in which are kept the chalk, and the white cloths which we use instead of the ordinary erasers.

Above the blackboards are hung attractive pictures, chosen carefully, representing simple scenes in which children would naturally be interested. Among the pictures in our "Children's Houses" in Rome we have hung a copy of Raphael's "Madonna della Seggiola," and this picture we have chosen as the emblem of the "Children's Houses." For indeed, these "Children's Houses" represent not only social progress, but universal human progress, and are closely related to the elevation of the idea of motherhood, to the progress of woman and to the protection of her offspring. In this beautiful conception, Raphael has not only shown us the Madonna as a Divine Mother holding in her arms the babe who is greater than she, but by the side of this symbol of all motherhood, he has placed the figure of St. John, who represents humanity. So in Raphael's picture we see humanity rendering homage to maternity,—maternity, the sublime fact in the definite triumph of humanity. In addition to this beautiful symbolism, the picture has a value as being one of the greatest works of art of Italy's greatest artist. And if the day shall come when the "Children's Houses" shall be established throughout the world, it is our wish that this picture of Raphael's shall have its place in each of the schools, speaking eloquently of the country in which they originated.

The children, of course, cannot comprehend the symbolic significance of the "Madonna of the Chair," but they will see something more beautiful than that which they feel in more ordinary pictures, in which they see mother, father, and children. And the constant companionship with this picture will awaken in their heart a religious impression.

This, then, is the environment which I have selected for the children we wish to educate.

I know the first objection which will present itself to the minds of persons accustomed to the old-time methods of discipline;—the children in these schools, moving about, will overturn the little tables and chairs, producing noise and disorder; but this is a prejudice which has long existed in the minds of those dealing with little children, and for which there is no real foundation.

Swaddling clothes have for many centuries been considered necessary to the new-born babe, walking-chairs to the child who is learning to walk. So in the school, we still believe it necessary to have heavy desks and chairs fastened to the floor. All these things are based upon the idea that the child should grow in immobility, and upon the strange prejudice that, in order to execute any educational movement, we must maintain a special position of the body;—as we believe that we must assume a special position when we are about to pray.

Our little tables and our various types of chairs are all light and easily transported, and we permit the child to *select* the position which he finds most comfortable. He can *make himself comfortable* as well as seat himself in his own place. And this freedom is not only an external sign of liberty, but a means of education. If by an awkward movement a child upsets a chair, which falls noisily to the floor, he will have an evident proof of his own incapacity; the same movement had it taken place amid stationary benches would have passed unnoticed by him. Thus the child has some means by which he can correct himself, and having done so he will have before him the actual proof of the power he has gained: the little tables and chairs remain firm and silent each in its own place. It is plainly seen that the *child has learned to command his movements*.

In the old method, the proof of discipline attained lay in a fact entirely contrary to this; that is, in the immobility and silence of the child himself. Immobility and silence which *hindered* the child from learning to move with grace and with discernment, and left him so untrained, that, when he found himself in an environment where the benches and chairs were not nailed to the floor, he was not able to move about without overturning the lighter pieces of furniture. In the "Children's Houses" the child will not only learn to move gracefully and properly, but will come to understand the reason for such deportment. The ability to move which he acquires here will be of use to him all his life. While he is still a child, he becomes capable of conducting himself correctly, and yet, with perfect freedom.

The Directress of the Casa dei Bambini at Milan constructed under one of the windows a long, narrow shelf upon which she placed the little tables containing the metal geometric forms used in the first lessons in design. But the shelf was too narrow, and it often happened that the children in selecting the pieces which they wished to use would allow one of the little tables to fall to the floor, thus upsetting with great noise all the metal pieces which it held. The directress intended to have the shelf changed, but the carpenter was slow in coming, and while waiting for him she discovered that the children had learned to handle these materials so carefully that in spite of the narrow and sloping shelf, the little tables no longer fell to the floor.

The children, by carefully directing their movements, had overcome the defect in this piece of furniture. The simplicity or imperfection of external objects often serves to develop the *activity* and the dexterity of the pupils. This has been one of the surprises of our method as applied in the "Children's Houses."

It all seems very logical, and now that it has been actually tried and put into words, it will no doubt seem to everyone as simple as the egg of Christopher Columbus.

NOTE

1. Incidentally, I may say, that I have invented a means of bathing children contemporaneously, without having a large bath. In order to manage this, I thought of having a long trough with supports at the bottom, on which small, separate tubs could rest, with rather large holes in the bottom. The little tubs are filled from the large trough, into which the water runs and then goes into all the little tubs together, by the law of the levelling of liquids, going through

the holes in the bottom. When the water is settled, it does not pass from tub to tub, and the children will each have their own bath. The emptying of the trough brings with it the simultaneous emptying of the little tubs, which being of light metal, will be easily moved from the bottom of the big tub, in order to clean it. It is not difficult to imagine arranging a cork for the hole at the bottom. These are only projects for the future!

5
Discipline

The pedagogical method of *observation* has for its base the *liberty* of the child; and *liberty is activity*.

Discipline must come through liberty. Here is a great principle which is difficult for followers of common-school methods to understand. How shall one obtain *discipline* in a class of free children? Certainly in our system, we have a concept of discipline very different from that commonly accepted. If discipline is founded upon liberty, the discipline itself must necessarily be *active*. We do not consider an individual disciplined only when he has been rendered as artificially silent as a mute and as immovable as a paralytic. He is an individual *annihilated*, not *disciplined*.

We call an individual disciplined when he is master of himself, and can, therefore, regulate his own conduct when it shall be necessary to follow some rule of life. Such a concept of *active discipline* is not easy either to comprehend or to apply. But certainly it contains a great *educational* principle, very different from the old-time absolute and undiscussed coercion to immobility.

A special technique is necessary to the teacher who is to lead the child along such a path of discipline, if she is to make it possible for him to continue in this way all his life, advancing indefinitely toward perfect self-mastery. Since the child now learns to *move* rather than to *sit still*, he prepares himself not for the school, but for life; for he becomes able, through habit and through practice, to perform easily and correctly the simple acts of social or community life. The discipline to which the child habituates himself here is, in its character, not limited to the school environment but extends to society.

The liberty of the child should have as its *limit* the collective interest; as its *form*, what we universally consider good breeding. We must, therefore, check in the child whatever offends or annoys others, or whatever tends toward rough or ill-bred acts. But all the rest,—every manifestation having a useful scope,—whatever it be, and under whatever form it expresses itself, must not only be permitted, but must be *observed* by the teacher. Here lies the essential point; from her scientific preparation, the teacher must bring not only the capacity, but the desire, to observe natural phenomena. In our system, she must become a passive, much more than an active, influence, and her passivity shall be composed of anxious scientific curiosity, and of absolute *respect* for the phenomenon which she wishes to observe. The teacher must understand and *feel* her position of *observer*: the *activity* must lie in the *phenomenon*.

Such principles assuredly have a place in schools for little children who are exhibiting the first psychic manifestations of their lives. We cannot know the consequences of suffocating a *spontaneous action* at the time when the child is just beginning to be active: perhaps we suffocate *life itself*. Humanity shows itself in all its intellectual splendour during this tender age as the sun shows itself at the dawn, and the flower in the first unfolding of the petals; and we must *respect* religiously, reverently, these first indications of individuality. If any educational act is to be efficacious, it will be only that which tends to *help* toward the complete unfolding of this life. To be thus helpful it is necessary rigorously to avoid the *arrest of spontaneous movements and the imposition of arbitrary tasks*. It is of course understood, that here we do not speak of useless or dangerous acts, for these must be *suppressed, destroyed*.

Actual training and practice are necessary to fit for this method teachers who have not been prepared for scientific observation, and such training is especially necessary to those who have been accustomed to the old domineering methods of the common school. My experiences in training teachers for the work in my schools did much to convince me of the great distance between these methods and those. Even an intelligent teacher, who understands the principle, finds much difficulty in putting it into practice. She can not understand that her new task is apparently *passive*, like that of the astronomer who sits immovable before the telescope while the worlds whirl through space. This idea, that *life acts of itself*, and that in order to study it, to divine its secrets or to direct its activity, it is necessary to observe it and to understand it without intervening—this idea, I say, is very difficult for anyone to *assimilate* and *to put into practice*.

The teacher has too thoroughly learned to be the one free activity of the school; it has for too long been virtually her duty to suffocate the activity of her pupils. When in the first days in one of the "Children's Houses" she does not obtain order and silence, she looks about her embarrassed as if asking the public to excuse her, and calling upon those present to testify to her innocence. In vain do we repeat to her that the disorder of the first moment is necessary. And finally, when we oblige her to do nothing but *watch*, she asks if she had not better resign, since she is no longer a teacher.

But when she begins to find it her duty to discern which are the acts to hinder and which are those to observe, the teacher of the old school feels a great void within herself and begins to ask if she will not be inferior to her new task. In fact, she who is not prepared finds herself for a long time abashed and impotent; whereas the broader the teacher's scientific culture and practice in experimental psychology, the sooner will come for her the marvel of unfolding life, and her interest in it.

Notari, in his novel, "My Millionaire Uncle," which is a criticism of modern customs, gives with that quality of vividness which is peculiar to him, a most eloquent example of the old-time methods of discipline. The "uncle" when a child was guilty of such a number of disorderly acts that he practically upset the whole town, and in desperation he was confined in a school.

Here "Fufu," as he was called, experiences his first wish to be kind, and feels the first moving of his soul when he is near to the pretty little Fufetta, and learns that she is hungry and has no luncheon.

"He glanced around, looked at Fufetta, rose, took his little lunch basket, and without saying a word placed it in her lap.

"Then he ran away from her, and, without knowing why he did so, hung his head and burst into tears.

"My uncle did not know how to explain to himself the reason for this sudden outburst.

"He had seen for the first time two kind eyes full of sad tears, and he had felt moved within himself, and at the same time a great shame had rushed over him; the shame of eating near to one who had nothing to eat.

"Not knowing how to express the impulse of his heart, nor what to say in asking her to accept the offer of his little basket, nor how to invent an excuse to justify his offering it to her, he remained the victim of this first deep movement of his little soul.

"Fufetta, all confused, ran to him quickly. With great gentleness she drew away the arm in which he had hidden his face.

"'Do not cry, Fufu,' she said to him softly, almost as if pleading with him. She might have been speaking to her beloved rag doll, so motherly and intent was her little face, and so full of gentle authority, her manner.

"Then the little girl kissed him, and my uncle yielding to the influence which had filled his heart, put his arms around her neck, and, still silent and sobbing, kissed her in return. At last, sighing deeply, he wiped from his face and eyes the damp traces of his emotion, and smiled again.

"A strident voice called out from the other end of the courtyard:

"'Here, here, you two down there—be quick with you; inside, both of you!'

"It was the teacher, the guardian. She crushed that first

gentle stirring in the soul of a rebel with the same blind brutality that she would have used toward two children engaged in a fight.

"It was the time for all to go back into the school—and everybody had to obey the rule."

Thus I saw my teachers act in the first days of my practice school in the "Children's Houses." They almost involuntarily recalled the children to immobility without *observing* and *distinguishing* the nature of the movements they repressed. There was, for example, a little girl who gathered her companions about her and then, in the midst of them, began to talk and gesticulate. The teacher at once ran to her, took hold of her arms, and told her to be still; but I, observing the child, saw that she was playing at being teacher or mother to the others, and teaching them the morning prayer, the invocation to the saints, and the sign of the cross: she already showed herself as a *director*. Another child, who continually made disorganised and misdirected movements, and who was considered abnormal, one day, with an expression of intense attention, set about moving the tables. Instantly they were upon him to make him stand still because he made too much noise. Yet this was one of the *first manifestations*, in this child, of *movements* that were *co-ordinated* and *directed toward a useful end*, and it was therefore an action that should have been respected. In fact, after this the child began to be quiet and happy like the others whenever he had any small objects to move about and to arrange upon his desk.

It often happened that while the directress replaced in the boxes various materials that had been used, a child would draw near, picking up the objects, with the evident desire of imitating the teacher. The first impulse was to send the child back to her place with the remark, "Let it alone; go to your seat." Yet the child expressed by this act a desire to be useful; the time, with her, was ripe for a lesson in order.

One day, the children had gathered themselves, laughing and talking, into a circle about a basin of water containing some floating toys. We had in the school a little boy barely two and a half years old. He had been left outside the circle, alone, and it was easy to see that he was filled with intense curiosity. I watched him from a distance with great interest; he first drew near to the other children and tried to force his way among them, but he was not strong enough to do this, and he then stood looking about him. The expression of thought on his little face was intensely interesting. I wish that I had had a camera so that I might have photographed him. His eye lighted upon a little chair, and evidently he made up his mind to place it behind the group of children and then to climb up on it. He began to move toward the chair, his face illuminated with hope, but at that moment the teacher seized him brutally (or, perhaps, she would have said, gently) in her arms, and lifting him up above the heads of the other children showed him the basin of water, saying, "Come, poor little one, you shall see too!"

Undoubtedly the child, seeing the floating toys, did not experience the joy that he was about to feel through conquering the obstacle with his own force. The sight of those objects could be of no advantage to him, while his intelligent efforts would have developed his inner powers.

The teacher *hindered* the child, in this case, from educating himself, without giving him any compensating good in return. The little fellow had been about to feel himself a conqueror, and he found himself held within two imprisoning arms, impotent. The expression of joy, anxiety, and hope, which had interested me so much faded from his face and left on it the stupid expression of the child who knows that others will act for him.

When the teachers were weary of my observations, they began to allow the children to do whatever they pleased. I saw children with their feet on the tables, or with their fingers in their noses, and no intervention was made to correct them. I saw others push their companions, and I saw dawn in the faces of these an expression of violence; and not the slightest attention on the part of the teacher. Then I had to intervene to show with what absolute rigour it is necessary to hinder, and little by little suppress, all those things which we must not do, so that the child may come to discern clearly between good and evil.

If discipline is to be lasting, its foundations must be laid in this way and these first days are the most difficult for the directress. The first idea that the child must acquire, in order to be actively disciplined, is that of the difference between *good* and *evil*; and the task of the educator lies in seeing that the child does not confound *good* with *immobility*, and *evil* with *activity*, as often happens in the case of the old-time discipline. And all this because our aim is to discipline *for activity, for work, for good*; not for *immobility*, not for *passivity*, not for *obedience*.

A room in which all the children move about usefully, intelligently, and voluntarily, without committing any rough or rude act, would seem to me a classroom very well disciplined indeed.

To seat the children in rows, as in the common schools, to assign to each little one a place, and to propose that they shall sit thus quietly observant of the order of the whole class as an assemblage—this can be attained later, as *the starting place* of *collective education*. For also, in life, it sometimes happens that we must all remain seated and quiet; when, for example, we attend a concert or a lecture. And we know that even to us, as grown people, this costs no little sacrifice.

If we can, when we have established individual discipline, arrange the children, sending each one to *his own place, in order*, trying to make them understand the idea that thus placed they look well, and that it is a *good thing* to be thus placed in order, that it is a *good and pleasing arrangement in the room*, this ordered and tranquil adjustment of theirs—then their remaining in their places, *quiet* and *silent*, is the result of a species of *lesson*, not an *imposition*. To make them understand the idea, without calling their attention too forcibly to the practice, to have them *assimilate a principle of collective order*—that is the important thing.

If, after they have understood this idea, they rise, speak, change to another place, they no longer do this without knowing and without thinking, but they do it because they *wish* to rise, to speak, etc.; that is, from that *state of repose and order*, well understood, they depart in order to undertake *some voluntary action*; and knowing that there are actions which are prohibited, this will give them a new impulse to remember to discriminate between good and evil.

The movements of the children from the state of order become always more co-ordinated and perfect with the passing of the days; in fact, they learn to reflect upon their own acts. Now (with the idea of order understood by the children) the observation of the way in which the children pass from the first disordered movements to those which are spontaneous and ordered—this is the book of the teacher; this is the book which must inspire her actions; it is the only one in which she must read and study if she is to become a real educator.

For the child with such exercises makes, to a certain extent, a selection of his own *tendencies*, which were at first confused in the unconscious disorder of his movements. It is remarkable how clearly *individual differences* show themselves, if we proceed in this way; the child, conscious and free, *reveals himself*.

There are those who remain quietly in their seats, apathetic, or drowsy; others who leave their places to quarrel, to fight, or to overturn the various blocks and toys, and then there are those others who set out to fulfil a definite and determined act—moving a chair to some particular spot and sitting down in it, moving one of the unused tables and arranging upon it the game they wish to play.

Our idea of liberty for the child cannot be the simple concept of liberty we use in the observation of plants, insects, etc.

The child, because of the peculiar characteristics of helplessness with which he is born, and because of his qualities as a social individual is circumscribed by *bonds* which *limit* his activity.

An educational method that shall have *liberty* as its basis must intervene to help the child to a conquest of these various obstacles. In other words, his training must be such as shall help him to diminish, in a rational manner, the *social bonds*, which limit his activity.

Little by little, as the child grows in such an atmosphere, his spontaneous manifestations will become more *clear, with the clearness of truth*, revealing his nature. For all these reasons, the first form of educational intervention must tend to lead the child toward independence.

INDEPENDENCE

No one can be free unless he is independent: therefore, the first, active manifestations of the child's individual liberty must be so guided that through this activity he may arrive at independence. Little children, from the moment in which they are weaned, are making their way toward independence.

What is a weaned child? In reality it is a child that has become independent of the mother's breast. Instead of this one source of nourishment he will find various kinds of food; for him the means of existence are multiplied, and he can to some extent make a selection of his food, whereas he was at first limited absolutely to one form of nourishment.

Nevertheless, he is still dependent, since he is not yet able to walk, and cannot wash and dress himself, and since he is not yet able to *ask* for things in a language which is clear and easily understood. He is still in this period to a great extent the *slave* of everyone. By the age of three, however, the child should have been able to render himself to a great extent *independent* and free.

That we have not yet thoroughly assimilated the highest concept of the term *independence*, is due to the fact that the social form in which we live is still *servile*. In an age of civilisation where servants exist, the concept of that *form of life* which is *independence* cannot take root or develop freely. Even so in the time of slavery, the concept of liberty was distorted and darkened.

Our servants are not our dependents, rather it is we who are dependent upon them.

It is not possible to accept universally as a part of our social structure such a deep human error without feeling the general effects of it in the form of moral inferiority. We often believe ourselves to be independent simply because no one commands us, and because we command others; but the nobleman who needs to call a servant to his aid is really a dependent through his own inferiority. The paralytic who cannot take off his boots because of a pathological fact, and the prince who dare not take them off because of a social fact, are in reality reduced to the same condition.

Any nation that accepts the idea of servitude and believes that it is an advantage for man to be served by man, admits servility as an instinct, and indeed we all too easily lend ourselves to *obsequious service*, giving to it such complimentary names as *courtesy, politeness, charity*.

In reality, *he who is served is limited* in his independence. This concept will be the foundation of the dignity of the man of the future; "I do not wish to be served, *because* I am not an impotent." And this idea must be gained before men can feel themselves to be really free.

Any pedagogical action, if it is to be efficacious in the training of little children, must tend to *help* the children to advance upon this road of independence. We must help them to learn to walk without assistance, to run, to go up and down stairs, to lift up fallen objects, to dress and undress themselves, to bathe themselves, to speak distinctly, and to express their own needs clearly. We must give such help as shall make it possible for children to achieve the satisfaction of their own individual aims and desires. All this is a part of education for independence.

We habitually *serve* children; and this is not only an act of servility toward them, but it is dangerous, since it tends to suffocate their useful, spontaneous activity. We are inclined to believe that children are like puppets, and we wash them and feed them as if they were dolls. We do not stop to think that the child *who does not do, does not know how to do*. He must, nevertheless, do these things, and nature has furnished him with the physical means for carrying on these various activities, and with the intellectual means for learning how to do them. And our duty toward him is, in every case, that of *helping him* to make a conquest of such useful acts as nature intended he should perform for himself. The mother who feeds her child without making the least effort to teach him to hold the spoon for himself and to try to find his mouth with it, and who does not at least eat herself, inviting the child to look and see how she does it, is not a good mother. She offends the fundamental human dignity of her son,—she treats him as if he were a doll, when he is, instead, a man confided by nature to her care.

Who does not know that to *teach* a child to feed himself, to wash and dress himself, is a much more tedious and difficult work, calling for infinitely greater patience, than feeding, washing and dressing the child one's self? But the former is the work of an educator, the latter is the easy and inferior work of a servant. Not only is it easier for the mother, but it is very dangerous for the child, since it doses the way and puts obstacles in the path of the life which is developing.

The ultimate consequences of such an attitude on the part of the parent may be very serious indeed. The grand gentleman who has too many servants not only grows constantly more and more dependent upon them, until he is, finally, actually their slave, but his muscles grow weak through inactivity and finally lose their natural capacity for action. The mind of one who does not work for that which he needs, but commands it from others, grows heavy and sluggish. If such a man should some day awaken to the fact of his inferior position and should wish to regain once more his own independence, he would find that he had no longer the force to do so. These dangers should be presented to the parents of the privileged social classes, if their children are to use independently and for right the special power which is theirs. Needless help is an actual hindrance to the development of natural forces.

Oriental women wear trousers, it is true, and European

women, petticoats; but the former, even more than the latter, are taught as a part of their education the art of *not moving*. Such an attitude toward woman leads to the fact that man works not only for himself, but for woman. And the woman wastes her natural strength and activity and languishes in slavery. She is not only maintained and served, she is, besides, diminished, belittled, in that individuality which is hers by right of her existence as a human being. As an individual member of society, she is a cypher. She is rendered deficient in all those powers and resources which tend to the preservation of life. Let me illustrate this:

A carriage containing a father, mother, and child, is going along a country road. An armed brigand stops the carriage with the well-known phrase, "Your money or your life." Placed in this situation, the three persons in the carriage act in very different ways. The man, who is a trained marksman, and who is armed with a revolver, promptly draws, and confronts the assassin. The boy, armed only with the freedom and lightness of his own legs, cries out and betakes himself to flight. The woman, who is not armed in any way whatever, neither artificially nor naturally (since her limbs, not trained for activity, are hampered by her skirts), gives a frightened gasp, and sinks down unconscious.

These three diverse reactions are in close relation to the state of liberty and independence of each of the three individuals. The swooning woman is she whose cloak is carried for her by attentive cavaliers, who are quick to pick up any fallen object that she may be spared all exertion.

The peril of servilism and dependence lies not only in that "useless consuming of life," which leads to helplessness, but in the development of individual traits which indicate all too plainly a regrettable perversion and degeneration of the normal man. I refer to the domineering and tyrannical behaviour with examples of which we are all only too familiar. The domineering habit develops side by side with helplessness. It is the outward sign of the state of feeling of him who conquers through the work of others. Thus it often happens that the master is a tyrant toward his servant. It is the spirit of the task-master toward the slave.

Let us picture to ourselves a clever and proficient workman, capable, not only of producing much and perfect work, but of giving advice in his workshop, because of his ability to control and direct the general activity of the environment in which he works. The man who is thus master of his environment will be able to smile before the anger of others, showing that great mastery of himself which comes from consciousness of his ability to do things. We should not, however, be in the least surprised to know that in his home this capable workman scolded his wife if the soup was not to his taste, or not ready at the appointed time. In his home, he is no longer the capable workman; the skilled workman here is the wife, who serves him and prepares his food for him. He is a serene and pleasant man where he is powerful through being efficient, but is domineering where he is served. Perhaps if he should learn how to prepare his soup he might become a perfect man! The man who, through his own efforts, is able to perform all the actions necessary for his comfort and development in life, conquers himself, and in doing so multiplies his abilities and perfects himself as an individual.

We must make of the future generation, *powerful men*, and by that we mean men who are independent and free.

ABOLITION OF PRIZES AND OF EXTERNAL FORMS OF PUNISHMENT

Once we have accepted and established such principles, the abolition of prizes and external forms of punishment will follow naturally. Man, disciplined through liberty, begins to desire the true and only prize which will never belittle or disappoint him,—the birth of human power and liberty within that inner life of his from which his activities must spring.

In my own experience I have often marvelled to see how true this is. During our first months in the "Children's Houses," the teachers had not yet learned to put into practice the pedagogical principles of liberty and discipline. One of them, especially, busied herself, when I was absent, in *remedying* my ideas by introducing a few of those methods to which she had been accustomed. So, one day when I came in unexpectedly, I found one of the most intelligent of the children wearing a large Greek cross of silver, hung from his neck by a fine piece of white ribbon, while another child was seated in an armchair which had been conspicuously placed in the middle of the room.

The first child had been rewarded, the second was being punished. The teacher, at least while I was present, did not interfere in any way, and the situation remained as I had found it. I held my peace, and placed myself where I might observe quietly.

The child with the cross was moving back and forth, carrying the objects with which he had been working, from his table to that of the teacher, and bringing others in their place. He was busy and happy. As he went back and forth he passed by the armchair of the child who was being punished. The silver cross slipped from his neck and fell to the floor, and the child in the armchair picked it up, dangled it on its white ribbon, looking at it from all sides, and then said to his companion: "Do you see what you have dropped?" The child turned and looked at the trinket with an air of indifference; his expression seemed to say; "Don't interrupt me," his voice replied "I don't care." "Don't you care, really?" said the punished one calmly. "Then I will put it on myself." And the other replied, "Oh, yes, put it on," in a tone that seemed to add, "and leave me in peace!"

The boy in the armchair carefully arranged the ribbon so that the cross lay upon the front of his pink apron where he could admire its brightness and its pretty form, then he settled himself more comfortably in his little chair and rested his arms with evident pleasure upon the arms of the chair. The affair remained thus, and was quite just. The dangling cross could satisfy the child who was being punished, but not the active child, content and happy with his work.

One day I took with me on a visit to another of the "Children's Houses" a lady who praised the children highly and who, opening a box she had brought, showed them a number of shining medals, each tied with a bright red ribbon. "The mistress," she said "will put these on the breasts of those children who are the cleverest and the best."

As I was under no obligation to instruct this visitor in my methods, I kept silence, and the teacher took the box. At that moment, a most intelligent little boy of four, who was seated quietly at one of the little tables, wrinkled his forehead in an act of protest and cried out over and over again;—"Not to the boys, though, not to the boys!"

What a revelation! This little fellow already knew that he stood among the best and strongest of his class, although no one had ever revealed this fact to him, and he did not wish to be offended by this prize. Not knowing how to defend his dignity, he invoked the superior quality of his masculinity!

As to punishments, we have many times come in contact with children who disturbed the others without paying any attention to our corrections. Such children were at once examined by the physician. When the case proved to be that of a normal child, we placed one of the little tables in a corner of the room, and in this way isolated the child; having him sit in a comfortable little armchair, so placed that he might see his companions at work, and giving him those games and toys to which he was most attracted. This isolation almost always succeeded in calming the child; from his position he could see the entire assembly of his companions, and the way in which they carried on their work was an *object lesson* much more efficacious than any words of the teacher could possibly have been. Little by little, he would come to see the advantages of being one of the company working so busily before his eyes, and he would really wish to go back and do as the others did. We have in this way led back again to discipline all the children who at first seemed to rebel against it. The isolated child was always made the object of special care, almost as if he were ill.

I myself, when I entered the room, went first of all directly to him, caressing him, as if he were a very little child. Then I turned my attention to the others, interesting myself in their work, asking questions about it as if they had been little men. I do not know what happened in the soul of these children whom we found it necessary to discipline, but certainly the conversion was always very complete and lasting. They showed great pride in learning how to work and how to conduct themselves, and always showed a very tender affection for the teacher and for me.

THE BIOLOGICAL CONCEPT OF LIBERTY IN PEDAGOGY

From a biological point of view, the concept of *liberty* in the education of the child in his earliest years must be understood as demanding those conditions adapted to the most favourable *development* of his entire individuality. So, from the physiological side as well as from the mental side, this includes the free development of the brain. The educator must be as one inspired by a deep *worship of life*, and must, through this reverence, *respect*, while he observes with human interest, the *development* of the child life. Now, child life is not an abstraction; *it is the life of individual children*. There exists only one real biological manifestation: the *living individual*; and toward single individuals, one by one observed, education must direct itself. By education must be understood the active *help* given to the normal expansion of the life of the child. The child is a body which grows, and a soul which develops,—these two forms, physiological and psychic, have one eternal font, life itself. We must neither mar nor stifle the mysterious powers which lie within these two forms of growth, but we must *await from them* the manifestations which we know will succeed one another.

Environment is undoubtedly a *secondary* factor in the phenomena of life; it can modify in that it can help or hinder, but it can never *create*. The modern theories of evolution, from Naegeli to De Vries, consider throughout the development of the two biological branches, animal and vegetable, this interior factor as the essential force in the transformation of the species and in the transformation of the individual. The origins of the *development*, both in the species and in the individual, *lie within*. The child does not grow *because* he is nourished, *because* he breathes, *because* he is placed in conditions of temperature to which he is adapted; he grows because the potential life within him develops, making itself visible; because the fruitful germ from which his life has come develops itself according to the biological destiny which was fixed for it by heredity. Adolescence does not come *because* the child laughs, or dances, or does gymnastic exercises, or is well nourished; but because he has arrived at that particular physiological state. Life makes itself manifest,—life creates, life gives:—and is in its turn held within certain limits and bound by certain laws which are insuperable. The *fixed* characteristics of the species do not change,—they can only vary.

This concept, so brilliantly set forth by De Vries in his Mutation Theory, illustrates also the limits of education. We can act on the *variations* which are in relation to the environment, and whose limits vary slightly in the species and in the individual, but we cannot act upon the *mutations*. The mutations are bound by some mysterious tie to the very font of life itself, and their power rises superior to the modifying elements of the environment.

A species, for example, cannot *mutate* or change into another species through any phenomenon of *adaptation*, as, on the other hand, a great human genius cannot be suffocated by any limitation, nor by any false form of education.

The *environment* acts more strongly upon the individual life the less fixed and strong this individual life may be. But environment can act in two opposite senses, favouring life, and stifling it. Many species of palm, for example, are splendid in the tropical regions, because the climatic conditions are favourable to their development, but many species of both animals and plants have become extinct in regions to which they were not able to adapt themselves.

Life is a superb goddess, always advancing, overthrowing the obstacles which environment places in the way of her triumph. This is the basic or fundamental truth,—whether it be a question of species or of individuals, there persists always the forward march of those victorious ones in whom this mysterious life-force is strong and vital.

It is evident that in the case of humanity, and especially in the case of our civil humanity, which we call society, the important and imperative question is that of the *care,* or perhaps we might say, the *culture* of human life.

6

How the Lessons Should be Given

"Let all thy words be counted."

Dante, Inf., canto X

Given the fact that, through the régime of liberty the pupils can manifest their natural tendencies in the school, and that with this in view we have prepared the environment and the materials (the objects with which the child is to work), the teacher must not limit her action to *observation*, but must proceed to *experiment*.

In this method the lesson corresponds to an *experiment*. The more fully the teacher is acquainted with the methods of experimental psychology, the better will she understand how to give the lesson. Indeed, a special technique is necessary if the method is to be properly applied. The teacher must at least have attended the training classes in the "Children's Houses," in order to acquire a knowledge of the fundamental principles of the method and to understand their application. The most difficult portion of this training is that which refers to the method for discipline.

In the first days of the school the children do not learn the idea of collective order; this idea follows and comes as a result of those disciplinary exercises through which the child learns to discern between good and evil. This being the case, it is evident that, at the outset the teacher *cannot give* collective lessons. Such lessons, indeed, will always be *very rare*, since the children being free are not obliged to remain in their places quiet and ready to listen to the teacher, or to watch what she is doing. The collective lessons, in fact, are of very secondary importance, and have been almost abolished by us.

CHARACTERISTICS OF THE INDIVIDUAL LESSONS: CONCISENESS, SIMPLICITY, OBJECTIVITY

The lessons, then, are individual, and *brevity* must be one of their chief characteristics. Dante gives excellent advice to teachers when he says, "Let thy words be counted." The more carefully we cut away useless words, the more perfect will become the lesson. And in preparing the lessons which she is to give, the teacher must pay special attention to this point, counting and weighing the value of the words which she is to speak.

Another characteristic quality of the lesson in the "Children's Houses" is its *simplicity*. It must be stripped of all that is not absolute truth. That the teacher must not lose herself in vain words, is included in the first quality of conciseness; this second, then, is closely related to the first: that is, the carefully chosen words must be the most simple it is possible to find, and must refer to the truth.

The third quality of the lesson is its *objectivity*. The lesson must be presented in such a way that the personality of the teacher shall disappear. There shall remain in evidence only the *object* to which she wishes to call the attention of the child. This brief and simple lesson must be considered by the teacher as an explanation of the object and of the use which the child can make of it.

In the giving of such lessons the fundamental guide must be the *method of observation*, in which is included and understood the liberty of the child. So the teacher shall *observe* whether the child interests himself in the object, how he is interested in it, for how long, etc., even noticing the expression of his face. And she must take great care not to offend the principles of liberty. For, if she provokes the child to make an unnatural effort, she will no longer know what is the *spontaneous* activity of the child. If, therefore, the lesson rigorously prepared in this brevity, simplicity and truth is not understood by the child, is not accepted by him as an explanation of the object,—the teacher must be warned of two things:—first, not to *insist* by repeating the lesson; and second, *not to make the child feel that he has made a mistake*, or that he is not understood, because in doing so she will cause him to make an effort to understand, and will thus alter the natural state which must be used by her in making her psychological observation. A few examples may serve to illustrate this point.

Let us suppose, for example, that the teacher wishes to teach to a child the two colours, red and blue. She desires to attract the attention of the child to the object. She says, therefore, "Look at this." Then, in order to teach the colours, she says, showing him the red, "This is *red*," raising her voice a little and pronouncing the word "red" slowly and clearly; then showing him the other colour, "This is *blue*." In order to make sure that the child has understood, she says to him, "Give me the red,"—"Give me the blue." Let us suppose that the child in following this last direction makes a mistake. The teacher does not repeat and does not insist; she smiles, gives the child a friendly caress and takes away the colours.

Teachers ordinarily are greatly surprised at such simplicity. They often say, "But everybody knows how to do that!" Indeed, this again is a little like the egg of Christopher Columbus, but the truth is that not everyone knows how to do this simple thing (to give a lesson with such simplicity). To *measure* one's own activity, to make it conform to these standards of clearness, brevity and truth, is practically a very difficult matter. Especially is this true of teachers prepared by the old-time methods, who have learned to labour to deluge the child with useless, and often, false words. For example, a teacher who had taught in the public schools often reverted to collectivity. Now in giving a collective lesson much importance is necessarily given to the simple thing which is to be taught, and it is necessary to oblige all the children to follow the teacher's explanation, when perhaps not all of them are disposed to give their attention to the particular lesson in hand. The teacher has perhaps commenced her lesson in this way:—"Children, see if you can guess what I have in my hand!" She knows that the children cannot guess, and she therefore attracts their attention by means of a falsehood. Then she probably says,—"Children, look out at the sky. Have you ever looked at it before? Have you never noticed it at night when it is all shining with stars? No! Look at my apron. Do you know what colour it is? Doesn't it seem to you the same colour as the sky? Very well then, look at this colour I have in my hand. It is the same colour as the sky and my apron. It is *blue*. Now look around you a little and see if you can find something in the room which is blue. And do you know what colour cherries are, and the colour of the burning coals in the fireplace, etc., etc."

Now in the mind of the child after he has made the useless effort of trying to guess there revolves a confused mass of ideas,—the sky, the apron, the cherries, etc. It will be difficult for him to extract from all this confusion the idea which it was the scope of the lesson to make clear to him; namely, the recognition of the two colours, blue and red. Such a work of selection is almost impossible for the mind of a child who is not yet able to follow a long discourse.

I remember being present at an arithmetic lesson where the children were being taught that two and three make five. To this end, the teacher made use of a counting board having coloured beads strung on its thin wires. She arranged, for example, two beads on the top line, then on a lower line three, and at the bottom five beads. I do not remember very clearly the development of this lesson, but I do know that the teacher found it necessary to place beside the two beads on the upper wire a little cardboard dancer with a blue skirt, which she christened on the spot the name of one of the children in the class, saying, "This is Mariettina." And then beside the other three beads she placed a little dancer dressed in a different colour, which she called "Gigina." I do not know exactly how the teacher arrived at the demonstration of the same, but certainly she talked for a long time with these little dancers, moving them about, etc. If *I* remember the dancers more clearly than I do the arithmetic process, how must it have been with the children? If by such a method they were able to learn that two and three make five, they must have made a tremendous mental effort, and the teacher must have found it necessary to talk with the little dancers for a long time.

In another lesson a teacher wished to demonstrate to the children the difference between noise and sound. She began by telling a long story to the children. Then suddenly someone in league with her knocked noisily at the door. The teacher stopped and cried out—"What is it! What's happened! What is the matter! Children, do you know what this person at the door has done? I can no longer go on with my story, I cannot remember it any more. I will have to leave it unfinished. Do you know what has happened? Did you hear! Have you understood? That was a noise, that is a noise. Oh! I would much rather play with this little baby (taking up a mandolin which she had dressed up in a table cover). Yes, dear baby, I had rather play with you. Do you see this baby that I am holding in my arms?" Several children replied, "It isn't a baby." Others said, "It's a mandolin." The teacher went on—"No, no, it is a baby, really a baby. I love this little baby. Do you want me to show you that it is a baby? Keep very, very quiet then. It seems to me that the baby is crying. Or, perhaps it is talking, or perhaps it is going to say papa or mamma." Putting her hand under the cover, she touched the strings of the mandolin. "There! did you hear the baby cry! Did you hear it call out?" The children cried out—"It's a mandolin, you touched the strings, you made it play." The teacher then replied, "Be quiet, be quiet, children. Listen to what I am going to do." Then she uncovered the mandolin and began to play on it, saying, "This is sound."

To suppose that the child from such a lesson as this shall come to understand the difference between noise and sound is ridiculous. The child will probably get the impression that the teacher wished to play a joke, and that she is rather foolish, because she lost the thread of her discourse when she was interrupted by noise, and because she mistook a mandolin for a baby. Most certainly, it is the figure of the teacher herself that is impressed upon the child's mind through such a lesson, and not the object for which the lesson was given.

To obtain a *simple lesson* from a teacher who has been prepared according to the ordinary methods, is a very difficult task. I remember that, after having explained the material fully and in detail, I called upon one of my teachers to teach, by means of the geometric insets, the difference between a square and a triangle. The task of the teacher was simply to fit a square and a triangle of wood into the empty spaces made to receive them. She should then have shown the child how to follow with his finger the contours of the wooden pieces and of the frames into which they fit, saying, meanwhile, "This is a square—this is a triangle." The teacher whom I had called upon began by having the child touch the square, saying, "This is a line,—another,—another,—and another. There are four lines: count them with your little finger and tell me how many there are. And the corners,—count the corners, feel them with your little finger. See, there are four corners too. Look at this piece well. It is a square." I corrected the teacher, telling her that in this way she was not teaching the child to recognise a form, but was giving him an idea of sides, of angles, of number, and that this was a very different thing from that which she was to teach in this lesson. "But," she said, trying to justify herself, "it is the same thing." It is not, however, the same thing. It is the geometric analysis and the mathematics of the thing. It would be possible to have an idea of the form of the quadrilateral without knowing how to count to four, and, therefore, without appreciating the number of sides and angles. The sides and the angles are abstractions which in themselves do not exist; that which does exist is this piece of wood of a determined form. The elaborate explanations of the teacher not only confused the child's mind, but bridged over the distance that lies between the concrete and the abstract, between the form of an object and the mathematics of the form.

Let as suppose, I said to the teacher, that an architect shows you a dome, the form of which interests you. He can follow one of two methods in showing you his work: he can call attention to the beauty of line, the harmony of the proportions, and may then take you inside the building and up into the cupola itself, in order that you may appreciate the relative proportion of the parts in such a way that your impression of the cupola as a whole shall be founded on general knowledge of its parts, or he can have you count the windows, the wide or narrow cornices, and can, in fact, make you a design showing the construction; he can illustrate for you the static laws and write out the algebraic formulæ necessary in the calculation of such laws. In the first place, you will be able to retain in your mind the form of the cupola; in the second, you will have understood nothing, and will come away with the impression that the architect fancied himself speaking to a fellow engineer, instead of to a traveller whose object was to become familiar with the beautiful things about him. Very much the same thing happens if we, instead of saying to the child, "This is a square," and by simply having him touch the contour establish materially the idea of the form, proceed rather to a geometrical analysis of the contour.

Indeed, we should feel that we are making the child precocious if we taught him the geometric forms in the plane, presenting at the same time the mathematical concept, but we do not believe that the child is too immature to appreciate the simple *form*; on the contrary, it is no effort for a child to look at a square window or table,—he sees all these forms about him in his daily life. To call his attention to a determined form is to clarify the impression he has already received of it, and to fix the idea of it. It is very much as if, while we are looking absent-mindedly at the shore of a lake, an artist should suddenly say to us—"How beautiful the curve is that the shore makes there under the shade of that cliff." At his words, the view which we have been observing almost unconsciously, is impressed upon our minds as if it had been illuminated by a sudden ray of sunshine, and we experience the joy of having crystallised an impression which we had before only imperfectly felt.

And such is our duty toward the child: to give a ray of light and to go on our way.

I may liken the effects of these first lessons to the impressions of one who walks quietly, happily, through a wood, alone, and thoughtful, letting his inner life unfold freely. Suddenly, the chime of a distant bell recalls him to himself, and in that awakening he feels more strongly than before the peace and beauty of which he has been but dimly conscious.

To stimulate life,—leaving it then free to develop, to unfold,—herein lies the first task of the educator. In such a delicate task, a great art must suggest the moment, and limit the intervention, in order that we shall arouse no perturbation, cause no deviation, but rather that we shall help the soul which is coming into the fulness of life, and which shall live from its *own forces*. This *art* must accompany the *scientific method*.

When the teacher shall have touched, in this way, soul for soul, each one of her pupils, awakening and inspiring the life within them as if she were an invisible spirit, she will then possess each soul, and a sign, a single word from her shall suffice; for each one will feel her in a living and vital way, will recognise her and will listen to her. There will come a day when the directress herself shall be filled with wonder to see that all the children obey her with gentleness and affection, not only ready, but intent, at a sign from her. They will look toward her who has made them live, and will hope and desire to receive from her, new life.

Experience has revealed all this, and it is something which forms the chief source of wonder for those who visit the "Children's Houses." Collective discipline is obtained as if by magic force. Fifty or sixty children from two and a half years to six years of age, all together, and at a single time know how to hold their peace so perfectly that the absolute silence seems that of a desert. And, if the teacher, speaking in a low voice, says to the children, "Rise, pass several times around the room on the tips of your toes and then come back to your place in silence" all together, as a single person, the children rise, and follow the order with the least possible noise. The teacher with that one voice has spoken to each one; and each child hopes from her intervention to receive some light and inner happiness. And feeling so, he goes forth intent and obedient like an anxious explorer, following the order in his own way.

In this matter of discipline we have again something of the egg of Christopher Columbus. A concert-master must prepare his scholars one by one in order to draw from their collective work great and beautiful harmony; and each artist must perfect himself as an individual before he can be ready to follow the voiceless commands of the master's baton.

How different is the method which we follow in the public schools! It is as if a concert-master taught the same monotonous and sometimes discordant rhythm contemporaneously to the most diverse instruments and voices.

Thus we find that the most disciplined members of society are the men who are best trained, who have most thoroughly perfected themselves, but this is the training or the perfection acquired through contact with other people. The perfection of the collectivity cannot be that material and brutal solidarity which comes from mechanical organisation alone.

In regard to infant psychology, we are more richly endowed with prejudices than with actual knowledge bearing upon the subject. We have, until the present day, wished to dominate the child through force, by the imposition of external laws, instead of making an interior conquest of the child, in order to direct him as a human soul. In this way, the children have lived beside us without being able to make us know them. But if we cut away the artificiality with which we have enwrapped them, and the violence through which we have foolishly thought to discipline them, they will reveal themselves to us in all the truth of child nature.

Their gentleness is so absolute, so sweet, that we recognise in it the infancy of that humility which can remain oppressed by every form of yoke, by every injustice; and child love and *knowledge* is such that it surpasses every other love and makes us think that in very truth humanity must carry within it that passion which pushes the minds of men to the successive conquest of thought, making easier from century to century the yokes of every form of slavery.

7

Exercises of Practical Life

PROPOSED WINTER SCHEDULE OF HOURS IN THE "CHILDREN'S HOUSES"

Opening at Nine O'clock—Closing at Four O'clock

9-10. Entrance. Greeting. Inspection as to personal cleanliness. Exercises of practical life; helping one another to take off and put on the aprons. Going over the room to see that everything is dusted and in order. Language: Conversation period: Children give an account of the events of the day before. Religious exercises.

10-11. Intellectual exercises. Objective lessons interrupted by short rest periods. Nomenclature, Sense exercises.

11-11:30. Simple gymnastics: Ordinary movements done gracefully, normal position of the body, walking, marching in line, salutations, movements for attention, placing of objects gracefully.

11:30-12. Luncheon: Short prayer.

12-1. Free games.

1-2. Directed games, if possible, in the open air. During this period the older children in turn go through with the exercises of practical life, cleaning the room, dusting, putting the material in order. General inspection for cleanliness: Conversation.

2-3. Manual work. Clay modelling, design, etc.

3-4. Collective gymnastics and songs, if possible in the open air. Exercises to develop forethought: Visiting, and caring for, the plants and animals.

As soon as a school is established, the question of schedule arises. This must be considered from two points of view; the length of the school-day and the distribution of study and of the activities of life.

I shall begin by affirming that in the "Children's Houses," as in the school for deficients, the hours may be very long, occupying the entire day. For poor children, and especially for the "Children's Houses" annexed to workingmen's tenements, I should advise that the school-day should be from nine in the morning to five in the evening in winter, and from eight to six in summer. These long hours are necessary, if we are to follow a directed line of action which shall be helpful to the growth of the child. It goes without saying, that in the case of little children such a long school-day should be interrupted by at least an hour's rest in bed. And here lies the great practical difficulty. At present we must allow our little ones to sleep in their seats in a wretched position, but I foresee a time, not distant, when we shall be able to have a quiet, darkened room where the children may sleep in low-swung hammocks. I should like still better to have this nap taken in the open air.

In the "Children's Houses" in Rome we send the little ones to their own apartments for the nap, as this can be done without their having to go out into the streets.

It must be observed that these long hours include not only the nap, but the luncheon. This must be considered in such schools as the "Children's Houses," whose aim is to help and to direct the growth of children in such an important period of development as that from three to six years of age.

The "Children's House" is a garden of child culture, and we most certainly do not keep the children for so many hours in school with the idea of making students of them!

The first step which we must take in our method is to *call* to the pupil. We call now to his attention, now to his interior life, now to the life he leads with others. Making a comparison which must not be taken in a literal sense,—it is necessary to proceed as in experimental psychology or anthropology when one makes an experiment,—that is, after having prepared the instrument (to which in this case the environment may correspond) we prepare the subject. Considering the method as a whole, we must begin our work by preparing the child for the forms of social life, and we must attract his attention to these forms.

In the schedule which we outlined when we established the first "Children's House," but which we have never followed entirely, (a sign that a schedule in which the material is distributed in arbitrary fashion is not adapted to the régime of liberty) we begin the day with a series of exercises of practical life, and I must confess that these exercises were the only part of the programme which proved thoroughly stationary. These exercises were such a success that they formed the beginning of the day in all of the "Children's Houses." First:

Cleanliness.
Order.
Poise.
Conversation.

As soon as the children arrive at school we make an inspection for cleanliness. If possible, this should be carried on in the presence of the mothers, but their attention should not be called to it directly. We examine the hands, the nails, the neck, the ears, the face, the teeth; and care is given to the tidiness of the hair. If any of the garments are torn or soiled or ripped, if the buttons are lacking, or if the shoes are not clean, we call the attention of the child to this. In this way, the children become accustomed to observing themselves and take an interest in their own appearance.

The children in our "Children's Houses" are given a bath in turn, but this, of course, can not be done daily. In the class, however, the teacher, by using a little washstand with small pitchers and basins, teaches the children to take a partial bath: for example, they learn how to wash their hands and clean their nails. Indeed, sometimes we teach them how to take a foot-bath. They are shown especially how to wash their ears and eyes with great care. They are taught to brush their teeth and rinse their mouths carefully. In all of this, we call their attention to the different parts of the body which they are washing, and to the different means which we use in order to cleanse them: clear water for the eyes, soap and water for the hands, the brush for the teeth, etc. We teach the big ones to help the little ones, and, so, encourage the younger children to learn quickly to take care of themselves.

After this care of their persons, we put on the little aprons. The children are able to put these on themselves, or, with the help of each other. Then we begin our visit about the schoolroom. We notice if all of the various materials are in order and if they are clean. The teacher shows the children how to clean out the little corners where dust has accumulated, and shows them how to use the various objects necessary in cleaning a room,—dust-cloths, dust-brushes, little brooms, etc. All of this, when the children are allowed *to do it by themselves*, is very quickly accomplished. Then the children go each to his own place. The teacher explains to them that the normal position is for each child to be seated in his own place, in silence, with his feet together on the floor, his hands resting on the table, and his head erect. In this way she teaches them poise and equilibrium. Then she has them rise on their feet in order to sing the hymn, teaching them that in rising and sitting down it is not necessary to be noisy. In this way the children learn to move about the furniture with poise and with care. After this we have a series of exercises in which the children learn to move gracefully, to go and come, to salute each other, to lift objects carefully, to receive various objects from each other politely. The teacher calls attention with little exclamations to a child who is clean, a room which is well ordered, a class seated quietly, a graceful movement, etc.

From such a starting point we proceed to the free teaching. That is, the teacher will no longer make comments to the children, directing them how to move from their seats, etc., she will limit herself to correcting the disordered movements.

After the directress has talked in this way about the attitude of the children and the arrangement of the room, she invites the children to talk with her. She questions them concerning what they have done the day before, regulating her inquiries in such a way that the children need not report the intimate happenings of the family but their individual behaviour, their games, attitude to parents, etc. She will ask if they have been able to go up the stairs without getting them muddy, if they have spoken politely to their friends who passed, if they have helped their mothers, if they have shown in their family what they have learned at school, if they have played in the street, etc. The conversations are longer on Monday after the vacation, and on that day the children are invited to tell what they have done with the family; if they have gone away from home, whether they have eaten things not usual for children to eat, and if this is the case we urge them not to eat these things and try to teach them that they are bad for them. Such conversations as these encourage the *unfolding* or development of language and are of great educational value, since the directress can prevent the children from recounting happenings in the house or in the neighbourhood, and can select, instead, topics which are adapted to pleasant conversation, and in this way can teach the children those things which it is desirable to talk about; that is, things with which we occupy ourselves in life, public events, or things which have happened in the different houses, perhaps, to the children themselves—as baptism, birthday parties, any of which may serve for occasional conversation. Things of this sort will encourage children to describe, themselves. After this morning talk we pass to the various lessons.

8

Refection—The Child's Diet

In connection with the exercises of practical life, it may be fitting to consider the matter of refection.

In order to protect the child's development, especially in neighbourhoods where standards of child hygiene are not yet prevalent in the home, it would be well if a large part at least of the child's diet could be entrusted to the school. It is well known today that the diet must be adapted to the physical nature of the child; and as the medicine of children is not the medicine of adults in reduced doses, so the diet must not be that of the adult in lesser quantitative proportions. For this reason I should prefer that even in the "Children's Houses" which are situated in tenements and from which little ones, being at home, can go up to eat with the family, school refection should be instituted. Moreover, even in the case of rich children, school refection would always be advisable until a scientific course in cooking shall have introduced into the wealthier families the habit of specialising in children's food.

The diet of little children must be rich in fats and sugar: the first for reserve matter and the second for plastic tissue. In fact, sugar is a stimulant to tissues in the process of formation.

As for the *form* of preparation, it is well that the alimentary substances should always be minced, because the child has not yet the capacity for completely masticating the food, and his stomach is still incapable of fulfilling the function of mincing food matter.

Consequently, soups, purées, and meat balls, should constitute the ordinary form of dish for the child's table.

The nitrogenous diet for a child from two or three years of

age ought to be constituted chiefly of milk and eggs, but after the second year broths are also to be recommended. After three years and a half meat can be given; or, in the case of poor children, vegetables. Fruits are also to be recommended for children.

Perhaps a detailed summary on child diet may be useful, especially for mothers.

Method of Preparing Broth for Little Children. (Age three to six; after that the child may use the common broth of the family). The quantity of meat should correspond to 1 gramme for every cubic centimetre of broth and should be put in cold water. No aromatic herbs should be used, the only wholesome condiment being salt. The meat should be left to boil for two hours. Instead of removing the grease from the broth it is well to add butter to it, or, in the case of the poor, a spoonful of olive oil; but substitutes for butter, such as margerine, etc., should never be used. The broth must be prepared *fresh*; it would be well, therefore, to put the meat on the fire two hours before the meal, because as soon as broth is cool there begins to take place a separation of chemical substances, which are injurious to the child and may easily cause diarrhea.

Soups. A very simple soup, and one to be highly recommended for children, is bread boiled in salt water or in broth and abundantly seasoned with oil. This is the classic soup of poor children and an excellent means of nutrition. Very like this, is the soup which consists of little cubes of bread toasted in butter and allowed to soak in the broth which is itself fat with butter. Soups of grated bread also belong in this class.

Pastine,[1] especially the glutinous pastine, which are of the same nature, are undoubtedly superior to the others for digestibility, but are accessible only to the privileged social classes.

The poor should know how much more wholesome is a broth made from remnants of stale bread, than soups of coarse spaghetti—often dry and seasoned with meat juice. Such soups are most indigestible for little children.

Excellent soups are those consisting of purées of vegetables (beans, peas, lentils). To-day one may find in the shops dried vegetables especially adapted for this sort of soups. Boiled in salt water, the vegetables are peeled, put to cool and passed through a sieve (or simply compressed, if they are already peeled). Butter is then added, and the paste is stirred slowly into the boiling water, care being taken that it dissolves and leaves no lumps.

Vegetable soups can also be seasoned with pork. Instead of broth, sugared milk may be the base of vegetable purées.

I strongly recommend for children a soup of rice boiled in broth or milk; also cornmeal broth, provided it be seasoned with abundant butter, but not with cheese. (The porridge form—polenta, really cornmeal mush, is to be highly recommended on account of the long cooking.)

The poorer classes who have no meat-broth can feed their children equally well with soups of boiled bread and porridge seasoned with oil.

Milk and Eggs. These are foods which not only contain nitrogenous substances in an eminently digestible form, but they have the so-called *enzymes* which facilitate assimilation into the tissues, and, hence, in a particular way, favour the growth of the child. And they answer so much the better this last most important condition if they are *fresh* and *intact*, keeping in themselves, one may say, the life of the animals which produced them.

Milk fresh from the cow, and the egg while it is still warm, are assimilable to the highest degree. Cooking, on the other hand, makes the milk and eggs lose their special conditions of assimilability and reduces the nutritive power in them to the simple power of any nitrogenous substance.

To-day, consequently, there are being founded *special dairies for children* where the milk produced is sterile; the rigorous cleanliness of the surroundings in which the milk-producing animals live, the sterilisation of the udder before milking, of the hands of the milker, and of the vessels which are to contain the milk, the hermetic sealing of these last, and the refrigerating bath immediately after the milking, if the milk is to be carried far,—otherwise it is well to drink it warm, procure a milk free from bacteria which, therefore, has no need of being sterilised by boiling, and which preserves intact its natural nutritive powers.

As much may be said of eggs; the best way of feeding them to a child is to take them still warm from the hen and have him eat them just as they are, and then digest them in the open air. But where this is not practicable, eggs must be chosen fresh, and barely heated in water, that is to say, prepared *à la coque*.

All other forms of preparation, milk-soup, omelettes, and so forth, do, to be sure, make of milk and eggs an excellent food, more to be recommended than others; but they take away the specific properties of assimilation which characterise them.

Meat. All meats are not adapted to children, and even their preparation must differ according to the age of the child. Thus, for example, children from three to five years of age ought to eat only more or less finely-ground meats, whereas at the age of five children are capable of grinding meat completely by mastication; at that time it is well to *teach the child accurately how to masticate* because he has a tendency to swallow food quickly, which may produce indigestion and diarrhea.

This is another reason why school-refection in the "Children's Houses" would be a very serviceable as well as convenient institution, as the whole diet of the child could then be rationally cared for in connection with the educative system of the Houses.

The meats most adapted to children are so-called white meats, that is, in the first place, chicken, then veal; also the light flesh of fish, (sole, pike, cod).

After the age of four, filet of beef may also be introduced into the diet, but never heavy and fat meats like that of the pig, the capon, the eel, the tunny, etc., which are to be *absolutely excluded* along with mollusks and crustaceans, (oysters, lobsters), from the child's diet.

Croquettes made of finely ground meat, grated bread, milk, and beaten eggs, and fried in butter, are the most wholesome preparation. Another excellent preparation is to mould into balls the grated meat, with sweet fruit-preserve, and eggs beaten up with sugar.

At the age of five, the child may be given breast of roast fowl, and occasionally veal cutlet or filet of beef.

Boiled meat must never be given to the child, because meat is deprived of many stimulating and even nutritive properties by boiling and rendered less digestible.

Nerve Feeding Substances. Besides meat a child who has reached the age of four may be given fried brains and sweetbreads, to be combined, for example, with chicken croquettes.

Milk Foods. All cheeses are to be excluded from the child's diet.

The only milk product suitable to children from three to six years of age is fresh butter.

Custard. Custard is also to be recommended provided it be *freshly prepared*, that is immediately before being eaten, and *with very fresh* milk and eggs: if such conditions cannot be rigorously fulfilled, it is preferable to do without custard, which is not a necessity.

Bread. From what we have said about soups, it may be inferred that bread is an *excellent food* for the child. It should be well selected; the crumb is not very digestible, but it can be utilised, when it is dry, to make a bread broth; but if one is to give the child simply a piece of bread to eat, it is well to offer him the crust, the end of the loaf. Bread sticks are excellent for those who can afford them.

Bread contains many nitrogenous substances and is very rich in starches, but is lacking in fats; and as the fundamental substances of diet are, as is well known, three in number, namely, proteids, (nitrogenous substances), starches, and fats, bread is not a complete food; it is necessary therefore to offer the child buttered bread, which constitutes a complete food and may be considered as a sufficient and complete breakfast.

Green Vegetables. Children must never eat raw vegetables, such as salads and greens, but only cooked ones; indeed they are not to be highly recommended either cooked or raw, with the exception of spinach which may enter with moderation into the diet of children.

Potatoes prepared in a purée with much butter form, however, an excellent complement of nutrition for children.

Fruits. Among fruits there are excellent foods for children. They too, like milk and eggs, if freshly gathered, retain a *living* quality which aids assimilation.

As this condition, however, is not easily attainable in cities, it is necessary to consider also the diet of fruits which are not perfectly fresh and which, therefore, should be prepared and cooked in various ways. All fruits are not to be advised for children; the chief properties to be considered are the degree of *ripeness*, the *tenderness* and *sweetness* of the pulp, and its *acidity*. Peaches, apricots, grapes, currants, oranges, and mandarins, in their natural state, can be given to little children with great advantage. Other fruits, such as pears, apples, plums, should be cooked or prepared in syrup.

Figs, pineapples, dates, melons, cherries, walnuts, almonds, hazelnuts, and chestnuts, are excluded for various reasons from the diet of early childhood.

The preparation of fruit must consist in removing from it all indigestible parts, such as the peel, and also such parts as the child inadvertently may absorb to his detriment, as, for example, the seed.

Children of four or five should be taught early how carefully the seeds must be thrown away and how the fruits are peeled. Afterwards, the child so educated may be promoted to the honour of receiving a fine fruit intact, and he will know how to eat it properly.

The culinary preparation of fruits consists essentially in two processes: cooking, and seasoning with sugar.

Besides simple cooking, fruits may be prepared as marmalades and jellies, which are excellent but are naturally within the reach of the wealthier classes only. While jellies and marmalades may be allowed, candied fruits,—on the other hand,—*marrons glacés*, and the like, are absolutely excluded from the child's diet.

Seasonings. An important phase of the hygiene of child diet concerns seasonings—with a view to their rigorous limitation. As I have already indicated, sugar and some fat substances along with kitchen salt (sodium chloride) should constitute the principal part of the seasonings.

To these may be added *organic acids* (acetic acid, citric acid) that is, vinegar and lemon juice; this latter can be advantageously used on fish, on croquettes, on spinach, etc.

Other condiments suitable to little children are some aromatic vegetables like garlic and rue which disinfect the intestines and the lungs, and also have a direct anthelminthic action.

Spices, on the other hand, such as pepper, nutmeg, cinnamon, clove, and especially mustard, are to be absolutely abolished.

Drinks. The growing organism of the child is very rich in water, and, hence, needs a constant supply of moisture. Among the beverages, the best, and indeed the only one, to be unreservedly advised is pure fresh spring water. The rich children might be allowed the so-called table waters which are slightly alkaline, such as those of San Gemini, Acqua Claudia, etc., mixed with syrups, as, for example, syrup of black cherry.

It is now a matter of general knowledge that all fermented beverages, and those exciting to the nervous system, are injurious to children; hence, all alcoholic and caffeic beverages are absolutely eliminated from child diet. Not only liquors, but wine and beer, ought to be unknown to the child's taste, and coffee and tea should be inaccessible to childhood.

The deleterious action of alcohol on the child organism needs no illustration, but in a matter of such vital importance insistent repetition is never superfluous. Alcohol is a poison especially fatal to organisms in the process of formation. Not only does it arrest their total development (whence infantilism, idiocy), but also predisposes the child to nervous maladies (epilepsy, meningitis), and to maladies of the digestive organs, and metabolism (cirrhosis of the liver, dyspepsia, anaemia).

If the "Children's Houses" were to succeed in enlightening

the people on such truths, they would be accomplishing a very lofty hygienic work for the new generations.

Instead of coffee, children may be given roasted and boiled barley, malt, and especially chocolate which is an excellent child food, particularly when mixed with milk.

DISTRIBUTION OF THE MEALS

Another chapter of child diet concerns the distribution of the meals. Here, one principle must dominate, and must be diffused, among mothers, namely, that the children shall be kept to rigorous meal hours in order that they may enjoy good health and have excellent digestion. It is true that there prevails among the people (and it is one of the forms of maternal ignorance most fatal to children) the prejudice that children in order to grow well must be eating almost continuously, without regularity, nibbling almost habitually a crust of bread. On the contrary, the child, in view of the special delicacy of his digestive system, has more need of regular meals than the adult has. It seems to me that the "Children's Houses" with very prolonged programmes are, for this reason, suitable places for child culture, as they can direct the child's diet. *Outside of their regular meal hours, children should not eat.*

In a "Children's House" with a long programme there ought to be two meals, a hearty one about noon, and a light one about four in the afternoon.

At the hearty meal, there should be soup, a meat dish, and bread, and, in the case of rich children, also fruits or custard, and butter on the bread.

At the four o'clock meal there should be prepared a light lunch, which from a simple piece of bread can range to buttered bread, and to bread accompanied by a fruit marmalade, chocolate, honey, custard, etc. Crisp crackers, biscuits, and cooked fruits, etc., might also be usefully employed. Very suitably the lunch might consist of bread soaked in milk or an egg *à la coque* with bread sticks, or else of a simple cup of milk in which is dissolved a spoonful of Mellin's Food. I recommend

Mellin's Food very highly, not only in infancy, but also much later on account of its properties of digestibility and nutrition, and on account of its flavour, which is so pleasing to children.

Mellin's Food is a powder prepared from barley and wheat, and containing in a concentrated and pure state the nutritive substances proper to those cereals; the powder is slowly dissolved in hot water in the bottom of the same cup which is to be used for drinking the mixture, and very fresh milk is then poured on top.

The child would take the other two meals in his own home, that is, the morning breakfast and the supper, which latter must be *very light* for children so that shortly after they may be ready to go to bed. On these meals it would be well to give advice to mothers, urging them to help complete the hygienic work of the "Children's Houses," to the profit of their children.

The morning breakfast for the rich might be milk and chocolate, or milk and extract of malt, with crackers, or, better, with toasted bread spread with butter or honey; for the poor, a cup of fresh milk, with bread.

For the evening meal, a soup is to be advised (children should eat soups twice a day), and an egg *à la coque* or a cup of milk; or rice soup with a base of milk, and buttered bread, with cooked fruits, etc.

As for the alimentary rations to be calculated, I refer the reader to the special treatises on hygiene: although practically such calculations are of no great utility.

In the "Children's Houses," especially in the case of the poor, I should make extensive use of the vegetable soups and I should have cultivated in the garden plots vegetables which can be used in the diet, in order to have them plucked in their freshness, cooked, and enjoyed. I should try, possibly, to do the same for the fruits, and, by the raising of animals, to have fresh eggs and pure milk. The milking of the goats could be done directly by the larger children, after they had scrupulously washed their hands. Another important educative application which school-refection in the "Children's Houses" has to offer, and which concerns "practical life," consists in the preparing of the table, arranging the table linen, learning its nomenclature, etc. Later, I shall show how this exercise can gradually increase in difficulty and constitute a most important didactic instrument.

It is sufficient to intimate here that it is very important to teach the children to eat with cleanliness, both with respect to themselves and with respect to their surroundings (not to soil the napkins, etc.), and to use the table implements (which, at least, for the little ones, are limited to the spoon, and for the larger children extended to the fork and knife).

NOTE

1. Those very fine forms of vermicelli used in soups.

9

Muscular Education—Gymnastics

The generally accepted idea of gymnastics is, I consider, very inadequate. In the common schools we are accustomed to describe as gymnastics a species of collective muscular discipline which has as its aim that children shall learn to follow definite ordered movements given in the form of commands. The guiding spirit in such gymnastics is coercion, and I feel that such exercises repress spontaneous movements and impose others in their place. I do not know what the psychological authority for the selection of these imposed movements is. Similar movements are used in medical gymnastics in order to restore a normal movement to a torpid muscle or to give back a normal movement to a paralysed muscle. A number of chest movements which are given in the school are advised, for example, in medicine for those who suffer from intestinal torpidity, but truly I do not well understand what office such exercises can fulfil when they are followed by squadrons of normal children. In addition to these formal gymnastics we have those which are carried on in a gymnasium, and which are very like the first steps in the training of an acrobat. However, this is not the place for criticism of the gymnastics used in our common schools. Certainly in our case we are not considering such gymnastics. Indeed, many who hear me speak of gymnastics for infant schools very plainly show disapprobation and they will disapprove more heartily when they hear me speak of a gymnasium for little children. Indeed, if the gymnastic exercises and the gymnasium were those of the common schools, no one would agree more heartily than I in the disapproval expressed by these critics.

We must understand by *gymnastics* and in general by muscular education a series of exercises tending to *aid* the normal development of physiological movements (such as walking, breathing, speech), to protect this development, when the child shows himself backward or abnormal in any way, and to encourage in the children those movements which are useful in the achievement of the most ordinary acts of life; such as dressing, undressing, buttoning their clothes and lacing their shoes, carrying such objects as balls, cubes, etc. If there exists an age in which it is necessary to protect a child by means of a series of gymnastic exercises, between three and six years is undoubtedly the age. The special gymnastics necessary, or, better still, hygienic, in this period of life, refer chiefly to walking. A child in the general morphological growth of his body is characterised by having a torso greatly developed in comparison with the lower limbs. In the new-born child the length of the torso, from the top of the head to the curve of the groin, is equal to 68 per cent of the total length of the body. The limbs then are barely 32 per cent of the stature. During growth these relative proportions change in a most noticeable way; thus, for example, in the adult the torso is fully half of the entire stature and, according to the individual, corresponds to 51 or 52 per cent of it.

This morphological difference between the new-born child and the adult is bridged so slowly during growth that in the first years of the child's life the torso still remains tremendously developed as compared with the limbs. In one year the height of the torso corresponds to 65 per cent of the total stature, in two years to 63, in three years to 62.

At the age when a child enters the infant school his limbs are still very short as compared with his torso; that is, the length of his limbs barely corresponds to 38 per cent of the stature. Between the years of six and seven the proportion of the torso to the stature is from 57 to 56 per cent In such a period therefore the child not only makes a noticeable growth in height, (he measures indeed at the age of three years about 0.85 metre and at six years 1.05 metres) but, changing so greatly the relative proportions between the torso and the limbs, the latter make a most decided growth. This growth is related to the layers of cartilage which still exist at the extremity of the long bones and is related in general to the still incomplete ossification of the entire skeleton. The tender bones of the limbs must therefore sustain the weight of the torso which is then disproportionately large. We cannot, if we consider all these things, judge the manner of walking in little children by the standard set for our own equilibrium. If a child is not strong, the erect posture and walking are really sources of fatigue for him, and the long bones of the lower limbs, yielding to the weight of the body, easily become deformed and usually bowed. This is particularly the case among the badly nourished children of the poor, or among those in whom the skeleton structure, while not actually showing the presence of rickets, still seems to be slow in attaining normal ossification.

We are wrong then if we consider little children from this physical point of view as *little men*. They have, instead, characteristics and proportions that are entirely special to their age. The tendency of the child to stretch out on his back and kick his legs in the air is an expression of physical needs related to the proportions of his body. The baby loves to walk on all fours just because, like the quadruped animals, his limbs are short in comparison with his body. Instead of this, we divert these natural manifestations by foolish habits which we impose on the child. We hinder him from throwing himself on the earth, from stretching, etc., and we oblige him to walk with grown people and to keep up with them; and excuse ourselves by saying that we don't want him to become capricious and think he can do as he pleases! It is indeed a fatal error and one which has made bow-legs common among little children. It is well to enlighten the mothers on these important particulars of infant hygiene. Now we, with the gymnastics, can, and, indeed, should, help the child in his development by making our exercises correspond to the movement which he *needs to make*, and in this way save his limbs from fatigue.

One very simple means for helping the child in his activity

was suggested to me by my observation of the children themselves. The teacher was having the children march, leading them about the courtyard between the walls of the house and the central garden. This garden was protected by a little fence made of strong wires which were stretched in parallel lines, and were supported at intervals by wooden palings driven into the ground. Along the fence, ran a little ledge on which the children were in the habit of sitting down when they were tired of marching. In addition to this, I always brought out little chairs, which I placed against the wall. Every now and then, the little ones of two and one half and three years would drop out from the marching line, evidently being tired; but instead of sitting down on the ground or on the chairs, they would run to the little fence and catching hold of the upper line of wire they would walk along sideways, resting their feet on the wire which was nearest the ground. That this gave them a great deal of pleasure, was evident from the way in which they laughed as, with bright eyes, they watched their larger companions who were marching about. The truth was that these little ones had solved one of my problems in a very practical way. They moved themselves along on the wires, pulling their bodies sideways. In this way, they moved their limbs *without throwing upon them the weight of the body*. Such an apparatus placed in the gymnasium for little children, will enable them to fulfil the need which they feel of throwing themselves on the floor and kicking their legs in the air; for the movements they make on the little fence correspond even more correctly to the same physical needs. Therefore, I advise the manufacture of this little fence for use in children's playrooms. It can be constructed of parallel bars supported by upright poles firmly fixed on to the heavy base. The children, while playing upon this little fence, will be able to look out and see with, great pleasure what the other children are doing in the room.

Other pieces of gymnasium apparatus can be constructed upon the same plan, that is, having as their aim the furnishing of the child with a proper outlet for his individual activities. One of the things invented by Séguin to develop the lower limbs, and especially to strengthen the articulation of the knee in weak children, is the trampolino.

This is a kind of swing, having a very wide seat, so wide, indeed, that the limbs of the child stretched out in front of him are entirely supported by this broad seat. This little chair is hung from strong cords and is left swinging. The wall in front of it is reinforced by a strong smooth board against which the children press their feet in pushing themselves back and forth in the swing. The child seated in this swing exercises his limbs, pressing his feet against the board each time that he swings toward the wall. The board against which he swings may be erected at some distance from the wall, and may be so low that the child can see over the top of it. As he swings in this chair, he strengthens his limbs through the species of gymnastics limited to the lower limbs, and this he does without resting the weight of his body upon his legs. Other pieces of gymnastic apparatus, less important from the hygienic standpoint, but very amusing to the children, may be described briefly. "The Pendulum," a game which may be played by one child or by several, consists of rubber balls hung on a cord. The children seated in their little armchairs strike the ball, sending it from one to another. It is an exercise for the arms and for the spinal column, and is at the same time an exercise in which the eye gauges the distance of bodies in motion. Another game, called "The Cord," consists of a line, drawn on the earth with chalk, along which the children walk. This helps to order and to direct their free movements in a given direction. A game like this is very pretty, indeed, after a snowfall, when the little path made by the children shows the regularity of the line they have traced, and encourages a pleasant war among them in which each one tries to make his line in the snow the most regular.

The little round stair is another game, in which a little wooden stairway, built on the plan of the spiral, is used. This little stair is enclosed on one side by a balustrade on which the children can rest their hands. The other side is open and circular. This serves to habituate the children to climbing and descending stairs without holding on to the balustrade, and teaches them to move up and down with movements that are poised and self-controlled. The steps must be very low and very shallow. Going up and down on this little stair, the very smallest children can learn movements which they cannot follow properly in climbing ordinary stairways in their homes, in which the proportions are arranged for adults.

Another piece of gymnasium apparatus, adapted for the broad-jump, consists of a low wooden platform painted with various lines, by means of which the distance jumped may be gauged. There is a small flight of stairs which may be used in connection with this plane, making it possible to practise and to measure the high-jump.

I also believe that rope-ladders may be so adapted as to be suitable for use in schools for little children. Used in pairs, these would, it seems to me, help to perfect a great variety of movements, such as kneeling, rising, bending forward and backward, etc.; movements which the child, without the help of the ladder, could not make without losing his equilibrium. All of these movements are useful in that they help the child to acquire, first, equilibrium, then that co-ordination of the muscular movements necessary to him. They are, moreover, helpful in that they increase the chest expansion. Besides all this, such movements as I have described, reinforce the *hand* in its most primitive and essential action,*prehension;*—the movement which necessarily precedes all the finer movements of the hand itself. Such apparatus was successfully used by Séguin to develop the general strength and the movement of prehension in his idiotic children.

The gymnasium, therefore, offers a field for the most varied exercises, tending to establish the co-ordination of the movements common in life, such as walking, throwing objects, going up and down stairs, kneeling, rising, jumping, etc.

FREE GYMNASTICS

By free gymnastics I mean those which are given without any apparatus. Such gymnastics are divided into two classes:

directed and required exercises, and free games. In the first class, I recommend the march, the object of which should be not rhythm, but poise only. When the march is introduced, it is well to accompany it with the singing of little songs, because this furnishes a breathing exercise very helpful in strengthening

Dr. Montessori in the Garden of the School at Via Giusti

the lungs. Besides the march, many of the games of Froebel which are accompanied by songs, very similar to those which the children constantly play among themselves, may be used. In the free games, we furnish the children with balls, hoops, bean bags and kites. The trees readily offer themselves to the game of "Pussy wants a corner," and many simple games of tag.

(A) Children Three and One-half and Four Years Old Learning to Button and Lace. (B) Ribbon and Button Frames.
These are among the earliest exercises.

EDUCATIONAL GYMNASTICS

Under the name of educational gymnastics, we include two series of exercises which really form a part of other school work, as, for instance, the cultivation of the earth, the care of plants and animals (watering and pruning the plants, carrying the grain to the chickens, etc.). These activities call for various co-ordinated movements, as, for example, in hoeing, in getting down to plant things, and in rising; the trips which children make in carrying objects to some definite place, and in making a definite practical use of these objects, offer a field for very valuable gymnastic exercises. The scattering of minute objects, such as corn and oats, is valuable, and also the exercise of opening and closing the gates to the garden and to the chicken yard. All of these exercises are the more valuable in that they are carried on in the open air. Among our educational gymnastics we have exercises to develop co-ordinated movements of the fingers, and these prepare the children for the exercises of practical life, such as dressing and undressing themselves. The didactic material which forms the basis of these last named gymnastics is very simple, consisting of wooden frames, each mounted with two pieces of cloth, or leather, to be fastened and unfastened by means of the buttons and buttonholes, hooks and eyes, eyelets and lacings, or automatic fastenings.

In our "Children's Houses" we use ten of these frames, so constructed that each one of them illustrates a different process in dressing or undressing.

One: mounted with heavy pieces of wool which are to be fastened by means of large bone buttons—corresponds to children's dresses.

Two: mounted with pieces of linen to be fastened with pearl buttons—corresponds to a child's underwear.

Three: leather pieces mounted with shoe buttons—in fastening these leather pieces the children make use of the button-hook—corresponds to a child's shoes.

Four: pieces of leather which are laced together by means

of eyelets and shoe laces.

Five: two pieces of cloth to be laced together. (These pieces are boned and therefore correspond to the little bodices worn by the peasants in Italy.)

Six: two pieces of stuff to be fastened by means of large hooks and eyes.

Seven: two pieces of linen, to be fastened by means of small hooks and worked eyelets.

Eight: two pieces of cloth to be fastened by means of broad coloured ribbon, which is to be tied into bows.

Nine: pieces of cloth laced together with round cord, on the same order as the fastenings on many of the children's underclothes.

Ten: two pieces to be fastened together by means of the modern automatic fasteners.

Through the use of such toys, the children can practically analyse the movements necessary in dressing and undressing themselves, and can prepare themselves separately for these movements by means of repeated exercises. We succeed in teaching the child to dress himself without his really being aware of it, that is, without any direct or arbitrary command we have led him to this mastery. As soon as he knows how to do it, he begins to wish to make a practical application of his ability, and very soon he will be proud of being sufficient unto himself, and will take delight in an ability which makes his body free from the hands of others, and which leads him the sooner to that modesty and activity which develops far too late in those children of to-day who are deprived of this most practical form of education. The fastening games are very pleasing to the little ones, and often when ten of them are using the frames at the same time, seated around the little tables, quiet and serious, they give the impression of a workroom filled with tiny workers.

RESPIRATORY GYMNASTICS

The purpose of these gymnastics is to regulate the respiratory movements: in other words, to teach the *art of breathing*. They also help greatly the correct formation of the child's *speech habits*. The exercises which we use were introduced into school literature by Professor Sala. We have chosen the simple exercises described by him in his treatise, "Cura della Balbuzie."[1] These include a number of respiratory gymnastic exercises with which are co-ordinated muscular exercises. I give here an example:

Mouth wide open, tongue held flat, hands on hips.

Breathe deeply, lift the shoulders rapidly, lowering the diaphragm.

Expel breath slowly, lowering shoulders slowly, returning to normal position.

The directress should select or devise simple breathing exercises, to be accompanied with arm movements, etc.

Exercises for proper use of *lips, tongue, and teeth*. These exercises teach the movements of the lips and tongue in the pronunciation of certain fundamental consonant sounds, reinforcing the muscles, and making them ready for these movements. These gymnastics prepare the organs used in the formation of language.

In presenting such exercises we begin with the entire class, but finish by testing the children individually. We ask the child to pronounce, *aloud* and with *force,* the first syllable of a word. When all are intent upon putting the greatest possible force into this, we call each child separately, and have him repeat the word. If he pronounces it correctly, we send him to the right, if badly, to the left. Those who have difficulty with the word, are then encouraged to repeat it several times. The teacher takes note of the age of the child, and of the particular defects in the movements of the muscles used in articulating. She may then touch the muscles which should be used, tapping, for example, the curve of the lips, or even taking hold of the child's tongue and placing it against the dental arch, or showing him clearly the movements which she herself makes when pronouncing the syllable. She must seek in every way to aid the normal development of the movements necessary to the exact articulation of the word.

As the basis for these gymnastics we have the children

pronounce the words: *pane—fame—tana—zina—stella—rana—gatto*.

In the pronunciation of *pane*, the child should repeat with much force, *pa, pa, pa*, thus exercising the muscles producing orbicular contraction of the lips.

In *fame* repeating *fa, fa, fa*, the child exercises the movements of the lower lip against the upper dental arch.

In *tana*, having him repeat *ta, ta, ta*, we cause him to exercise the movement of the tongue against the upper dental arch.

In *zina*, we provoke the contact of the upper and lower dental arches.

With *stella* we have him repeat the whole word, bringing the teeth together, and holding the tongue (which has a tendency to protrude) close against the upper teeth.

In *rana* we have him repeat *r, r, r*, thus exercising the tongue in the vibratory movements. In *gatto* we hold the voice upon the guttural *g*.

NOTE

1. "Cura della Balbuzie e del Difetti di Pronunzia." Sala. Ulrico Hoepli, Publisher, Milan, Italy.

10

Nature in Education—Agricultural Labour: Culture of Plants and Animals

Itard, in a remarkable pedagogical treatise: "*Des premiers développements du jeune sauvage de l'Aveyron*," expounds in detail the drama of a curious, gigantic education which attempted to overcome the psychical darkness of an idiot and at the same time to snatch a man from primitive nature.

The savage of the Aveyron was a child who had grown up in the natural state: criminally abandoned in a forest where his assassins thought they had killed him, he was cured by natural means, and had survived for many years free and naked in the wilderness, until, captured by hunters, he entered into the civilised life of Paris, showing by the scars with which his miserable body was furrowed the story of the struggles with wild beasts, and of lacerations caused by falling from heights.

The child was, and always remained, mute; his mentality, diagnosed by Pinel as idiotic, remained forever almost inaccessible to intellectual education.

To this child are due the first steps of positive pedagogy. Itard, a physician of deaf-mutes and a student of philosophy, undertook his education with methods which he had already partially tried for treating defective hearing—believing at the beginning that the savage showed characteristics of inferiority, not because he was a degraded organism, but for want of education. He was a follower of the principles of Helvetius: "Man is nothing without the work of man"; that is, he believed in the omnipotence of education, and was opposed to the pedagogical principle which Rousseau had promulgated before the Revolution: "*Tout est bien sortant des mains de l'Auteur des choses, tout dégénère dans les mains de l'homme,"*—that is, the work of education is deleterious and spoils the man.

The savage, according to the erroneous first impression of Itard, demonstrated experimentally by his characteristics the truth of the former assertion. When, however, he perceived, with the help of Pinel, that he had to do with an idiot, his philosophical theories gave place to the most admirable, tentative, experimental pedagogy.

Itard divides the education of the savage into two parts. In the first, he endeavours to lead the child from natural life to social life; and in the second, he attempts the intellectual education of the idiot. The child in his life of frightful abandonment had found one happiness; he had, so to speak, immersed himself in, and unified himself with, nature, taking delight in it—rains, snow, tempests, boundless space, had been his sources of entertainment, his companions, his love. Civil life is a renunciation of all this: but it is an acquisition beneficent to human progress. In Itard's pages we find vividly described the moral work which led the savage to civilisation, multiplying the needs of the child and surrounding him with loving care. Here is a sample of the admirably patient work of Itard as *observer of the spontaneous expressions* of his pupil: it can most truly give teachers, who are to prepare for the experimental method, an idea of the patience and the self-abnegation necessary in dealing with a phenomenon which is to be observed:

"When, for example, he was observed within his room, he was seen to be lounging with oppressive monotony, continually directing his eyes toward the window, with his gaze wandering in the void. If on such occasions a sudden storm blew up, if the sun, hidden behind the clouds, peeped out of a sudden, lighting the atmosphere brilliantly, there were loud bursts of laughter and almost convulsive joy. Sometimes, instead of these expressions of joy, there was a sort of frenzied rage: he would twist his arms, put his clenched fists upon his eyes, gnashing his teeth and becoming dangerous to those about him.

"One morning, when the snow fell abundantly while he

was still in bed, he uttered a cry of joy upon awaking, leaped from his bed, ran to the window and then to the door; went and came impatiently from one to the other; then ran out undressed as he was into the garden. There, giving vent to his joy with the shrillest of cries, he ran, rolled in the snow, gathered it up in handfuls, and swallowed it with incredible avidity.

"But his sensations at sight of the great spectacles of nature did not always manifest themselves in such a vivid and noisy manner. It is worthy of note that in certain cases they were expressed by a quiet regret and melancholy. Thus, it was when the rigour of the weather drove everybody from the garden that the savage of the Aveyron chose to go there. He would walk around it several times and finally sit down upon the edge of the fountain.

"I have often stopped for *whole hours*, and with indescribable pleasure, to watch him as he sat thus—to see how his face, inexpressive or contracted by grimaces, gradually assumed an expression of sadness, and of melancholy reminiscence, while his eyes were fixed upon the surface of the water into which from time to time he would throw a few dead leaves.

"If when there was a full moon, a sheaf of mild beams penetrated into his room, he rarely failed to wake and to take his place at the window. He would remain there *for a large part of the night*, erect, motionless, with his head thrust forward, his eyes fixed on the countryside lighted by the moon, plunged in a sort of contemplative ecstasy, the immobility and silence of which were only interrupted at long intervals by a breath as deep as a sigh, which died away in a plaintive sound of lamentation."

Elsewhere, Itard relates that the boy did not know the *walking gait* which we use in civilised life, but only the *running gait*, and tells how he, Itard, ran after him at the beginning, when he took him out into the streets of Paris, rather than violently check the boy's running.

The gradual and gentle leading of the savage through all the manifestations of social life, the early adaptation of the teacher to the pupil rather than of the pupil to the teacher, the successive attraction to a new life which was to win over the child by its charms, and not be imposed upon him violently so that the pupil should feel it as a burden and a torture, are as many precious educative expressions which may be generalised and applied to the education of children.

I believe that there exists no document which offers so poignant and so eloquent a contrast between the life of nature and the life of society, and which so graphically shows that society is made up solely of renunciations and restraints. Let it suffice to recall the run, checked to a walk, and the loud-voiced cry, checked to the modulations of the ordinary speaking voice.

And, yet, without any violence, leaving to social life the task of charming the child little by little, Itard's education triumphs. It is true that civilised life is made by renunciation of the life of nature; it is almost the snatching of a man from the lap of earth; it is like snatching the new-born child from its mother's breast; but it is also a new life.

In Itard's pages we see the final triumph of the love of man over the love of nature: the savage of the Aveyron ends by *feeling* and preferring the affection of Itard, the caresses, the tears shed over him, to the joy of immersing himself voluptuously in the snow, and of contemplating the infinite expanse of the sky on a starry night: one day after an attempted escape into the country, he returns of his own accord, humble and repentant, to find his good soup and his warm bed.

It is true that man has created enjoyments in social life and has brought about a vigorous human love in community life. But nevertheless he still belongs to nature, and, especially when he is a child, he must needs draw from it the forces necessary to the development of the body and of the spirit. We have intimate communications with nature which have an influence, even a material influence, on the growth of the body. (For example, a physiologist, isolating young guinea pigs from terrestrial magnetism by means of insulators, found that they grew up with rickets.)

In the education of little children Itard's educative drama is repeated: we must prepare man, who is one among the living creatures and therefore belongs to nature, for social life, because social life being his own peculiar work, must also correspond to the manifestation of his natural activity.

But the advantages which we prepare for him in this social life, in a great measure escape the little child, who at the beginning of his life is a predominantly vegetative creature.

To soften this transition in education, by giving a large part of the educative work to nature itself, is as necessary as it is not to snatch the little child suddenly and violently from its mother and to take him to school; and precisely this is done in the "Children's Houses," which are situated within the tenements where the parents live, where the cry of the child reaches the mother and the mother's voice answers it.

Nowadays, under the form of child hygiene, this part of education is much cultivated: children are allowed to grow up in the open air, in the public gardens, or are left for many hours half naked on the seashore, exposed to the rays of the sun. It has been understood, through the diffusion of marine and Apennine colonies, that the best means of invigorating the child is to immerse him in nature.

Short and comfortable clothing for children, sandals for the feet, nudity of the lower extremities, are so many liberations from the oppressive shackles of civilisation.

It is an obvious principle that we should sacrifice to natural liberties in education only as much as is *necessary* for the acquisition of the greater pleasures which are offered by civilisation without *useless sacrifices*.

But in all this progress of modern child education, we have not freed ourselves from the prejudice which denies children spiritual expression and spiritual needs, and makes us consider them only as amiable vegetating bodies to be cared for, kissed, and set in motion. The *education* which a good mother or a good modern teacher gives today to the child who, for example, is running about in a flower garden is the counsel *not to touch the flowers*, not to tread on the grass; as if it were sufficient for the child to satisfy the physiological needs of his body by moving his legs and breathing fresh air.

But if for the physical life it is necessary to have the child exposed to the vivifying forces of nature, it is also necessary for his psychical life to place the soul of the child in contact with creation, in order that he may lay up for himself treasure from the directly educating forces of living nature. The method for arriving at this end is to set the child at agricultural labour, guiding him to the cultivation of plants and animals, and so to the intelligent contemplation of nature.

Already, in England Mrs. Latter has devised the *basis* for a method of child education by means of *gardening* and *horticulture*. She sees in the contemplation of developing life the basis of religion, since the soul of the child may go from the creature to the Creator. She sees in it also the point of departure for intellectual education, which she limits to drawing from life as a step toward art, to the ideas about plants, insects, and seasons, which spring from agriculture, and to the first notions of household life, which spring from the cultivation and the culinary preparation of certain alimentary products that children later serve upon the table, providing afterwards also for the washing of the utensils and tableware.

Mrs. Latter's conception is too one-sided; but her institutions, which continue to spread in England, undoubtedly complete the natural *education* which, up to this time limited to the physical side, has already been so efficacious in invigorating the bodies of English children. Moreover, her experience offers a positive corroboration of the practicability of agricultural teaching in the case of little children.

As for deficients, I have seen agriculture applied on a large scale to their education at Paris by the means which the kindly spirit of Baccelli tried to introduce into the elementary schools when he attempted to institute the "little educative gardens." In every *little garden* are sown different agricultural products, demonstrating practically the proper method and the proper time for seeding and for crop gathering, and the period of development of the various products; the manner of preparing the soil, of enriching it with natural or chemical manures, etc. The same is done for ornamental plants and for gardening, which is the work yielding the best income for deficients, when they are of an age to practise a profession.

But this side of education, though it contains, in the first place, an objective method of intellectual culture, and, in addition, a professional preparation, is not, in my opinion, to be taken into serious consideration for child education. The educational conception of this age must be solely that of aiding the psycho-physical development of the individual; and, this being the case, agriculture and animal culture contain in themselves precious means of moral education which can be analysed far more than is done by Mrs. Latter, who sees in them essentially a method of conducting the child's soul to religious feeling. Indeed, in this method, which is a progressive ascent, several gradations can be distinguished: I mention here the principal ones:

First. The child is initiated into observation of the phenomena of life. He stands with respect to the plants and animals in relations analogous to those in which the *observing*teacher stands towards him. Little by little, as interest and observation grow, his zealous care for the living creatures grows also, and in this way, the child can logically be brought to appreciate the care which the mother and the teacher take of him.

Second. The child is initiated into *foresight* by way of *auto-education*; when he knows that the life of the plants that have been sown depends upon his care in watering them, and that of the animals, upon his diligence in feeding them, without which the little plant dries up and the animals suffer hunger, the child becomes vigilant, as one who is beginning to feel a mission in life. Moreover, a voice quite different from that of his mother and his teacher calling him to his duties, is speaking here, exhorting him never to forget the task he has undertaken. It is the plaintive voice of the needy life which lives by his care. Between the child and the living creatures which he cultivates there is born a mysterious correspondence which induces the child to fulfil certain determinate acts without the intervention of the teacher, that is, leads him to an *auto-education.*

The rewards which the child reaps also remain between

him and nature: one fine day after long patient care in carrying food and straw to the brooding pigeons, behold the little ones! behold a number of chickens peeping about the setting hen which yesterday sat motionless in her brooding place! behold one day the tender little rabbits in the hutch where formerly dwelt in solitude the pair of big rabbits to which he had not a few times lovingly carried the green vegetables left over in his mother's kitchen!

I have not yet been able to institute in Rome the breeding of animals, but in the "Children's Houses" at Milan there are several animals, among them a pair of pretty little white American fowl that live in a diminutive and elegant *chalet*, similar in construction to a Chinese pagoda: in front of it, a little piece of ground inclosed by a rampart is reserved for the pair. The little door of the *chalet* is locked at evening, and the children take care of it in turn. With what delight they go in the morning to unlock the door, to fetch water and straw, and with what care they watch during the day, and at evening lock the door after having made sure that the fowl lack nothing! The teacher informs me that among all the educative exercises this is the most welcome, and seems also the most important of all. Many a time when the children are tranquilly occupied in tasks, each at the work he prefers, one, two, or three, get up silently, and go out to cast a glance at the animals to see if they need care. Often it happens that a child absents himself for a long time and the teacher surprises him watching enchantedly the fish gliding ruddy and resplendent in the sunlight in the waters of the fountain.

One day I received from the teacher in Milan a letter in which she spoke to me with great enthusiasm of a truly wonderful piece of news. The little pigeons were hatched. For the children it was a great festival. They felt themselves to some extent the parents of these little ones, and no artificial reward which had flattered their vanity would ever have provoked such a truly fine emotion. Not less great are the joys which vegetable nature provides. In one of the "Children's Houses" at Rome, where there was no soil that could be cultivated, there have been arranged, through the efforts of Signora Talamo, flower-pots all around the large terrace, and climbing plants near the walls. The children never forget to water the plants with their little watering-pots.

One day I found them seated on the ground, all in a circle, around a splendid red rose which had bloomed in the night; silent and calm, literally immersed in mute contemplation.

Third. The children are initiated into the virtue of *patience and into confident expectation,* which is a form of faith and of philosophy of life.

When the children put a seed into the ground, and wait until it fructifies, and see the first appearance of the shapeless plant, and wait for the growth and the transformations into flower and fruit, and see how some plants sprout sooner and some later, and how the deciduous plants have a rapid life, and the fruit-trees a slower growth, they end by acquiring a peaceful equilibrium of conscience, and absorb the first germs of that wisdom which so characterised the tillers of the soil in the time when they still kept their primitive simplicity.

Fourth. The children are inspired with a feeling for nature, which is maintained by the marvels of creation—that creation which *rewards* with a generosity not measured by the labour of those who help it to evolve the life of its creatures.

Even while at the work, a sort of correspondence arises between the child's soul and the lives which are developed under his care. The child loves naturally the manifestations of life: Mrs. Latter tells us how easily little ones are interested even in earthworms and in the movement of the larvæ of insects in manure, without feeling that horror which we, who have grown up isolated from nature, experience towards certain animals. It is well then, to develop this feeling of trust and confidence in living creatures, which is, moreover, a form of love, and of union with the universe.

But what most develops a feeling of nature is the *cultivation* of the *living* things, because they by their natural development give back far more than they receive, and show something like infinity in their beauty and variety. When the child has cultivated the iris or the pansy, the rose or the hyacinth, has placed in the soil a seed or a bulb and periodically watered it, or has planted a fruit-bearing shrub, and the blossomed flower and the ripened fruit offer themselves as a *generous gift* of nature, a rich reward for a small effort; it seems almost as if nature were answering with her gifts to the feeling of desire, to the vigilant love of the cultivator, rather than striking a balance with his material efforts.

It will be quite different when the child has to gather the *material* fruits of his labour: motionless, uniform objects, which are consumed and dispersed rather than increased and multiplied.

The difference between the products of nature and those of industry, between divine products and human products—it is this that must be born spontaneously in the child's conscience, like the determination of a fact.

But at the same time, as the plant must give its fruit, so man must give his labour.

Fifth. The child follows the natural way of development of the human race. In short, such education makes the evolution of the individual harmonise with that of humanity. Man passed from the natural to the artificial state through agriculture: when he discovered the secret of intensifying the production of the soil, he obtained the reward of civilisation.

The same path must be traversed by the child who is destined to become a civilised man.

The action of educative nature so understood is very practically accessible. Because, even if the vast stretch of ground and the large courtyard necessary for physical education are lacking, it will always be possible to find a few square yards of land that may be cultivated, or a little place where pigeons can make their nest, things sufficient for spiritual education. Even a pot of flowers at the window can, if necessary, fulfil the purpose.

In the first "Children's House" in Rome we have a vast courtyard, cultivated as a garden, where the children are free to run in the open air—and, besides, a long stretch of ground, which is planted on one side with trees, has a branching path in the middle, and on the opposite side, has broken ground for the cultivation of plants. This last, we have divided into so many portions, reserving one for each child.

While the smaller children run freely up and down the paths, or rest in the shade of the trees, the *possessors of the earth* (children from four years of age up), are sowing, or hoeing, watering or examining, the surface of the soil watching for the sprouting of plants. It is interesting to note the following fact: the little reservations of the children are placed along the wall of the tenement, in a spot formerly neglected because it leads to a blind road; the inhabitants of the house, therefore, had the habit of throwing from those windows every kind of offal, and at the beginning our garden was thus contaminated.

But, little by little, without any exhortation on our part, solely through the respect born in the people's mind for the children's labour, nothing more fell from the windows, except the loving glances and smiles of the mothers upon the soil which was the beloved possession of their little children.

11

Manual Labour—The Potter's Art and Building

Manual labour is distinguished from manual gymnastics by the fact that the object of the latter is to exercise the hand, and the former, to *accomplish a determinate work*, being, or simulating, a socially useful object. The one perfects the individual, the other enriches the world; the two things are, however, connected because, in general, only one who has perfected his own hand can produce a useful product.

I have thought wise, after a short trial, to exclude completely Froebel's exercises, because weaving and sewing on cardboard are ill adapted to the physiological state of the child's visual organs where the powers of the accommodation of the eye have not yet reached complete development; hence, these exercises cause an *effort* of the organ which may have a fatal influence on the development of the sight. The other little exercises of Froebel, such as the folding of paper, are exercises of the hand, not work.

There is still left plastic work,—the most rational among all the exercises of Froebel,—which consists in making the child reproduce determinate objects in clay.

In consideration, however, of the system of liberty which I proposed, I did not like to make the children *copy* anything, and, in giving them clay to fashion in their own manner, I did not direct the children to *produce useful things*; nor was I accomplishing an educative result, in as much as plastic work, as I shall show later, serves for the study of the psychic individuality of the child in his spontaneous manifestations, but not for his education.

I decided therefore to try in the "Children's Houses" some

very interesting exercises which I had seen accomplished by an artist, Professor Randone, in the "School of Educative Art" founded by him. This school had its origin along with the society for young people, called *Giovinezza Gentile*, both school and society having the object of educating youth in gentleness towards their surroundings—that is, in respect for objects, buildings, monuments: a really important part of civil education, and one which interested me particularly on account of the "Children's Houses," since that institution has, as its fundamental aim, to teach precisely this respect for the walls, for the house, for the surroundings.

Very suitably, Professor Randone had decided that the society of *Giovinezza Gentile* could not be based upon sterile theoretical preachings of the principles of citizenship, or upon moral pledges taken by the children; but that it must proceed from an artistic education which should lead the youth to appreciate and love, and consequently respect, objects and especially monuments and historic buildings. Thus the "School of Educative Art" was inspired by a broad artistic conception including the reproduction of objects which are commonly met in the surroundings; the history and pre-history of their production, and the illustration of the principal civic monuments which, in Rome, are in large measure composed of archaeological monuments. In order the more directly to accomplish his object, Professor Randone founded his admirable school in an opening in one of the most artistic parts of the walls of Rome, namely, the wall of Belisarius, overlooking the Villa Umberto Primo—a wall which has been entirely neglected by the authorities and by no means respected by the citizens, and upon which Randone lavished care, decorating it with graceful hanging gardens on the outside, and locating within it the School of Art which was to shape the *Giovinezza Gentile*.

Here Randone has tried, very fittingly, to rebuild and revive a form of art which was once the glory of Italy and of Florence—the potter's art, that is, the art of constructing vases.

The archaeological, historical, and artistic importance of the vase is very great, and may be compared with the numismatic art. In fact the first object of which humanity felt the need was the *vase*, which came into being with the utilisation of fire, and before the discovery of the *production* of fire. Indeed the first food of mankind was cooked in a vase.

One of the things most important, ethnically, in judging the civilisation of a primitive people is the grade of perfection attained in *pottery*; in fact, the *vase* for domestic life and the *axe* for social life are the first sacred symbols which we find in the prehistoric epoch, and are the religious symbols connected with the temples of the gods and with the cult of the dead. Even to-day, religious cults have sacred vases in their Sancta Sanctorum.

People who have progressed in civilisation show their feeling for art and their æsthetic feeling also in *vases* which are multiplied in almost infinite form, as we see in Egyptian, Etruscan, and Greek art.

The vase then comes into being, attains perfection, and is multiplied in its uses and its forms, in the course of human civilisation; and the history of the vase follows the history of humanity itself. Besides the civil and moral importance of the vase, we have another and practical one, its literal *adaptability* to every modification of form, and its susceptibility to the most diverse ornamentation; in this, it gives free scope to the individual genius of the artist.

Thus, when once the handicraft leading to the construction of vases has been learned (and this is the part of the progress in the work, learned from the direct and graduated instruction of the teacher), anyone can modify it according to the inspiration of his own æsthetic taste and this is the artistic, individual part of the work. Besides this, in Randone's school the use of the potter's wheel is taught, and also the composition of the mixture for the bath of majolica ware, and baking the pieces in the furnace, stages of manual labour which contain an industrial culture.

Another work in the School of Educative Art is the manufacture of diminutive bricks, and their baking in the furnace, and the construction of diminutive *walls* built by the same processes which the masons use in the construction of houses, the bricks being joined by means of mortar handled with a trowel. After the simple construction of the wall,—which is very amusing for the children who build it, placing brick on brick, superimposing row on row,—the children pass to the construction of real *houses,*—first, resting on the ground, and, then, really constructed with foundations, after a previous excavation of large holes in the ground by means of little hoes and shovels. These little houses have openings corresponding to windows and doors, and are variously ornamented in their façades by little tiles of bright and multi-coloured majolica: the tiles themselves being manufactured by the children.

Thus the children learn to *appreciate* the objects and constructions which surround them, while a real manual and artistic labour gives them profitable exercise.

Such is the manual training which I have adopted in the "Children's Houses"; after two or three lessons the little pupils are already enthusiastic about the construction of vases, and they preserve very carefully their own products, in which they take pride. With their plastic art they then model little objects, eggs or fruits, with which they themselves fill the vases. One of the first undertakings is the simple vase of red clay filled with eggs of white clay; then comes the modelling of the vase with one or more spouts, of the narrow-mouthed vase, of the vase with a handle, of that with two or three handles, of the tripod, of the amphora.

For children of the age of five or six, the work of the potter's wheel begins. But what most delights the children is the work of building a wall with little bricks, and seeing a little house, the fruit of their own hands, rise in the vicinity of the ground in which are growing plants, also cultivated by them. Thus the age of childhood epitomises the principal primitive labours of humanity, when the human race, changing from the nomadic to the stable condition, demanded of the earth its fruit, built itself shelter, and devised vases to cook the foods yielded by the fertile earth.

12

Education of the Senses

In a pedagogical method which is experimental the education of the senses must undoubtedly assume the greatest importance. Experimental psychology also takes note of movements by means of sense measurements.

Pedagogy, however, although it may profit by psychometry is not designed to *measure* the sensations, but *educate* the senses. This is a point easily understood, yet one which is often confused. While the proceedings of esthesiometry are not to any great extent applicable to little children, the *education* of the *senses* is entirely possible.

We do not start from the conclusions of experimental psychology. That is, it is not the knowledge of the average sense conditions according to the age of the child which leads us to determine the educational applications we shall make. We start essentially from a method, and it is probable that psychology will be able to draw its conclusions from pedagogy so understood, and not *vice versa*.

The method used by me is that of making a pedagogical experiment with a didactic object and awaiting the spontaneous reaction of the child. This is a method in every way analogous to that of experimental psychology.

I make use of a material which, at first glance, may be confused with psychometric material. Teachers from Milan who had followed the course in the Milan school of experimental psychology, seeing my material exposed, would recognise among it, measures of the perception of colour, hardness, and weight, and would conclude that, in truth, I brought no new contribution to pedagogy since these instruments were already known to them.

But the great difference between the two materials lies in this: The esthesiometer carries within itself the possibility of *measuring;* my objects on the contrary, often do not permit a measure, but are adapted to cause the child to *exercise* the senses.

In order that an instrument shall attain such a pedagogical end, it is necessary that it shall not *weary* but shall *divert* the child. Here lies the difficulty in the selection of didactic material. It is known that the psychometric instruments are great *consumers of energy*—for this reason, when Pizzoli wished to apply them to the education of the senses, he did not succeed because the child was annoyed by them, and became tired. Instead, *the aim of education is to develop the energies.*

Psychometric instruments, or better, the instruments of *esthesiometry*, are prepared in their differential gradations upon the laws of Weber, which were in truth drawn from experiments made upon adults.

With little children, we must proceed to the making of trials, and must select the didactic materials in which they show themselves to be interested.

This I did in the first year of the "Children's Houses" adopting a great variety of stimuli, with a number of which I had already experimented in the school for deficients.

Much of the material used for deficients is abandoned in the education of the normal child—and much that is used has been greatly modified. I believe, however, that I have arrived at a *selection of objects* (which I do not here wish to speak of in the technical language of psychology as stimuli) representing the minimum *necessary* to a practical sense education.

These objects constitute the *didactic system* (or set of didactic materials) used by me. They are manufactured by the House of Labour of the Humanitarian Society at Milan.

A description of the objects will be given as the educational scope of each is explained. Here I shall limit myself to the setting forth of a few general considerations.

First. The difference in the reaction between deficient and normal children, in the presentation of didactic material made up of graded stimuli. This difference is plainly seen from the fact that the same didactic material used with deficients *makes education possible,* while with normal children it *provokes auto-education.*

This fact is one of the most interesting I have met with in all my experience, and it inspired and rendered possible the method of *observation* and *liberty*.

Let us suppose that we use our first object,—a block in which solid geometric forms are set. Into corresponding holes in the block are set ten little wooden cylinders, the bases diminishing gradually about the millimetres. The game consists in taking the cylinders out of their places, putting them on the table, mixing them, and then putting each one back in its own place. The aim is to educate the eye to the differential perception of dimensions.

With the deficient child, it would be necessary to begin with exercises in which the stimuli were much more strongly contrasted, and to arrive at this exercise only after many others had preceded it.

With normal children, this is, on the other hand, the first object which we may present, and out of all the didactic material this is the game preferred by the very little children of two and a half and three years. Once we arrived at this exercise with a deficient child, it was necessary continually and actively to recall his attention, inviting him to look at the block and showing him the various pieces. And if the child once succeeded in placing all the cylinders properly, he stopped, and the game was finished. Whenever the deficient child committed an error, it was necessary to correct it, or to urge him to correct it himself, and when he was able to correct an error he was usually quite indifferent.

Now the normal child, instead, takes spontaneously a lively interest in this game. He pushes away all who would interfere, or offer to help him, and wishes to be alone before his problem.

It had already been noted that little ones of two or three years take the greatest pleasure in arranging small objects, and this experiment in the "Children's Houses" demonstrates the truth of this assertion.

Now, and here is the important point, the normal child

attentively observes the relation between the size of the opening and that of the object which he is to place in the mould, and is greatly interested in the game, as is clearly shown by the expression of attention on the little face.

If he mistakes, placing one of the objects in an opening that is small for it, he takes it away, and proceeds to make various trials, seeking the proper opening. If he makes a contrary error, letting the cylinder fall into an opening that is a little too large for it, and then collects all the successive cylinders in openings just a little too large, he will find himself at the last with the big cylinder in his hand while only the smallest opening is empty. The didactic material *controls every error*. The child proceeds to correct himself, doing this in various ways. Most often he feels the cylinders or shakes them, in order to recognise which are the largest. Sometimes, he sees at a glance where his error lies, pulls the cylinders from the places where they should not be, and puts those left out where they belong, then replaces all the others. The normal child always repeats the exercise with growing interest.

Indeed, it is precisely in these errors that the educational importance of the didactic material lies, and when the child with evident security places each piece in its proper place, he has outgrown the exercise, and this piece of material becomes useless to him.

This self-correction leads the child to concentrate his attention upon the differences of dimensions, and to compare the various pieces. It is in just this comparison that the*psycho-sensory* exercise lies.

There is, therefore, no question here of teaching the child the *knowledge* of the dimensions, through the medium of these pieces. Neither is it our aim that the child shall know how to use, *without an error*, the material presented to him thus performing the exercises well.

That would place our material on the same basis as many others, for example that of Froebel, and would require again the *active* work of the *teacher*, who busies herself furnishing knowledge, and making haste to correct every error in order that the child may *learn the use of the objects.*

Here instead it is the work of the child, the auto-correction, the auto-education which acts, for the *teacher must not interfere* in the *slightest* way. No teacher can furnish the child with the *agility which he acquires* through gymnastic *exercises*: it is necessary that the pupil perfect himself through his own efforts. It is very much the same with the *education of the senses.*

It might be said that the same thing is true of every form of education; a man is not what he is because of the teachers he has had, but because of what he has done.

One of the difficulties of putting this method into practice with teachers of the old school, lies in the difficulty of preventing them from intervening when the little child remains for some time puzzled before some error, and with his eyebrows drawn together and his lips puckered, makes repeated efforts to correct himself. When they see this, the old-time teachers are seized with pity, and long, with an almost irresistible force, to help the child. When we prevent this intervention, they burst into words of compassion for the little scholar, but he soon shows in his smiling face the joy of having surmounted an obstacle.

Normal children repeat such exercises many times. This repetition varies according to the individual. Some children after having completed the exercise five or six times are tired of it. Others will remove and replace the pieces at least *twenty times,* with an expression of evident interest. Once, after I had watched a little one of four years repeat this exercise sixteen times, I had the other children sing in order to distract her, but she continued unmoved to take out the cylinders, mix them up and put them back in their places.

An intelligent teacher ought to be able to make most interesting individual psychological observations, and, to a certain point, should be able to measure the length of time for which the various stimuli held the attention.

In fact, when the child educates himself, and when the control and correction of errors is yielded to the didactic material, there *remains for the teacher nothing but to observe.* She must then be more of a psychologist than a teacher, and this shows the importance of a scientific preparation on the part of the teacher.

Indeed, with my methods, the teacher teaches *little* and observes *much*, and, above all, it is her function to direct the psychic activity of the children and their physiological development. For this reason I have changed the name of teacher into that of directress.

At first this name provoked many smiles, for everyone asked whom there was for this teacher to direct, since she had no assistants, and since she must leave her little scholars *in liberty*. But her direction is much more profound and important than that which is commonly understood, for this teacher directs *the life and the soul.*

Second. The education of the senses has, as its aim, the refinement of the differential perception of stimuli by means of repeated exercises.

There exists a *sensory culture*, which is not generally taken into consideration, but which is a factor in esthesiometry.

For example, in the mental *tests* which are used in France, or in a series of tests which De Sanctis has established for the *diagnosis* of the intellectual status, I have often seen used *cubes of different sizes placed at varying distances*. The child was to select the *smallest* and the *largest*, while the chronometer measured the time of reaction between the command and the execution of the act. Account was also taken of the errors. I repeat that in such experiments the factor of *culture* is forgotten and by this I mean *sensory culture*.

Our children have, for example, among the didactic material for the education of the senses, a series of ten cubes. The first has a base of ten centimetres, and the others decrease, successively, one centimetre as to base, the smallest cube having a base of one centimetre. The exercise consists in throwing the blocks, which are pink in colour, down upon a green carpet, and then building them up into a little tower, placing the largest cube as the base, and then placing the others in order of size until the little cube of one centimetre is placed at the top.

The little one must each time select, from the blocks scattered upon the green carpet, "the largest" block. This game is most entertaining to the little ones of two years and a half, who, as soon as they have constructed the little tower, tumble it down with little blows of the hand, admiring the pink cubes as they lie scattered upon the green carpet. Then, they begin again the construction, building and destroying a definite number of times.

If we were to place before these tests one of my children from three to four years, and one of the children from the first elementary (six or seven years old), my pupil would undoubtedly manifest a shorter period of reaction, and would not commit errors. The same may be said for the tests of the chromatic sense, etc.

This educational method should therefore prove interesting to students of experimental psychology as well as to teachers.

In conclusion, let me summarize briefly: Our didactic material renders auto-education possible, permits a methodical education of the senses. Not upon the ability of the teacher does such education rest, but upon the didactic system. This presents objects which, first, attract the spontaneous attention of the child, and, second, contain a rational gradation of stimuli.

We must not confuse the *education* of the senses, with the concrete ideas which may be gathered from our environment by means of the senses. Nor must this education of the senses be identical in our minds with the language through which is given the nomenclature corresponding to the concrete idea, nor with the acquisition of the abstract idea of the exercises.

Let us consider what the music master does in giving instruction in piano playing. He teaches the pupil the correct position of the body, gives him the idea of the notes, shows him the correspondence between the written notes and the touch and the position of the fingers, and then he leaves the child to perform the exercise by himself. If a pianist is to be made of this child, there must, between the ideas given by the teacher and the musical exercises, intervene long and patient application to those exercises which serve to give agility to the articulation of the fingers and of the tendons, in order that the co-ordination of special muscular movements shall become automatic, and that the muscles of the hand shall become strong through their repeated use.

The pianist must, therefore, *act for himself*, and the more his natural tendencies lead him to *persist* in these exercises the greater will be his success. However, without the direction of the master the exercise will not suffice to develop the scholar into a true pianist.

The directress of the "Children's House" must have a clear idea of the two factors which enter into her work—the guidance of the child, and the individual exercise.

Only after she has this concept clearly fixed in her mind, may she proceed to the application of a *method* to *guide* the spontaneous education of the child and to impart necessary notions to him.

In the opportune quality and in the manner of this intervention lies the *personal art* of the *educator*.

For example, in the "Children's House" in the Prati di Castello, where the pupils belong to the middle-class, I found, a month after the opening of the school, a child of five years who already knew how to compose any word, as he knew the alphabet perfectly—he had learned it in two weeks. He knew how to write on the blackboard, and in the exercises in free design he showed himself not only to be an observer, but to have some intuitive idea of perspective, drawing a house and chair very cleverly. As for the exercises of the chromatic sense, he could mix together the eight gradations of the eight colours which we use, and from this mass of sixty-four tablets, each wound with silk of a different colour or shade, he could rapidly separate the eight groups. Having done this, he would proceed with ease to arrange each colour series in perfect gradation. In this game the child would almost cover one of the little tables with a carpet of finely-shaded colours. I made the experiment, taking him to the window and showing him in full daylight one of the coloured tablets, telling him to look at it well, so that he might be able to remember it. I then sent him to the table on which all the gradations were spread out, and asked him to find the tablet like the one at which he had looked. He committed only very slight errors, often choosing the exact shade but more often the one next it, rarely a tint two grades removed from the right one. This boy had then a power of discrimination and a colour memory which were almost prodigious. Like all the other children, he was exceedingly fond of the colour exercises. But when I asked the name of the white colour spool, he hesitated for a long time before replying uncertainly "white." Now a child of such intelligence should have been able, even without the special intervention of the teacher, to learn the name of each colour.

The directress told me that having noticed that the child had great difficulty in retaining the nomenclature of the colours, she had up until that time left him to exercise himself freely with the games for the colour sense. At the same time he had developed rapidly a power over written language, which in my method as presented through a series of problems to be solved. These problems are presented as sense exercises. This child was, therefore, most intelligent. In him the discriminative sensory perceptions kept pace with great intellectual activities—attention and judgment. But his *memory for names* was inferior.

The directress had thought best not to interfere, as yet, in the teaching of the child. Certainly, the education of the child was a little disordered, and the directress had left the spontaneous explanation of his mental activities excessively free. However desirable it may be to furnish a sense education as a basis for intellectual ideas, it is nevertheless advisable at the same time to associate the *language* with these *perceptions*.

In this connection I have found excellent for use with normal children *the three periods* of which the lesson according to Séguin consists:

First Period. The association of the sensory perception with the name.

For example, we present to the child, two colours, red and blue. Presenting the red, we say simply, "This is red," and presenting the blue, "This is blue." Then, we lay the spools upon the table under the eyes of the child.

Second Period. Recognition of the object corresponding to

the name. We Say to the child, "Give me the red," and then, "Give me the blue."

Third Period. The remembering of the name corresponding to the object. We ask the child, showing him the object, "What is this?" and he should respond, "Red."

Séguin insists strongly upon these three periods, and urges that the colours be left for several instants under the eyes of the child. He also advises us never to present the colour singly, but always two at a time, since the contrast helps the chromatic memory. Indeed, I have proved that there cannot be a better method for teaching colour to the deficients, who, with this method were able to learn the colours much more perfectly than normal children in the ordinary schools who have had a haphazard sense education. For normal children however there exists a *period preceding* the Three Periods of Séguin—a period which contains the real *sense education*. This is the acquisition of a fineness of differential perception, which can be obtained *only* through auto-education.

This, then, is an example of the great superiority of the normal child, and of the greater effect of education which such pedagogical methods may exercise upon the mental development of normal as compared with deficient children.

The association of the name with the stimulus is a source of great pleasure to the normal child. I remember, one day, I had taught a little girl, who was not yet three years old, and who was a little tardy in the development of language, the names of three colours. I had the children place one of their little tables near a window, and seating myself in one of the little chairs, I seated the little girl in a similar chair at my right.

I had, on the table, six of the colour spools in pairs, that is two reds, two blues, two yellows. In the First Period, I placed one of the spools before the child, asking her to find the one like it. This I repeated for all three of the colours, showing her how to arrange them carefully in pairs. After this I passed to the Three Periods of Séguin. The little girl learned to recognise the three colours and to pronounce the name of each.

She was so happy that she looked at me for a long time,

and then began to jump up and down. I, seeing her pleasure, said to her, laughing, "Do you know the colours?" and she replied, still jumping up and down, "Yes! YES!" Her delight was inexhaustible; she danced about me, waiting joyously for me to ask her the same question, that she might reply with the same enthusiasm, "Yes! Yes!"

Another important particular in the technique of sense education lies in *isolating the sense,* whenever this is possible. So, for example, the exercises on the sense of hearing can be given more successfully in an environment not only of silence, but even of darkness.

For the education of the senses in general, such as in the tactile, thermic, baric, and stereognostic exercises, we blindfold the child. The reasons for this particular technique have been fully set forth by psychology. Here, it is enough to note that in the case of normal children the blindfold greatly increases their interest, without making the exercises degenerate into noisy fun, and without having the child's attention attracted more to the *bandage* than to the sense-stimuli upon which we wish to *focus* the attention.

For example, in order to test the acuteness of the child's sense of hearing (a most important thing for the teacher to know), I use an empiric test which is coming to be used almost universally by physicians in the making of medical examinations. This test is made by modulating the voice, reducing it to a whisper. The child is blindfolded, or the teacher may stand behind him, speaking his name, in *a whisper* and from varying distances. I establish a *solemn silence* in the schoolroom, darken the windows, have the children bow their heads upon their hands which they hold in front of their eyes. Then I call the children by name, one by one, in a whisper, lighter for those who are nearer me, and more clearly for those farther away. Each child awaits, in the darkness, the faint voice which calls him, listening intently, ready to run with keenest joy toward the mysterious and much, desired call.

The normal child may be blindfolded in the games where, for example, he is to recognise various weights, for this does help him to intensify and concentrate his attention upon the baric stimuli which he is to test. The blindfold adds to his pleasure, since he is proud of having been able to guess.

The effect of these games upon deficient children is very different. When placed in darkness, they often go to sleep, or give themselves up to disordered acts. When the blindfold is used, they fix their attention upon the bandage itself, and change the exercise into a game, which does not fulfil the end we have in view with the exercise.

We speak, it is true, of *games* in education, but it must be made clear that we understand by this term a free activity, ordered to a definite end; not disorderly noise, which distracts the attention.

The following pages of Itard give an idea of the patient experiments made by this pioneer in pedagogy. Their lack of success was due largely to errors which successive experiments have made it possible to correct, and in part to the mentality of his subject.

"IV: In this last experiment it was not necessary, as in the one preceding, to demand that the pupil repeat the sounds which he perceived. This double work, distributing his attention, was outside the plane of my purpose, which was to educate each organ separately. I, therefore, limited myself to following the simple perception of sounds. To be certain of this result, I placed my pupil in front of me with his eyes blinded, his fists closed, and had him extend a finger every time that I made a sound. He understood this arrangement, and as soon as the sound reached his ear, the finger was raised, with a species of impetuosity, and often, with demonstrations of joy which left no doubt as to the pleasure the pupil took in these bizarre lessons. Indeed, whether it be that he found a real pleasure in the sound of the human voice, or that he had at last conquered the annoyance he at first felt on being deprived of the light for so long a time, the fact remains that more than once, during the intervals of rest, he came to me with his blindfold in his hand, holding it over his eyes, and jumping with joy when he felt my hands tying it about his head.

"V: Having thoroughly assured myself, through such experiments as the one described above, that all sounds of the voice, whatever their intensity, were perceived by Vittorio, I proceeded to the attempt of making him compare these sounds. It was no longer a case of simply noting the sounds of the voice, but of perceiving the differences and of appreciating all these modifications and varieties of tone which go to make up the music of the word. Between this task and the preceding there stretched a prodigious difference, especially for a being whose development was dependent upon gradual effort, and who advanced toward civilisation only because I led thitherward so gently that he was unconscious of the progress. Facing the difficulty now presented, I had need to arm myself more strongly than ever with patience and gentleness, encouraged by the hope that once I had surmounted this obstacle all would have been done for the sense of hearing.

"We began with the comparison of the vowel sounds, and here, too, made use of the hand to assure ourselves as to the result of our experiments. Each one of the fingers was made the sign of one of the five vowels. Thus the thumb represented A and was to be raised whenever this vowel was pronounced; the index finger was the sign for E; the middle finger for I; and so on.

"VI: Not without fatigue, and not for a long time, was I able to give a distinct idea of the vowels. The first to be clearly distinguished was O, and then followed A. The three others presented much greater difficulty, and were for a long time confused. At last, however, the ear began to perceive distinctly, and, then, there returned in all their vivacity, those demonstrations of joy of which I have spoken. This continued until the pleasure taken in the lessons began to be boisterous, the sounds became confused, and the finger was raised indiscriminately. The outbursts of laughter became indeed so excessive that I lost patience! As soon as I placed the blindfold over his eyes the shouts of laughter began."

Itard, finding it impossible to continue his educational work, decided to do away with the blindfold, and, indeed, the shouts ceased, but now the child's attention was distracted by the slightest movement about him. The blindfold was necessary, but the boy had to be made to understand that he must not laugh so much and that he was having a lesson. The corrective means of Itard and their touching results are worth reporting here!

"I wished to intimidate him with my manner, not being able to do so with my glance. I armed myself with a tambourine and struck it lightly whenever he made a mistake. But he mistook this correction for a joke, and his joy became more noisy than ever. I then felt that I must make the correction a little more severe. It was understood, and I saw, with a mixture of pain and pleasure, revealed in the darkened face of this boy the fact that the feeling of injury surpassed the unhappiness of the blow. Tears came from beneath the blindfold, he urged me to take it off, but, whether from embarrassment or fear, or from some inner preoccupation, when freed from the bandage he still kept his eyes tightly closed. I could not laugh at the doleful expression of his face, the closed eyelids from between which trickled an occasional tear! Oh, in this moment, as in many others, ready to renounce my task, and feeling that the time I had consecrated to it was lost, how I regretted ever having known this boy, and bow severely I condemned the barren and inhuman curiosity of the men who in order to make scientific advancement had torn him away from a life, at least innocent and happy!"

Here also is demonstrated the great educative superiority of scientific pedagogy for normal children.

Finally, one particular of the technique consists in the *distribution of the stimuli*. This will be treated more fully in the description of the didactic system (materials) and of the sense education. Here it is enough to say that one should proceed from *few stimuli strongly contrasting, to many stimuli in gradual differentiation always more fine and imperceptible*. So, for example, we first present, together, red and blue; the shortest rod beside the longest; the thinnest beside the thickest, etc., passing from these to the delicately differing tints, and to the discrimination of very slight differences in length and size.

13

Education of the Senses and Illustrations of the Didactic Material: General Sensibility; the Tactile, Thermic, Baric, and Stereognostic Senses

The education of the tactile and the thermic senses go together, since the warm bath, and heat in general, render the tactile sense more acute. Since to exercise the tactile sense it is necessary to *touch*, bathing the hands in warm water has the additional advantage of teaching the child a principle of cleanliness—that of not touching objects with hands that are not clean. I therefore apply the general notions of practical life, regarding the washing of the hands, care of the nails, to the exercises preparatory to the discrimination of tactile stimuli.

The limitation of the exercises of the tactile sense to the cushioned tips of the fingers, is rendered necessary by practical life. It must be made a necessary phase of *education* because it prepares for a life in which man exercises and uses the tactile sense through the medium of these finger tips. Hence, I have the child wash his hands carefully with soap, in a little basin; and in another basin I have him rinse them in a bath of tepid water. Then I show him how to dry and rub his hands gently, in this way preparing for the regular bath. I next teach the child how to *touch*, that is, the manner in which he should touch surfaces. For this it is necessary to take the finger of the child and to draw *it very, very lightly* over the surface.

Another particular of the technique is to teach the child to hold his eyes closed while he touches, encouraging him to do this by telling him that he will be able to feel the differences better, and so leading him to distinguish, without the help of sight, the change of contact. He will quickly learn, and will show that he enjoys the exercise. Often after the introduction of such exercises, it is a common thing to have a child come to you, and, closing his eyes, touch with great delicacy the palm of your hand or the cloth of your dress, especially any silken or velvet trimmings. They do verily *exercise* the tactile sense. They enjoy

The Cloister School of the Franciscan Nuns in Rome
Children playing a game with tablets of coloured silk

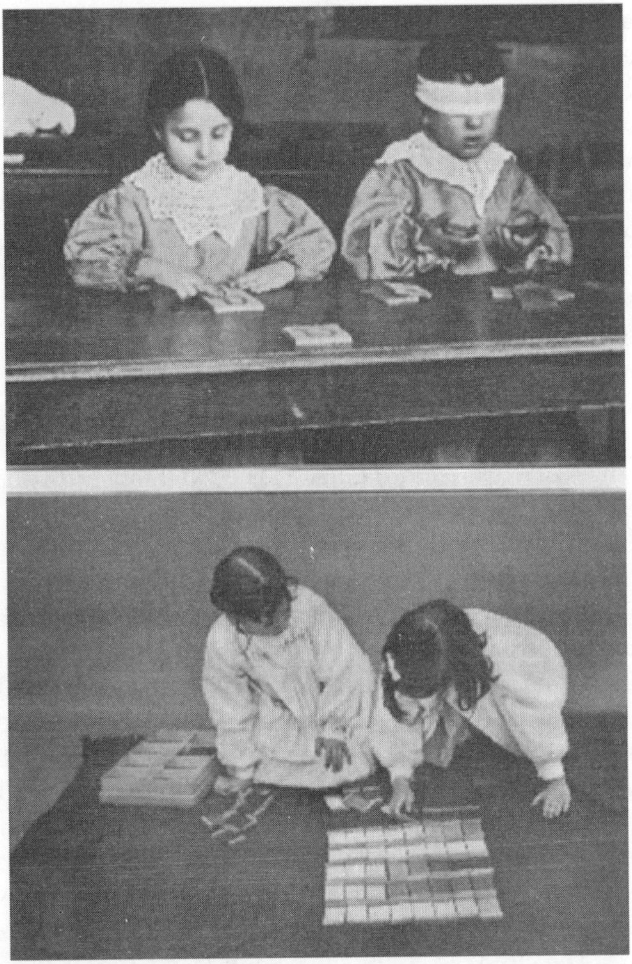

(a) Girl Touching a Letter and Boy Telling Objects by Weight. (b) Arranging Tablets of Silk in Their Chromatic Order. There are eight colours, and eight shades of each colour, making sixty-four gradations in all.

keenly touching any soft pleasant surface, and become exceedingly keen in discriminating between the differences in the sandpaper cards.

The Didactic Material consists of; *a*—a rectangular wooden board divided into two equal rectangles, one covered with very smooth paper, or having the wood polished until a smooth surface is obtained; the other covered with sandpaper, *b*—a tablet like the preceding covered with alternating strips of smooth paper and sandpaper.

I also make use of a collection of paper slips, varying through many grades from smooth, fine cardboard to coarsest sandpaper. The stuffs described elsewhere are also used in these lessons.

As to the Thermic Sense, I use a set of little metal bowls, which are filled with water at different degrees of temperature. These I try to measure with a thermometer, so that there may be two containing water of the same temperature.

I have designed a set of utensils which are to be made of very light metal, and filled with water. These have covers, and to each is attached a thermometer. The bowl touched from the outside gives the desired impression of heat.

I also have the children put their hands into cold, tepid, and warm water, an exercise which they find most diverting. I should like to repeat this exercise with the feet, but I have not bad an opportunity to make the trial.

For the education of the baric sense (sense of weight), I use with great success little wooden tablets, six by eight centimetres, having a thickness of 1/2 centimetre. These tablets are in three different qualities of wood, wistaria, walnut, and pine. They weigh respectively, 24, 18, and 12 grammes, making them differ in weight by 6 grammes. These tablets should be very smooth; if possible, varnished in such a way that every roughness shall be eliminated, but so that the natural colour of the wood shall remain. The child, *observing* the colour, *knows* that they are of differing weights, and this offers a means of controlling the exercise. He takes two of the tablets in his hands, letting them rest upon the palm at the base of his outstretched fingers. Then he moves his hands up and down in order to gauge the weight. This movement should come to be, little by little, almost insensible. We lead the child to make his distinction purely through the difference in weight, leaving out the guide of the different colours, and closing his eyes. He learns to do this of himself, and takes great interest in "guessing."

The game attracts the attention of those near, who gather in a circle about the one who has the tablets, and who take turns in *guessing*. Sometimes the children spontaneously make use of the blindfold, taking turns, and interspersing the work with peals of joyful laughter.

EDUCATION OF THE STEREOGNOSTIC SENSE

The education of this sense leads to the recognition of objects through feeling, that is, through the simultaneous help of the tactile and muscular senses.

Taking this union as a basis, we have made experiments which have given marvellously successful educational results. I feel that for the help of teachers these exercises should be described.

The first didactic material used by us is made up of the bricks and cubes of Froebel. We call the attention of the child to the form of the two solids, have him feel them carefully and accurately, with his eyes open, repeating some phrase serving to fix his attention upon the particulars of the forms presented. After this the child is told to place the cubes to the right, the bricks to the left, always feeling them, and without looking at them. Finally the exercise is repeated, by the child blindfolded. Almost all the children succeed in the exercise, and after two or three times, are able to eliminate every error. There are twenty-four of the bricks and cubes in all, so that the attention may be held for some time through this "game"—but undoubtedly the child's pleasure is greatly increased by the fact of his being watched by a group of his companions, all interested and eager.

One day a directress called my attention to a little girl of three years, one of our very youngest pupils, who had repeated this exercise perfectly. We seated the little girl comfortably in an armchair, close to the table. Then, placing the twenty-four objects before her upon the table, we mixed them, and calling the child's attention to the difference in form, told her to place the cubes to the right and the bricks to the left. When she was blindfolded she began the exercise as taught by us, taking an object in each hand, feeling each and putting it in its right place. Sometimes she took two cubes, or two bricks, sometimes she found a brick in the right hand, a cube in the left. The child had to recognise the form, and to remember throughout the exercise the proper placing of the different objects. This seemed to me very difficult for a child of three years.

But observing her I saw that she not only performed the exercise easily, but that the movements with which we had taught her to feel the form were superfluous. Indeed the instant she had taken the two objects in her hands, if it so happened that she had taken a cube with the left hand and a brick in the right, she *exchanged* them *immediately*, and *then* began the laborious feeling the form which we had taught and which she perhaps, believed to be obligatory. But the objects had been recognised by her through *the first light touch*, that is, the *recognition* was *contemporaneous* to *the taking*.

Continuing my study of the subject, I found that this little girl was possessed of a remarkable *functional ambidexterity*—I should be very glad to make a wider study of this phenomenon having in view the desirability of a simultaneous education of both hands.

I repeated the exercise with other children and found that they *recognise* the objects before feeling their contours. This was particularly true of the *little ones*. Our educational methods in this respect furnished a remarkable exercise in associative gymnastics, leading to a rapidity of judgment which was truly surprising and had the advantage of being perfectly adapted to very young children.

These exercises of the stereognostic sense may be multiplied in many ways—they amuse the children who find delight in the recognition of a stimulus, as in the thermic exercises; for example—they may raise any small objects, toy soldiers, little balls, and, above all, the various *coins* in common use. They come to discriminate between small forms varying very slightly, such as corn, wheat, and rice.

They are very proud of *seeing without eyes*, holding out their hands and crying, "Here are my eyes!" "I can see with my hands!" Indeed, our little ones walking in the ways we have planned, make us marvel over their unforeseen progress, surprising us daily. Often, while they are wild with delight over some new conquest,—we watch, in deepest wonder and meditation.

EDUCATION OF THE SENSES OF TASTE AND SMELL

This phase of sense education is most difficult, and I have not as yet had any satisfactory results to record. I can only say that the exercises ordinarily used in the tests of psychometry do not seem to me to be practical for use with young children.

The olfactory sense in children is not developed to any great extent, and this makes it difficult to attract their attention by means of this sense. We have made use of one test which has not been repeated often enough to form the basis of a method. We have the child smell fresh violets, and jessamine flowers. We then blindfold him, saying, "Now we are going to present you with flowers." A little friend then holds a bunch of violets under the child's nose, that he may guess the name of the flower. For greater or less intensify we present fewer flowers, or even one single blossom.

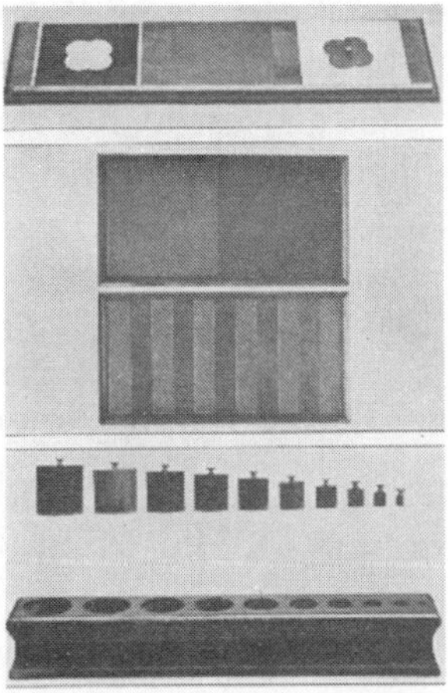

(a) Drawing Table and Inset. (b) Wooden Tablets: These are partly covered with sandpaper to give rough and smooth surfaces. (c) Solid Insets: With these the child, working by himself, learns to differentiate objects according to thickness, height, and size.

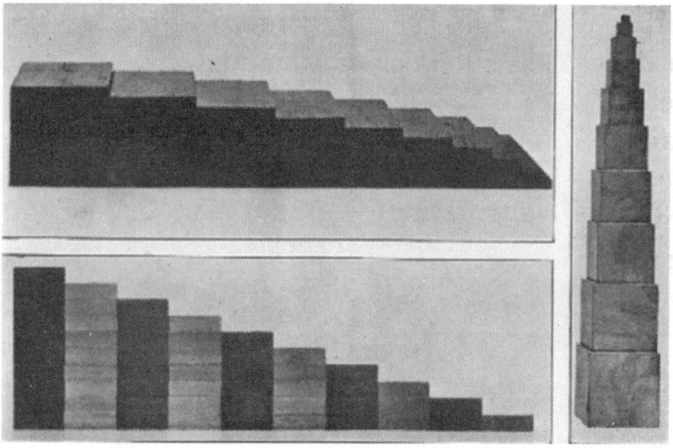

(a) Broad Stair. (b) Long Stair. (c) Tower.
Blocks by which children are taught thickness, length, size.

But this part of education, like that of the sense of taste, can be obtained by the child during the luncheon hour;—when he can learn to recognise various odours.

As to taste, the method of touching the tongue with various solutions, bitter or acid, sweet, salty, is perfectly applicable. Children of four years readily lend themselves to such games, which serve as a reason for showing them how to rinse their mouths perfectly. The children enjoy recognising various flavours, and learn, after each test, to fill a glass with tepid water, and carefully rinse their months. In this way the exercise for the sense of taste is also an exercise in hygiene.

EDUCATION OF THE SENSE OF VISION

I. Differential Visual Perception of Dimensions

First. Solid Insets: This material consists of three solid blocks of wood each 55 centimetres long, 6 centimetres high and 8 centimetres wide. Each block contains ten wooden pieces, set into corresponding holes. These pieces are cylindrical in shape and are to be handled by means of a little wooden or brass button which is fixed in the centre of the top. The cases of cylinders are in appearance much like the cases of weights used by chemists. In the first set of the series, the cylinders are all of equal height

(55 millimetres) but differ in diameter. The smallest cylinder has a diameter of 1 centimetre, and the others increase in diameter at the rate of 1/2 centimetre. In the second set, the cylinders are all of equal diameter, corresponding to half the diameter of the largest cylinder in the preceding series—(27 millimetres). The cylinders in this set differ in height, the first being merely a little disk only a centimetre high, the others increase 5 millimetres each, the tenth one being 55 millimetres high. In the third set, the cylinders differ both in height and diameter, the first being 1 centimetre high and 1 centimetre in diameter and each succeeding one increasing 1/2 centimetre in height and diameter. With these insets, the child, working by himself, learns to differentiate objects according to *thickness*, according to *height*, and according to *size*.

In the schoolroom, these three sets may be played with by three children gathered about a table, an exchange of games adding variety. The child takes the cylinders out of the moulds, mixes them upon the table, and then puts each back into its corresponding opening. These objects are made of hard pine, polished and varnished.

Second. Large pieces in graded dimensions:—There are three sets of blocks which come under this head, and it is desirable to have two of each of these sets in every school.

(*a*) Thickness: this set consists of objects which vary from *thick* to *thin*. There are ten quadrilateral prisms, the largest of which has a base of 10 centimetres, the others decreasing by 1 centimetre. The pieces are of equal length, 20 centimetres. These prisms are stained a dark brown. The child mixes them, scattering them over the little carpet, and then puts them in order, placing one against the other according to the graduations of thickness, observing that the length shall correspond exactly. These blocks, taken from the first to the last, form a species of *stair*, the steps of which grow broader toward the top. The child may begin with the thinnest piece or with the thickest, as suits his pleasure. The control of the exercise is not *certain*, as it was in the solid cylindrical insets. There, the large cylinders could not enter the small opening, the taller ones would project beyond the top of the block, etc. In this game of the Big Stair, the *eye* of the child can easily recognise an error, since if he mistakes, the *stair* is irregular, that is, there will be a high step, behind which, the step which should have ascended, decreases.

(*b*) Length: Long and Short Objects:—This set consists of *ten rods*. These are four-sided, each face being 3 centimetres. The first rod is a metre long, and the last a decimetre. The intervening rods decrease, from first to last, 1 decimetre each. Each space of 1 decimetre is painted alternately *red* or *blue*. The rods, when placed close to each other, must be so arranged that the colours correspond, forming so many transverse stripes—the whole set when arranged has the appearance of a rectangular triangle made up of organ pipes, which decrease on the side of the hypothenuse.

The child arranges the rods which have first been scattered and mixed. He puts them together according to the graduation of length, and observes the correspondence of colours. This exercise also offers a very evident control of error, for the regularity of the decreasing length of the stairs along the hypothenuse will be altered if the rods are not properly placed.

This most important set of blocks will have its principal application in arithmetic, as we shall see. With it, one may count from one to ten and may construct the addition and other tables, and it may constitute the first steps in the study of the decimal and metric system.

(*c*) Size: Objects, Larger and Smaller:—This set is made up of ten wooden cubes painted in rose-coloured enamel. The largest cube has a base of 10 centimetres, the smallest, of 1 centimetre, the intervening ones decrease 1 centimetre each. A little green cloth carpet goes with these blocks. This may be of oilcloth or cardboard. The game consists of building the cubes up, one upon another, in the order of their dimensions, constructing a little tower of which the largest cube forms the base and the smallest the apex. The carpet is placed on the floor, and the cubes are scattered upon it. As the tower is built upon the carpet, the child goes through the exercise of kneeling, rising, etc. The control is given by the irregularity of the tower as it decreases toward the apex. A cube misplaced reveals itself, because it breaks the line. The most common error made by the children in playing with these blocks at first, is that of placing the second cube as the base and placing the first cube upon it, thus confusing the two largest blocks. I have noted that the same error was made by deficient children in the repeated trials I made with the tests of De Sanctis. At the question, "Which is the largest?" the child would take, not the largest, but that nearest it in size.

Any of these three sets of blocks may be used by the children in a slightly different game. The pieces may be mixed upon a carpet or table, and then put in order upon another table at some distance. As he carries each piece, the child must walk without letting his attention wander, since he must remember the dimensions of the piece for which he is to look among the mixed blocks.

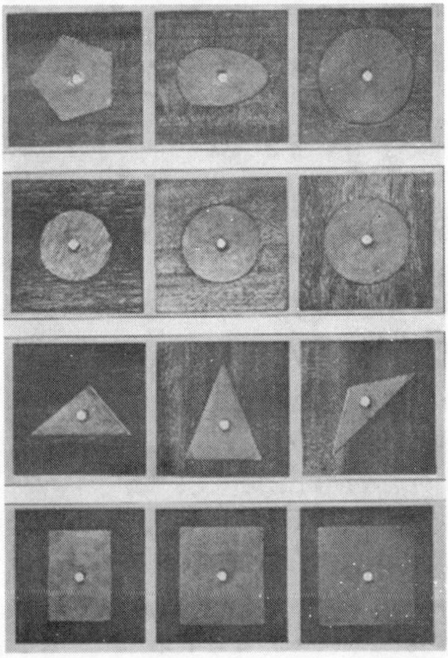

A Few of the Many Geometric Insets of Wood Used to Teach Form

The games played in this way are excellent for children of four or five years; while the simple work of arranging the pieces in order upon the same carpet where they have been mixed is more adapted to the little ones between three and four years of age. The construction of the tower with the pink cubes is very attractive to little ones of less than three years, who knock it down and build it up time after time.

(a) Geometric Insets of Wood, and Frame. The frame furnishes the control necessary for exactness of work. (b) Cabinet (For storing geometric inset frames.)

II. Differential Visual Perception of Form and Visual-tactile-muscular Perception

Didactic Material. Plane geometric *insets of wood*: The idea of these insets goes back to Itard and was also applied by Séguin.

In the school for deficients I had made and applied these insets in the same form used by my illustrious predecessors. In these there were two large tablets of wood placed one above the other and fastened together. The lower board was left solid, while the upper one was perforated by various geometric figures. The game consisted in placing in these openings the corresponding wooden figures which, in order that they might be easily handled, were furnished with a little brass knob.

In my school for deficients, I had multiplied the games calling for these insets, and distinguished between those used to teach colour and those used to teach form. The insets for teaching colour were all circles, those used for teaching form were all painted blue. I had great numbers of these insets made in graduations of colour and in an infinite variety of form. This material was most expensive and exceedingly cumbersome.

In many later experiments with normal children, I have, after many trials, completely excluded the plane geometric insets as an aid to the teaching of colour, since this material offers no control of errors, the child's task being that of *covering* the forms before him.

I have kept the geometric insets, but have given them a new and original aspect. The form in which they are now made was suggested to me by a visit to the splendid manual training school in the Reformatory of St. Michael in Rome. I saw there wooden models of geometric figures, which could be set into corresponding frames or placed above corresponding forms. The scope of these materials was to lead to exactness in the making of the geometric pieces in regard to control of dimension and form; the *frame* furnishing the *control* necessary for the exactness of the work.

This led me to think of making modifications in my geometric insets, making use of the frame as well as of the inset I therefore made a rectangular tray, which measured 30x20 centimetres. This tray was painted a dark blue and was surrounded by a dark frame. It was furnished with a cover so arranged that it would contain six of the square frames with their insets. The advantage of this tray is that the forms may be changed, thus allowing us to present any combination we choose. I have a number of blank wooden squares which make it possible to present as few as two or three geometric forms at a time, the other spaces being filled in by the blanks. To this material I have added a set of white cards, 10 centimetres square. These cards form a series presenting the geometric forms in other aspects. In the *first* of the series, the form is cut from blue paper and mounted upon the card. In the *second* box of cards, the *contour* of the same figures is mounted in the same blue paper, forming an outline one centimetre in width. On the *third* set of cards the contour of the geometric form is *outlined by a blank line*. We have then the tray, the collection of small frames with their corresponding insets, and the set of the cards in three series.

Some of the Card Forms used in the exercises
with the three series of cards.

I also designed a case containing six trays. The front of this box may be lowered when the top is raised and the trays may be drawn out as one opens the drawers of a desk. Each *drawer* contains six of the small frames with their respective insets. In the first drawer I keep the four plain wooden squares and two frames, one containing a rhomboid, and the other a trapezoid. In the second, I have a series consisting of a square, and five rectangles of the same length, but varying in width. The third drawer contains six circles which diminish in diameter. In the fourth are six triangles, in the fifth, five polygons from a pentagon to a decagon. The sixth drawer contains six curved figures (an ellipse, an oval, etc., and a flower-like figure formed by four crossed arcs).

Exercise with the Insets. This exercise consists in presenting to the child the large frame or tray in which we may arrange the figures as we wish to present them. We proceed to take out the insets, mix them upon the table, and then invite the child to put them back in place. This game may be played by even the younger children and holds the attention for a long period, though not for so long a time as the exercise with the cylinders. Indeed, I have never seen a child repeat this exercise more than five or six times. The child, in fact, expends much energy upon this exercise. He must *recognise* the form and must look at it carefully.

At first many of the children only succeed in placing the insets after many attempts, trying for example to place a triangle in a trapezoid, then in a rectangle, etc. Or when they have taken a rectangle, and recognise where it should go, they will still place it with the long side of the inset across the short side of the opening, and will only after many attempts, succeed in placing it. After three or four successive lessons, the child recognises the geometric figures with *extreme* facility and places the insets with a security which has a tinge of nonchalance, or of *slight contempt for an exercise that is too easy*. This is the moment in which the child may be led to a methodical observation of the forms. We change the forms in the frame and pass from contrasted frames to analogous ones. The exercise is easy for the child, who habituates himself to placing the pieces in their frames without errors or false attempts.

The first period of these exercises is at the time when the child is obliged to make repeated *trials* with figures that are strongly contrasted in form. The *recognition* is greatly helped by associating with the visual sense the muscular-tactile perception of the forms. I have the child touch[1] the contour of the piece with the *index finger* of *his right hand*, and then have him repeat this with the contour of the frame into which the pieces must fit. We succeed in making this a *habit* with the child. This is very easily attained, since all children love to *touch* things. I have already learned, through my work with deficient children, that among the various forms of sense memory that of the muscular sense is the most precocious. Indeed, many children who have not arrived at the point of recognising a *figure by looking at it*, could recognise it by *touching it*, that is, by computing the movements necessary to the following of its contour. The same is true of the greater number of normal children;—confused as to where to place a figure, they turn it about trying in vain to fit it in, yet as soon as they have touched the two contours of the piece and its frame, they succeed in placing it perfectly. Undoubtedly, the association of the *muscular-tactile* sense with that of *vision*, aids in a most remarkable way the perception of forms and fixes them in memory.

In such exercises, the control is absolute, as it was in the solid insets. The figure can only enter the corresponding frame. This makes it possible for the child to work by himself, and to accomplish a genuine sensory auto-education, in the visual perception of form.

Exercise with the three series of cards. First series. We give the child the wooden forms and the cards upon which the white figure is mounted. Then we mix the cards upon the table; the child must arrange them in a line upon his table (which he loves to do), and then place the corresponding wooden pieces upon the cards. Here the control lies in the eyes. The child must *recognise* this figure, and place the wooden piece upon it so perfectly that it will cover and hide the paper figure. The eye of the child here corresponds to the frame, which *materially* led him at first to bring the two pieces together. In addition to covering the figure, the child is to accustom himself to *touching* the contour of the mounted figures as a part of the exercise (the child always voluntarily follows those movements); and after he has placed the wooden inset he again touches the contour, adjusting with his finger the superimposed piece until it exactly covers the form beneath.

Second Series. We give a number of cards to the child together with the corresponding wooden insets. In this second series, the figures are repeated by an outline of blue paper. The child through these exercises is passing gradually from the *concrete* to the *abstract*. At first, he handled only *solid objects*. He then passed to a *plane figure*, that is, to the plane which in itself does not exist. He is now passing to the *line*, but this line does not represent for him the abstract contour of a plane figure. It is to him the *path which he has so often followed with his index finger*; this line is the *trace* of a *movement*. Following again the contour of the figure with his finger, the child receives the impression of actually leaving a trace, for the figure is covered by his finger and appears as he moves it. It is the eye now which guides the movement, but it must be remembered that this movement was *already prepared* for when the child touched the contours of the solid pieces of wood.

Third Series. We now present to the child the cards upon which the figures are drawn in black, giving him, as before, the corresponding wooden pieces. Here, he has actually passed to the *line*; that is, to an abstraction, yet here, too, there is the idea of the result of a movement.

This cannot be, it is true, the trace left by the finger, but, for example, that of a pencil which is guided by the hand in the same movements made before. These geometric figures in simple outline *have grown out* of a gradual series of representations which were concrete to vision and touch. These representations return to the mind of the child when he performs the exercise of superimposing the corresponding wooden figures.

III. Differential Visual Perception of Colours:—Education of the Chromatic Sense

In many of our *lessons on the colours*, we make use of pieces of brightly-coloured stuffs, and of balls covered with wool of different colours. The didactic material for the*education of the chromatic* sense is the following, which I have established after a long series of tests made upon normal children, (in the institute for deficients, I used as I have said above, the geometric insets). The present material consists of small flat tablets, which are wound with coloured wool or silk. These tablets have a little wooden border at each end which prevents the silk-covered card from touching the table. The child is also taught to take hold of the piece by these wooden extremities, so that he need not soil the delicate colours. In this way, we are able to use this material for a long time without having to renew it.

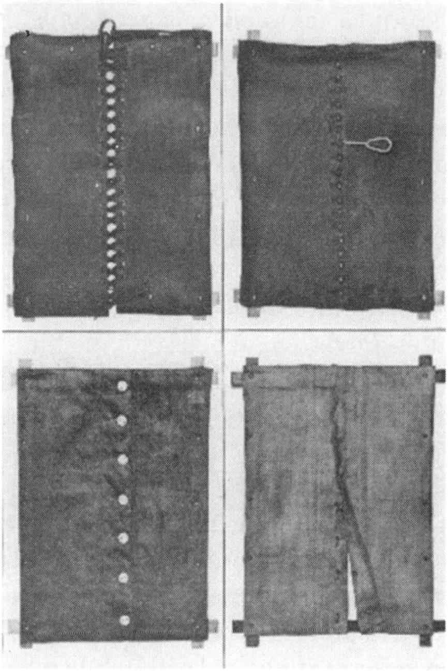

(a) Lacing. (b) Shoe Buttoning. (c) Buttoning of other Garments. (d) Hooks and Eyes. Frames illustrating the different processes of dressing and undressing.

I have chosen eight tints, and each one has with it eight gradations of different intensity of colour. There are, therefore, sixty-four colour-tablets in all. The eight tints selected are *black (from grey to white)*, *red*, *orange*, *yellow*, *green*, *blue*, *violet* and *brown*. We have duplicate boxes of these sixty-four colours, giving us two of each exercise. The entire set, therefore, consists of one hundred twenty-eight tablets. They are contained in two boxes, each divided into eight equal compartments so that one box may contain sixty-four tablets.

Exercises with the Colour-tablets. For the earliest of these exercises, we select three strong colours: for example, *red*, *blue*,

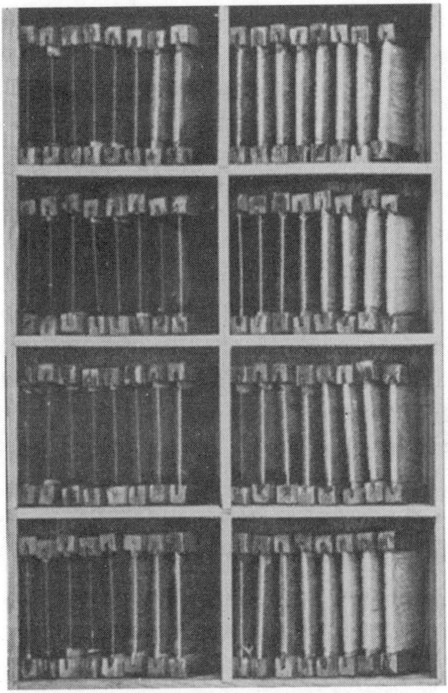

Tablets Wound with Coloured Silk

Used for educating the chromatic sense.

The tablets are shown in the boxes in which they are kept.

and *yellow*, in pairs. These six tablets we place upon the table before the child. Showing him one of the colours, we ask him to find its duplicate among the mixed tablets upon the table. In this way, we have him arrange the colour-tablets in a column, two by two, pairing them according to colour.

The number of tablets in this game may be increased until the eight colours, or sixteen tablets, are given at once. When the strongest tones have been presented, we may proceed to the presentation of lighter tones, in the same way. Finally, we present two or three tablets of the same colour, but of different tone, showing the child how to arrange these in order of gradation. In this way, the eight gradations are finally presented.

Following this, we place before the child the eight gradations of two different colours (red and blue); he is shown how to separate the groups and then arrange each group in gradation. As we proceed we offer groups of more nearly related colours; for example, blue and violet, yellow and orange, etc.

In one of the "Children's Houses," I have seen the following game played with the greatest success and interest, and with surprising *rapidity*. The directress places upon a table, about which the children are seated, as many colour groups as there are children, for example, three. She then calls each child's attention to the colour each is to select, or which she assigns to him. Then, she mixes the three groups of colours upon the table. Each child takes rapidly from the mixed heap of tablets all the gradations of his colour, and proceeds to arrange the tablets, which, when thus placed in a line, give the appearance of a strip of shaded ribbon.

In another "House," I have seen the children take the entire box, empty the sixty-four colour-tablets upon the table and after carefully mixing them, rapidly collect them into groups and arrange them in gradation, constructing a species of little carpet of delicately coloured and intermingling tints. The children very quickly acquire an ability before which we stand amazed. Children of three years are able to put all of the tints into gradation.

Experiments in Colour-memory. Experiments in colour-memory may be made by showing the child a tint, allowing him to look at it as long as he will, and then asking him to go to a distant table upon which all of the colours are arranged and to select from among them the tint similar to the one at which he has looked. The children succeed in this game remarkably, committing only slight errors. Children of five years enjoy this immensely, taking great pleasure in comparing the two spools and judging as to whether they have chosen correctly.

At the beginning of my work, I made use of an instrument invented by Pizzoli. This consisted of a small brown disk having a half-moon shape opening at the top. Various colours were made to pass behind this opening, by means of a rotary disk which was composed of strips of various colours. The teacher called the attention of the child to a certain colour, then turned the disk, asking him to indicate the same disk when it again showed itself in the opening. This exercise rendered the child inactive, preventing him from controlling the material. It is not, therefore, an instrument which can promote the *education* of the senses.

EXERCISE FOR THE DISCRIMINATION OF SOUNDS

It would be desirable to have in this connection the didactic material used for the "auricular education" in the principal institutions for deaf mutes in Germany and America. These exercises are an introduction to the acquisition of language, and serve in a very special way to centre the children's discriminative attention upon the "modulations of the sound of the human voice."

With very young children linguistic education must occupy a most important place. Another aim of such exercises is to educate the ear of the child to noises so that he shall accustom himself to distinguish every slight noise and compare it with *sounds*, coming to resent harsh or disordered noises. Such sense education has a value in that it exercises æsthetic taste, and may be applied in a most noteworthy way to practical discipline. We all know how the younger children disturb the order of the room by shouts, and by the noise of over-turned objects.

The rigorous scientific education of the sense of hearing is not practically applicable to the didactic method. This is true because the child cannot *exercise himself through his own activity* as he does for the other senses. Only one child at a time can work with any instrument producing the gradation of sounds. In other words, *absolute silence* is necessary for the discrimination of sounds.

Signorina Maccheroni, Directress, first of the "Children's House" in Milan and later in the one in Franciscan Convent at Rome, has invented and has had manufactured a series of thirteen bells hung upon a wooden frame. These bells are to all appearances, identical, but the vibrations brought about by a blow of a hammer produce the following thirteen notes:

The set consists of a double series of thirteen bells and there are four hammers. Having struck one of the bells in the first series, the child must find the corresponding sound in the second. This exercise presents grave difficulty, as the child does not know how to strike each time with the same force, and therefore produces sounds which vary in intensity. Even when the teacher strikes the bells, the children have difficulty in distinguishing between sounds. So we do not feel that this instrument in its present form is entirely practical.

For the discrimination of sounds, we use Pizzoli's series of little whistles. For the gradation of noises, we use small boxes filled with different substances, more or less fine (sand or pebbles). The noises are produced by shaking the boxes.

In the lessons for the sense of hearing I proceed as follows: I have the teachers establish silence in the usual way and then I *continue* the work, making the silence more profound. I say, "St! St!" in a series of modulations, now sharp and short, now prolonged and light as a whisper. The children, little by little, become fascinated by this. Occasionally I say, "More silent still—more silent."

I then begin the sibilant St! St! again, making it always lighter and repeating "More silent still," in a barely audible voice. Then I say still in a low whisper, "Now, I hear the clock, now I can hear the buzzing of a fly's wings, now I can hear the whisper of the trees in the garden."

The children, ecstatic with joy, sit in such absolute and complete silence that the room seems deserted; then I whisper, "Let us close our eyes." This exercise repeated, so habituates the children to immobility and to absolute silence that, when one of them interrupts, it needs only a syllable, a gesture to call him back immediately to perfect order.

In the silence, we proceeded to the production of sounds and noises, making these at first strongly contrasted, then, more nearly alike. Sometimes we present the comparisons between noise and sound. I believe that the best results can be obtained with the primitive means employed by Itard in 1805. He used the drum and the bell. His plan was a graduated series of drums for the noises,—or, better, for the heavy harmonic sounds, since these belong to a musical instrument,—and a series of bells. The diapason, the whistles, the boxes, are not attractive to the child, and do not educate the sense of hearing as do these other instruments. There is an interesting suggestion in the fact that the two great human institutions, that of hate (war), and that of love (religion), have adopted these two opposite instruments, the drum and the bell.

I believe that after establishing silence it would be educational to ring well-toned bells, now calm and sweet, now clear and ringing, sending their vibrations through the child's whole body. And when, besides the education of the ear, we have produced a *vibratory* education of the whole body, through these wisely selected sounds of the bells, giving a peace that pervades the very fibres of his being, then I believe these young bodies would be sensitive to crude noises, and the children would come to dislike, and to cease from making, disordered and ugly noises.

In this way one whose ear has been trained by a musical education suffers from strident or discordant notes. I need give no illustration to make clear the importance of such education for the masses in childhood. The new generation would be more calm, turning away from the confusion and the discordant sounds, which strike the ear to-day in one of the vile tenements where the poor live, crowded together, left by us to abandon themselves to the lower, more brutal human instincts.

Musical Education

This must be carefully guided by method. In general, we see little children pass by the playing of some great musicians as an animal would pass. They do not perceive the delicate complexity of sounds. The street children gather about the organ grinder, crying out as if to hail with joy the *noises* which will come instead of sounds.

For the musical education we must *create instruments* as well as music. The scope of such an instrument in addition to the discrimination of sounds, is to awaken a sense of rhythm, and, so to speak, to give the *impulse* toward calm and co-ordinate movements to those muscles already vibrating in the peace and tranquillity of immobility.

I believe that stringed instruments (perhaps some very much simplified harp) would be the most convenient. The stringed instruments together with the drum and the bells form the trio of the classic instruments of humanity. The harp is the instrument of "the intimate life of the individual." Legend places it in the hand of Orpheus, folk-lore puts it into fairy hands, and romance gives it to the princess who conquers the heart of a wicked prince.

The teacher who turns her back upon her scholars to play, (far too often badly), will never be the *educator* of their musical sense.

The child needs to be charmed in every way, by the glance as well as by the pose. The teacher who, bending toward them, gathering them about her, and leaving them free to stay or go, touches the chords, in a simple rhythm, puts herself in communication with them, *in relation with their very souls*. So much the better if this touch can be accompanied by her *voice*, and the children left free to follow her, no one being obliged to sing. In this way she can select as "adapted to education," those songs which were followed by all the children. So she may regulate the complexity of rhythm to various ages, for she will see now only the older children following the rhythm, now, also the little ones. At any rate, I believe that simple and primitive instruments are the ones best adapted to the awakening of music in the soul of the little child.

I have tried to have the Directress of the "Children's House" in Milan, who is a gifted musician, make a number of trials, and experiments, with a view to finding out more about the muscular capacity of young children. She has made many trials with the pianoforte, observing how the children *are not sensitive* to the musical *tone*, but only to the *rhythm*. On a basis of rhythm she arranged simple little dances, with the intention of studying the influence of the rhythm itself upon the co-ordination of muscular movements. She was greatly surprised to discover the *educational disciplinary* effect of such music. Her children, who had been led with great wisdom and art through liberty to a *spontaneous* ordering of their acts and movements, had nevertheless lived in the streets and courts, and had an almost universal habit of jumping.

Being a faithful follower of the method of liberty, and not considering that *jumping* was a wrong act, she had never corrected them.

She now noticed that as she multiplied and repeated the rhythm exercises, the children little by little left off their ugly jumping, until finally it was a thing of the past. The directress one day asked for an explanation of this change of conduct. Several little ones looked at her without saying anything. The older children gave various replies, whose meaning was the same.

"It isn't nice to jump."

"Jumping is ugly."

"It's rude to jump."

This was certainly a beautiful triumph for our method!

This experience shows that it is possible to educate the child's *muscular sense,* and it shows how exquisite the refinement of this sense may be as it develops in relation to the*muscular memory,* and side by side with the other forms of sensory memory.

Tests for Acuteness of Hearing

The only entirely successful experiments which we have made so far in the "Children's Houses" are those of the *clock,* and of the *lowered* or whispered *voice.* The trial is purely empirical, and does not lend itself to the measuring of the sensation, but it is, however, most useful in that it helps us to an approximate knowledge of the child's auditory acuteness.

The exercise consists in calling attention, when perfect silence has been established, to the ticking of the clock, and to all the little noises not commonly audible to the ear. Finally we call the little ones, one by one from an adjoining room, pronouncing each name in a low voice. In preparing for such an exercise it is necessary to *teach* the children the real meaning of *silence*.

Toward this end I have several *games* of *silence*, which help in a surprising way to strengthen the remarkable discipline of our children.

I call the children's attention to myself, telling them to see how silent I can be. I assume different positions; standing, sitting, and maintain each pose *silently, without movement*. A finger moving can produce a noise, even though it be imperceptible. We may breathe so that we may be heard. But I maintain *absolute* silence, which is not an easy thing to do. I call a child, and ask him to do as I am doing. He adjusts his feet to a better position, and this makes a noise! He moves an arm, stretching it out upon the arm of his chair; it is a noise. His breathing is not altogether silent, it is not tranquil, absolutely unheard as mine is.

During these manœuvres on the part of the child, and while my brief comments are followed by intervals of immobility and silence, the other children are watching and listening. Many of them are interested in the fact, which they have never noticed before; namely, that we make so many noises of which we are not conscious, and that there are *degrees of silence*. There is an absolute silence where nothing, *absolutely nothing* moves. They watch me in amazement when I stand in the middle of the room, so quietly that it is really as if "I were not." Then they strive to imitate me, and to do even better. I call attention here and there to a foot that moves, almost inadvertently. The attention of the child is called to every part of his body in an anxious eagerness to attain to immobility.

When the children are trying in this way, there is established a silence very different from that which we carelessly call by that name.

It seems as if life gradually vanishes, and that the room becomes, little by little, empty, as if there were no longer anyone in it. Then we begin to hear the tick-tock of the clock, and this sound seems to grow in intensity as the silence becomes absolute. From without, from the court which before seemed silent, there come varied noises, a bird chirps, a child passes. The children sit fascinated by that silence as if by some conquest of their own. "Here," says the directress, "here there is no longer anyone; the children have all gone away."

Having arrived at that point, we darken the windows, and tell the children to close their eyes, resting their heads upon their hands. They assume this position, and in the darkness the absolute silence returns.

"Now listen," we say. "A soft voice is going to call your name." Then going to a room behind the children, and standing within the open door, I call in a low voice, lingering over the syllables as if I were calling from across the mountains. This voice, almost occult, seems to reach the heart and to call to the soul of the child. Each one as he is called, lifts his head, opens his eyes as if altogether happy, then rises, silently seeking not to move the chair, and walks on the tips of his toes, so quietly that he is scarcely heard. Nevertheless his step resounds in the silence, and amid the immobility which persists.

Having reached the door, with a joyous face, he leaps into the room, choking back soft outbursts of laughter. Another child may come to hide his face against my dress, another, turning, will watch his companions sitting like statues silent and waiting. The one who is called feels that he is privileged, that he has received a gift, a prize. And yet they know that all will be called, "beginning with the most silent one in all the room." So each one tries to merit by his perfect silence the certain call. I once saw a little one of three years try to suffocate a sneeze, and succeed! She held her breath in her little breast, and resisted, coming out victorious. A most surprising effort!

This game delights the little ones beyond measure. Their intent faces, their patient immobility, reveal the enjoyment of a great pleasure. In the beginning, when the soul of the child was unknown to me, I had thought of showing them sweetmeats and little toys, promising to give them to the ones who were *called*, supposing that the gifts would be necessary to persuade the child to make the necessary effort. But I soon found that this was unnecessary.

The children, after they had made the effort necessary to maintain silence, enjoyed the sensation, took pleasure in the *silence* itself. They were like ships safe in a tranquil harbour, happy in having experienced something new, and to have won a victory over themselves. This, indeed, was their recompense. They *forgot* the promise of sweets, and no longer cared to take the toys, which I had supposed would attract them. I therefore abandoned that useless means, and saw, with surprise, that the game became constantly more perfect, until even children of three years of age remained immovable in the silence throughout the time required to call the entire forty children out of the room! It was then that I learned that the soul of the child has its own reward, and its peculiar spiritual pleasures. After such exercises it seemed to me that the children came closer to me, certainly they became more obedient, more gentle and sweet. We had, indeed, been isolated from the world, and had passed several minutes during which the communion between us was very close, I wishing for them and calling to them, and they receiving in the perfect silence the voice which was directed personally toward each one of them, crowning each in turn with happiness.

A Lesson in Silence

I am about to describe a lesson which *proved* most successful in teaching the perfect silence to which it is possible to attain. One day as I was about to enter one of the "Children's Houses," I met in the court a mother who held in her arms her little baby of four months. The little one was swaddled, as is still the custom among the people of Rome—an infant thus in the swaddling bands is called by us a *pupa*. This tranquil little one seemed the incarnation of peace. I took her in my arms, where she lay quiet and good. Still holding her I went toward the schoolroom, from which the children now ran to meet me. They always welcomed me thus, throwing their arms about me, clinging to my skirts, and almost tumbling me over in their eagerness. I smiled at them, showing them the "*pupa*." They understood and skipped about me looking at me with eyes brilliant with pleasure, but did not touch me through respect for the little one that I held in my arms.

I went into the schoolroom with the children clustered about me. We sat down, I seating myself in a large chair instead of, as usual, in one of their little chairs. In other words, I seated myself solemnly. They looked at my little one with a mixture of tenderness and joy. None of us had yet spoken a word. Finally I said to them, "I have brought you a little teacher." Surprised glances and laughter. "A little teacher, yes, because none of you know how to be quiet as she does." At this all the children changed their positions and became quiet. "Yet no one holds his limbs and feet as quietly as she." Everyone gave closer attention to the position of limbs and feet. I looked at them smiling, "Yes, but they can never be as quiet as hers. You move a little bit, but she, not at all; none of you can be as quiet as she." The children looked serious. The idea of the superiority of the little teacher seemed to have reached them. Some of them smiled, and seemed to say with their eyes that the swaddling bands deserved all the merit. "Not one of you can be silent, voiceless as she." General silence. "It is not possible to be as silent as she, because,—listen to her breathing—how delicate it is; come near to her on your tiptoes."

Several children rose, and came slowly forward on tiptoe, bending toward the baby. Great silence. "None of you can breathe so silently as she." The children looked about amazed, they had never thought that even when sitting quietly they were making noises, and that the silence of a little babe is more profound than the silence of grown people. They almost ceased to breathe. I rose. "Go out quietly, quietly," I said, "walk on the tips of your toes and make no noise." Following them I said, "And yet I still hear some sounds, but she, the baby, walks with me and makes no sound. She goes out silently!" The children smiled. They understood the truth and the jest of my words. I went to the open window, and placed the baby in the arms of the mother who stood watching us.

The little one seemed to have left behind her a subtle charm which enveloped the souls of the children. Indeed, there is in nature nothing more sweet than the silent breathing of a new-born babe. There is an indescribable majesty about this human life which in repose and silence gathers strength and newness of life. Compared to this, Wordsworth's description of the silent peace of nature seems to lose its force. "What calm, what quiet! The one sound the drip of the suspended oar." The children, too, felt the poetry and beauty in the peaceful silence of a new-born human life.

NOTE

1. Here and elsewhere throughout the book the word "touch" is used not only to express contact between the fingers and an object, but the moving of fingers or hand over an object or its outline.

14

General Notes on the Education of the Senses

I do not claim to have brought to perfection the method of sense training as applied to young children. I do believe, however, that it opens a new field for psychological research, promising rich and valuable results.

Experimental psychology has so far devoted its attention to *perfecting the instruments by which the sensations are measured.* No one has attempted the *methodical*preparation *of the individual for the sensations*. It is my belief that the development of psychometry will owe more to the attention given to the preparation of the *individual* than to the perfecting of the *instrument*.

But putting aside this purely scientific side of the question, the *education of the senses* must be of the greatest *pedagogical* interest.

Our aim in education in general is two-fold, biological and social. From the biological side we wish to help the natural development of the individual, from the social standpoint it is our aim to prepare the individual for the environment. Under this last head technical education may be considered as having a place, since it teaches the individual to make use of his surroundings. The education of the senses is most important from both these points of view. The development of the senses indeed precedes that of superior intellectual activity and the child between three and seven years is in the period of formation.

We can, then, help the development of the senses while they are in this period. We may graduate and adapt the stimuli just as, for example, it is necessary to help the formation of language before it shall be completely developed.

All education of little children must be governed by this principle—to help the natural *psychic* and *physical development* of the child.

The other aim of education (that of adapting the individual to the environment) should be given more attention later on when the period of intense development is past.

These two phases of education are always interlaced, but one or the other has prevalence according to the age of the child. Now, the period of life between the ages of three and seven years covers a period of rapid physical development. It is the time for the formation of the sense activities as related to the intellect The child in this age develops his senses. His attention is further attracted to the environment under the form of passive curiosity.

The stimuli, and not yet the reasons for things, attract his attention. This is, therefore, the time when we should methodically direct the sense stimuli, in such a way that the sensations which he receives shall develop in a rational way. This sense training will prepare the ordered foundation upon which he may build up a clear and strong mentality.

It is, besides all this, possible with the education of the senses to discover and eventually to correct defects which today pass unobserved in the school. Now the time comes when the defect manifests itself in an evident and irreparable inability to make use of the forces of life about him. (Such defects as deafness and near-sightedness.) This education, therefore, is physiological and prepares directly for intellectual education, perfecting the organs of sense, and the nerve-paths of projection and association.

But the other part of education, the adaptation of the individual to his environment, is indirectly touched. We prepare with our method the infancy of the *humanity of our time*. The men of the present civilisation are preeminently observers of their environment because they must utilise to the greatest possible extent all the riches of this environment.

The art of to-day bases itself, as in the days of the Greeks, upon observation of the truth.

The progress of positive science is based upon its observations and all its discoveries and their applications, which in the last century have so transformed our civic environment, were made by following the same line—that is, they have come through observation. We must therefore prepare the new generation for this attitude, which has become necessary in our modern civilised life. It is an indispensable means—man must be so armed if he is to continue efficaciously the work of our progress.

We have seen the discovery of the Roentgen Rays born of observation. To the same methods are due the discovery of Hertzian waves, and vibrations of radium, and we await wonderful things from the Marconi telegraph. While there has been no period in which thought has gained so much from positive study as the present century, and this same century promises new light in the field of speculative philosophy and upon spiritual questions, the theories upon the matter have themselves led to most interesting metaphysical concepts. We may say that in preparing the method of observation, we have also prepared the way leading to spiritual discovery.

The education of the senses makes men observers, and not only accomplishes the general work of adaptation to the present epoch of civilisation, but also prepares them directly for practical life. We have had up to the present time, I believe, a most imperfect idea of what is necessary in the practical living of life. We have always started from ideas, and have *proceeded thence* to *motor activities*; thus, for example, the method of education has always been to teach intellectually, and then to have the child follow the principles he has been taught. In general, when we are teaching, we talk about the object which interests us, and then we try to lead the scholar, when he has understood, to perform some kind of work with the object itself; but often the scholar who has understood the idea finds great difficulty in the execution of the work which we give him, because we have left out of his education a factor of the utmost importance, namely, the perfecting of the senses. I may, perhaps, illustrate this statement with a few examples. We ask the cook to buy only 'fresh fish.' She understands the idea, and tries to follow it in her marketing, but, if the cook has not been trained to recognise through sight and smell the signs which indicate freshness in the fish, she will not know how to follow the order we have given her.

Such a lack will show itself much more plainly in culinary operations. A cook may be trained in book matters, and may know exactly the recipes and the length of time advised in her cook book; she may be able to perform all the manipulations necessary to give the desired appearance to the dishes, but when it is a question of deciding from the odor of the dish the exact moment of its being properly cooked, or with the eye, or the taste, the time at which she must put in some given condiment, then she will make a mistake if her senses have not been sufficiently prepared.

She can only gain such ability through long practice, and such practice on the part of the cook is nothing else than a *belated education* of the senses—an education which often can never be properly attained by the adult. Thia is one reason why it is so difficult to find good cooks.

Something of the same kind is true of the physician, the student of medicine who studies theoretically the character of the pulse, and sits down by the bed of the patient with the best will in the world to read the pulse, but, if his fingers do not know how to read the sensations his studies will have been in vain. Before he can become a doctor, he must gain a *capacity for discriminating between sense stimuli.*

The same may be said for the *pulsations* of the *heart*, which the student studies in theory, but which the ear can learn to distinguish only through practice.

We may say the same for all the delicate vibrations and movements, in the reading of which the hand of the physician is too often deficient. The thermometer is the more indispensable to the physician the more his sense of touch is unadapted and untrained in the gathering of the thermic stimuli. It is well understood that the physician may be learned, and most intelligent, without being a good practitioner, and that to make a good practitioner long practice is necessary. In reality, this *long practice* is nothing else than a tardy, and often inefficient, *exercise* of the senses. After he has assimilated the brilliant theories, the physician sees himself forced to the unpleasant labor of the semiography, that is to making a record of the symptoms revealed by his observation of and experiments with the patients. He must do this if he is to receive from these theories any practical results.

Here, then, we have the beginner proceeding in a stereotyped way to tests of *palpation*, percussion, and auscultation, for the purpose of identifying the throbs, the resonance, the tones, the breathings, and the various sounds which *alone* can enable him to formulate a diagnosis. Hence the deep and unhappy discouragement of so many young physicians, and, above all, the loss of time; for it is often a question of lost years. Then, there is the immorality of allowing a man to follow a profession of so great responsibility, when, as is often the case, he is so unskilled and inaccurate in the taking of symptoms. The whole art of medicine is based upon an education of the senses; the schools, instead, *prepare* physicians through a study of the classics. All very well and good, but the splendid intellectual development of the physician falls, impotent, before the insufficiency of his senses.

One day, I heard a surgeon giving, to a number of poor mothers, a lesson on the recognition of the first deformities noticeable in little children from the disease of rickets. It was his hope to lead these mothers to bring to him their children who were suffering from this disease, while the disease was yet in the earliest stages, and when medical help might still be efficacious. The mothers understood the idea, but they did not know how to recognise these first signs of deformity, because they were lacking in the sensory education through which they might discriminate between signs deviating only slightly from the normal.

Therefore those lessons were useless. If we think of it for a minute, we will see that almost all the forms of adulteration in food stuffs are rendered possible by the torpor of the senses, which exists in the greater number of people. Fraudulent industry feeds upon the lack of sense education in the masses, as any kind of fraud is based upon the ignorance of the victim. We often see the purchaser throwing himself upon the honesty of the merchant, or putting his faith in the company, or the label upon the box. This is because purchasers are lacking in the capacity of judging directly for themselves. They do not know how to distinguish with their senses the different qualities of various substances. In fact, we may say that in many cases intelligence is rendered useless by lack of practice, and this practice is almost always sense education. Everyone knows in practical life the fundamental necessity of judging with exactness between various stimuli.

But very often sense education is most difficult for the adult, just as it is difficult for him to educate his hand when he wishes to become a pianist. It is necessary to begin the education of the senses in the formative period, if we wish to perfect this sense development with the education which is to follow. The education of the senses should be begun methodically in infancy, and should continue during the entire period of instruction which is to prepare the individual for life in society.

Aesthetic and moral education are closely related to this sensory education. Multiply the sensations, and develop the capacity of appreciating fine differences in stimuli, and we *refine* the sensibility and multiply man's pleasures.

Beauty lies in harmony, not in contrast; and harmony is refinement; therefore, there must be a fineness of the senses if we are to appreciate harmony. The æsthetic harmony of nature is lost upon him who has coarse senses. The world to him is narrow and barren. In life about us, there exist inexhaustible fonts of æsthetic enjoyment, before which men pass as insensible as the brutes seeking their enjoyment in those sensations which are crude and showy, since they are the only ones accessible to them.

Now, from the enjoyment of gross pleasures, vicious habits very often spring. Strong stimuli, indeed, do not render acute, but blunt the senses, so that they require stimuli more and more accentuated and more and more gross.

Onanism, so often found among normal children of the lower classes, alcoholism, fondness for watching sensual acts of adults—these things represent the enjoyment of those unfortunate ones whose intellectual pleasures are few, and whose senses are blunted and dulled. Such pleasures kill the man within the individual, and call to life the beast.

Indeed from the physiological point of view, the importance of the education of the senses is evident from an observation of the scheme of the diagrammatic arc which represents the functions of the nervous system. The external stimulus acts upon the organ of sense, and the impression is transmitted along the centripetal way to the nerve centre—the corresponding motor impulse is elaborated, and is transmitted along the centrifugal path to the organ of motion, provoking a movement. Although the arc represents diagrammatically the mechanism of reflex spinal actions, it may still be considered as a fundamental key explaining the phenomena of the more complex nervous mechanisms. Man, with the peripheral sensory system, gathers various stimuli from his environment. He puts himself thus in direct communication with his surroundings. The psychic life develops, therefore, in relation to the system of nerve centres; and human activity which is eminently social activity, manifests itself through acts of the individual—manual work, writing, spoken language, etc.—by means of the psychomotor organs.

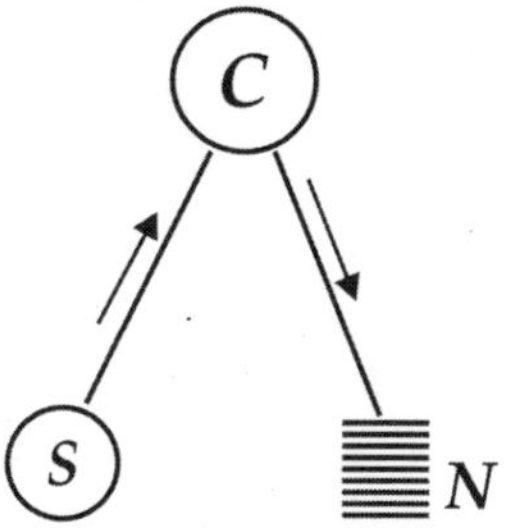

S–Sense, *C*–Nerve centre, *M*–Motor.

Education should guide and perfect the development of the three periods, the two peripheral and the central; or, better still, since the process fundamentally reduces itself to the nerve centres, education should give to psychosensory exercises the same importance which it gives to psychomotor exercises.

Otherwise, we *isolate* man from his *environment*. Indeed, when with *intellectual culture* we believe ourselves to have completed education, we have but made thinkers, whose tendency will be to live without the world. We have not made practical men. If, on the other hand, wishing through education to prepare for practical life; we limit ourselves to exercising the psychomotor phase, we lose sight of the chief end of education, which is to put man in direct communication with the external world.

Since *professional work* almost always requires man to make *use of his surroundings*, the technical schools are not forced to return to the very beginnings of education, sense exercises, in order to supply the great and universal lack.

15

Intellectual Education

"... To lead the child from the education of the senses to ideas."

Edward Séguin

The sense exercises constitute a species of auto-education, which, if these exercises be many times repeated, leads to a perfecting of the child's psychosensory processes. The directress must intervene to lead the child from sensations to ideas—from the concrete to the abstract, and to the association of ideas. For this, she should use a method tending to isolate the inner attention of the child and to fix it upon the perceptions—as in the first lessons his objective attention was fixed, through isolation, upon single stimuli.

The teacher, in other words, when she gives a lesson must seek to limit the field of the child's consciousness to the object of the lesson, as, for example, during sense education she isolated the sense which she wished the child to exercise.

For this, knowledge of a special technique is necessary. The educator must, *"to the greatest possible extent, limit his intervention; yet he must not allow the child to weary himself in an undue effort of auto-education."*

It is here, that the factor of individual limitation and differing degrees of perception are most keenly felt in the teacher. In other words, in the quality of this intervention lies the art which makes up the individuality of the teacher.

A definite and undoubted part of the teacher's work is that of teaching an exact nomenclature.

She should, in most cases, pronounce the necessary names

and adjectives without adding anything further. These words she should pronounce distinctly, and in a clear strong voice, so that the *various sounds* composing the word may be distinctly and plainly perceived by the child.

So, for example, touching the smooth and rough cards in the first tactile exercise, she should say, "This is smooth. This is rough," repeating the words with varying modulations of the voice, always letting the tones be clear and the enunciation very distinct. "Smooth, smooth, smooth. Rough, rough, rough."

In the same way, when treating of the sensations of heat and cold, she must say, "This is cold." "This is hot." "This is ice-cold." "This is tepid." She may then begin to use the generic terms, "heat," "more heat," "less heat," etc.

First. "The lessons in nomenclature must consist simply in provoking the association of the name with the object, or with the abstract idea which the name represents." Thus the*object* and the *name* must be united when they are received by the child's mind, and this makes it most necessary that no other word besides the name be spoken.

Second. The teacher must always *test* whether or not her lesson has attained the end she had in view, and her tests must be made to come within the restricted field of consciousness, provoked by the lesson on nomenclature.

The first test will be to find whether the name is still associated in the child's mind with the object. She must allow the necessary time to elapse, letting a short period of silence intervene between the lesson and the test. Then she may ask the child, pronouncing slowly and very clearly the name or the adjective she has taught: "Which is *smooth*? Which is *rough*?"

The child will point to the object with his finger, and the teacher will know that he has made the desired association. But if he has not done this, that is, if he makes a mistake, *she must not correct him*, but must suspend her lesson, to take it up again another day. Indeed, why correct him? If the child has not succeeded in associating the name with the object, the only way in which to succeed would be to *repeat* both the action of the sense stimuli and the *name*; in other words, to repeat the lesson. But when the child has failed, we should know that he was not at that instant ready for the psychic association which we wished to provoke in him, and we must therefore choose another moment.

If we should say, in correcting the child, "No, you have made a mistake," all these words, which, being in the form of a reproof, would strike him more forcibly than others (such as smooth or rough), would remain in the mind of the child, retarding the learning of the names. On the contrary, the *silence* which follows the error leaves the field of consciousness clear, and the next lesson may successfully follow the first. In fact, by revealing the error we may lead the child to make an undue *effort* to remember, or we may discourage him, and it is our duty to avoid as much as possible all unnatural effort and all depression.

Third. If the child has not committed any error, the teacher may provoke the *motor activity* corresponding to the idea of the object: that is, to the *pronunciation of the name*. She may ask him, "What is this?" and the child should respond, "Smooth." The teacher may then interrupt, teaching him how to pronounce the word correctly and distinctly, first, drawing a deep breath and, then, saying in a rather loud voice, "Smooth." When he does this the teacher may note his particular speech defect, or the special form of baby talk to which he may be addicted.

In regard to the *generalisation* of the ideas received, and by that I mean the application of these ideas to his environment, I do not advise any lessons of this sort for a certain length of time, even for a number of months. There will be children who, after having touched a few times the stuffs, or merely the smooth and rough cards, *will quite spontaneously touch the various surfaces about them*, repeating "Smooth! Rough! It is velvet! etc." In dealing with normal children, we must *await* this spontaneous investigation of the surroundings, or, as I like to call it, this *voluntary explosion* of the exploring spirit. In such cases, the children experience a joy at each *fresh discovery*. They are conscious of a sense of dignity and satisfaction which encourages them to seek for new sensations from their environment and to make themselves spontaneous *observers*.

The teacher should *watch* with the most solicitous care to see when and how the child arrives at this generalisation of ideas. For example, one of our little four-year-olds while running about in the court one day suddenly stood still and cried out, "Oh! the sky is blue!" and stood for some time looking up into the blue expanse of the sky.

One day, when I entered one of the "Children's Houses," five or six little ones gathered quietly about me and began caressing, lightly, my hands, and my clothing, saying, "It is smooth." "It is velvet." "This is rough." A number of others came near and began with serious and intent faces to repeat the same words, touching me as they did so. The directress wished to interfere to release me, but I signed to her to be quiet, and I myself did not move, but remained silent, admiring this spontaneous intellectual activity of my little ones. The greatest triumph of our educational method should always be this: *to bring about the spontaneous progress of the child*.

One day, a little boy, following one of our exercises in design, had chosen to fill in with coloured pencils the outline of a tree. To colour the trunk he laid hold upon a red crayon. The teacher wished to interfere, saying, "Do you think trees have red trunks?" I held her back and allowed the child to colour the tree red. This design was precious to us; it showed that the child was not yet an observer of his surroundings. *My way of treating this was to encourage the child to make use of the games for the chromatic sense.* He went daily into the garden with the other children, and could at any time see the tree trunks. When the sense exercises should have succeeded in attracting the child's spontaneous attention to colours about him, then, in some *happy moment* he would become aware that the tree trunks were not red, just as the other child during his play had become conscious of the fact that the sky was blue. In fact, the teacher continued to give the child outlines of trees to fill in. He one day chose a brown pencil with which to colour the trunk, and made the branches and leaves green. Later, he made the branches brown, also, using green only for the leaves.

Thus we have *the test* of the child's intellectual progress. We can not create observers by saying, "*observe*," but by giving them the power and the means for this observation, and these means are procured through education of the senses. Once we have *aroused* such activity, auto-education is assured, for refined well-trained senses lead us to a closer observation of the environment, and this, with its infinite variety, attracts the attention and continues the psychosensory education.

If, on the other hand, in this matter of sense education we single out definite concepts of the quality of certain objects, these very objects become associated with, or a part of, the training, which is in this way limited to those concepts taken and recorded. So the sense training remains unfruitful. When, for example, a teacher has given in the old way a lesson on the names of the colours, she has imparted an idea concerning that particular *quality*, but she has not educated the chromatic sense. The child will know these colours in a superficial way, forgetting them from time to time; and at best his appreciation of them will lie within the limits prescribed by the teacher. When, therefore, the teacher of the old methods shall have provoked the generalisation of the idea, saying, for example, "What is the colour of this flower!" "of this ribbon?" the attention of the child will in all probability remain torpidly fixed upon the examples suggested by her.

We may liken the child to a clock, and may say that with the old-time way it is very much as if we were to hold the wheels of the clock quiet and move the hands about the clock face with our fingers. The hands will continue to circle the dial just so long as we apply, through our fingers, the necessary motor force. Even so is it with that sort of culture which is limited to the work which the teacher does with the child. The new method, instead, may be compared to the process of winding, which sets the entire mechanism in motion.

This motion is in direct relation with the machine, and not with the work of winding. So the spontaneous psychic development of the child continues indefinitely and is in direct relation to the psychic potentiality of the child himself, and not with the work of the teacher. The movement, or the *spontaneous psychic activity* starts in our case from the education of the senses and is maintained by the observing intelligence. Thus, for example, the hunting dog receives his ability, not from the education given by his master, but from the *special acuteness* of his senses; and as soon as this physiological quality is applied to the right environment, the *exercise of hunting*, the increasing refinement of the sense perceptions, gives the dog the pleasure and then the passion for the chase. The same is true of the pianist who, refining at the same time his musical sense and the agility of his hand, comes to love more and more to draw new harmonies from the instrument. Thia double perfection proceeds until at last the pianist is launched upon a course which will be limited only by the personality which lies within him. Now a student of physics may know all the laws of harmony which form a part of his scientific culture, and yet he may not know how to follow a most simple musical composition. His culture, however vast, will be bound by the definite limits of his science. Our educational aim with very young children must be to*aid the spontaneous development of the mental, spiritual, and physical personality*, and not to make of the child a cultured individual in the commonly accepted sense of the term. So, after we have offered to the child such didactic material as is adapted to provoke the development of his senses, we must wait until the activity known as observation develops. And herein lies the *art of the educator*; in knowing how to measure the action by which we help the young child's personality to develop. To one whose attitude is right, little children soon reveal *profound individual differences* which call for very different kinds of help from the teacher. Some of them require almost no intervention on her part, while others demand actual *teaching*. It is necessary, therefore, that the teaching shall be rigorously guided by the principle of limiting to the greatest possible point the active intervention of the educator.

Here are a number of games and problems which we have used effectively in trying to follow this principle.

GAMES OF THE BLIND

The Games of the Blind are used for the most part as exercises in general sensibility as follows:

The Stuffs. We have in our didactic material a pretty little chest composed of drawers within which are arranged rectangular pieces of stuff in great variety. There are velvet, satin, silk, cotton, linen, etc. We have the child touch each of these pieces, teaching the appropriate nomenclature and adding something regarding the quality, as coarse, fine, soft. Then, we call the child and seat him at one of the tables where he can be seen by his companions, blindfold him, and offer him the stuffs one by one. He touches them, smooths them, crushes them between his fingers and decides, "It is velvet,—It is fine linen,—It is rough cloth," etc. This exercise provokes general interest. When we offer the child some unexpected foreign object, as, for example, a sheet of paper, a veil, the little assembly trembles as it awaits his response.

Weight. We place the child in the same position, call his attention to the tablets used for the education of the sense of weight, have him notice again the already well-known differences of weight, and then tell him to put all the dark tablets, which are the heavier ones, at the right, and all the light ones, which are the lighter, to the left. We then blindfold him and he proceeds to the game, taking each time two tablets. Sometimes he takes two of the same colour, sometimes two of different colours, but in a position opposite to that in which he must arrange them on his desk. These exercises are most exciting; when, for example, the child has in his hands two of the dark tablets and changes them from one hand to the other uncertain, and finally places them together on the right, the children watch in a state of intense eagerness, and a great sigh often expresses their final relief. The shouts of the audience when the entire game is followed without an error, gives the impression that their little friend *sees with his hands* the colours of the tablets.

Dimension and Form. We use games similar to the preceding one, having the child distinguish between different coins, the cubes and bricks of Froebel, and dry seeds, such as beans and peas. But such games never awaken the intense interest aroused by the preceding ones. They are, however, useful and serve to associate with the various objects those qualities peculiar to them, and also to fix the nomenclature.

APPLICATION OF THE EDUCATION OF THE VISUAL SENSE TO THE OBSERVATION OF THE ENVIRONMENT

Nomenclature. This is one of the most important phases of education. Indeed, nomenclature prepares for an *exactness* in the use of language which is not always met with in our schools. Many children, for example, use interchangeably the words thick and big, long and high. With the methods already described, the teacher may easily establish, by means of the didactic material, ideas which are very exact and clear, and may associate the proper word with these ideas.

Method of Using the Didactic Material

Dimensions. The directress, after the child has played for a long time with the three sets of solid insets and has acquired a security in the performance of the exercise, takes out all the cylinders of equal height and places them in a horizontal position on the table, one beside the other. Then she selects the two extremes, saying, "This is the *thickest*—This is the *thinnest*." She places them side by side so that the comparison may be more marked, and then taking them by the little button, she compares the bases, calling attention to the great difference. She then places them again beside each other in a vertical position in order to show that they are equal in height, and repeats several times, "thick—thin." Having done this, she should follow it with the test, asking, "Give me the thickest—Give me the thinnest," and finally she should proceed to the test of nomenclature, asking, "What is this?" In the lessons which follow this, the directress may take away the two extreme pieces and may repeat the lesson with the two pieces remaining at the extremities, and so on until she has used all the pieces. She may then take these up at random, saying, "Give me one a little thicker than this one," or "Give me one a little thinner than this one." With the second set of solid insets she proceeds in the same way. Here she stands the pieces upright, as each one has a base sufficiently broad to maintain it in this position, saying, "This is the highest" and "This is the lowest." Then placing the two extreme pieces side by side she may take them out of the line and compare the bases, showing that they are equal. From the extremes she may proceed as before, selecting each time the two remaining pieces most strongly contrasted.

With the third solid inset, the directress, when she has arranged the pieces in gradation, calls the child's attention to the first one, saying, "This is the largest," and to the last one, saying, "This is the smallest." Then she places them side by side and observes how they differ both in height and in base. She then proceeds in the same way as in the other two exercises.

Similar lessons may be given with the series of graduated prisms, of rods, and of cubes. The prisms are *thick* and *thin* and of equal *length*. The rods are *long* and *short* and of equal *thickness*. The cubes are *big* and *little* and differ in size and in height.

The application of these ideas to environment will come most easily when we measure the children with the anthropometer. They will begin among themselves to make comparisons, saying, "I am taller,—you are thicker." These comparisons are also made when the children hold out their little hands to show that they are clean, and the directress stretches hers out also, to show that she, too, has clean hands. Often the contrast between the dimensions of the hands calls forth laughter. The children make a perfect game of measuring themselves. They stand side by side; they look at each other; they decide. Often they place themselves beside grown persons, and observe with curiosity and interest the great difference in height.

Form. When the child shows that he can with security distinguish between the forms of the plane geometric insets, the directress may begin the lessons in nomenclature. She should begin with two strongly-contrasted forms, as the square and the circle, and should follow the usual method, using the three periods of Séguin. We do not teach all the names relative to the geometric figures, giving only those of the most familiar forms, such as square, circle, rectangle, triangle, oval. We now call attention to the fact that there are *rectangles which are narrow and long*, and others which are *broad and short*, while the *squares* are equal on all sides and can be only big and little. These things are most easily shown with the insets, for, though we turn the square about, it still enters its frame, while the rectangle, if placed across the opening, will not enter. The child is much interested in this exercise, for which we arrange in the frame a square and a series of rectangles, having the longest side equal to the side of the square, the other side gradually decreasing in the five pieces.

In the same way we proceed to show the difference between the oval, the ellipse, and the circle. The circle enters no matter how it is placed, or turned about; the ellipse does not enter when placed transversely, but if placed lengthwise will enter even if turned upside down. The oval, however, not only cannot enter the frame if placed transversely, but not even when turned upside down; it must be placed with the *large* curve toward the large part of the opening, and with the *narrow* curve toward the *narrow* portion of the opening.

The circles, *big* and *little*, enter their frames no matter how they are turned about. I do not reveal the difference between the oval and the ellipse until a very late stage of the child's education, and then not to all children, but only to those who show a special interest in the forms by choosing the game often, or by asking about the differences. I prefer that such differences should be recognised later by the child, spontaneously, perhaps in the elementary school.

It seems to many persons that in teaching these forms we are teaching *geometry*, and that this is premature in schools for such young children. Others feel that, if we wish to present geometric forms, we should use the *solids*, as being more concrete.

I feel that I should say a word here to combat such prejudices. To *observe* a geometric form is not to *analyse* it, and in the analysis geometry begins. When, for example, we speak to the child of sides and angles and explain these to him, even though with objective methods, as Froebel advocates (for example, the square has four sides and can be constructed with four sticks of equal length), then indeed we do enter the field of geometry, and I believe that little children are too immature for these steps. But the *observation of the form* cannot be too advanced for a child at this age. The plane of the table at which the child sits while eating his supper is probably a rectangle; the plate which contains his food is a circle, and we certainly do not consider that the child is too *immature* to be allowed to look at the table and the plate.

The insets which we present simply call the attention to a given *form*. As to the name, it is analogous to other names by which the child learns to call things. Why should we consider it premature to teach the child the words *circle, square, oval,* when in his home he repeatedly hears the word *round* used in connection with plates, etc. He will hear his parents speak of the *square* table, the *oval* table, etc., and these words in common use will remain for a long time *confused* in his mind and in his speech, if we do not interpose such help as that we give in the teaching of forms.

We should reflect upon the fact that many times a child, left to himself, makes an undue effort to comprehend the language of the adults and the meaning of the things about him. Opportune and rational instruction *prevents* such an effort, and therefore does not *weary*, but *relieves*, the child and satisfies his desire for knowledge. Indeed, he shows his contentment by various expressions of pleasure. At the same time, his attention is called to the word which, if he is allowed to pronounce badly, develops in him an imperfect use of the language.

This often arises from an effort on his part to imitate the careless speech of persons about him, while the teacher, by pronouncing clearly the word referring to the object which arouses the child's curiosity, prevents such effort and such imperfections.

Here, also, we face a widespread prejudice; namely, the belief that the child left to himself gives absolute repose to his mind. If this were so he would remain a stranger to the world, and, instead, we see him, little by little, spontaneously conquer various ideas and words. He is a traveller through life, who observes the new things among which he journeys, and who tries to understand the unknown tongue spoken by those about him. Indeed, he makes a great and *voluntary effort* to understand and to imitate. The instruction given to little children should be so directed as to *lessen this expenditure* of poorly directed effort, converting it instead into the enjoyment of conquest made easy and infinitely broadened. We are *the guides* of these travellers just entering the great world of human thought. We should see to it that we are intelligent and cultured guides, not losing ourselves in vain discourse, but illustrating briefly and concisely the work of art in which the traveller shows himself interested, and we should then respectfully allow him to observe it as long as he wishes to. It is our privilege to lead him to observe the most important and the most beautiful things of life in such a way that he does not lose energy and time in useless things, but shall find pleasure and satisfaction throughout his pilgrimage.

I have already referred to the prejudice that it is more suitable to present the geometric forms to the child in the *solid* rather than in the *plane*, giving him, for example, the *cube*, the *sphere*, the *prism*. Let us put aside the physiological side of the question showing that the visual recognition of the solid figure is more complex than that of the plane, and let us view the question only from the more purely pedagogical standpoint of *practical life*.

The greater number of objects which we look upon every day present more nearly the aspect of our plane geometric insets. In fact, doors, window-frames, framed pictures, the wooden or marble top of a table, are indeed *solid* objects, but with one of the dimensions greatly reduced, and with the two dimensions determining the form of the plane surface made most evident.

When the plane form prevails, we say that the window is rectangular, the picture frame oval, this table square, etc. *Solids having a determined form prevailing in the plane surface* are almost the only ones which come to our notice. And such solids are clearly represented by our *plane geometric insets*.

The child will *very often* recognise in his environment forms which he has learned in this way, but he will rarely recognise the *solid geometric forms*.

That the table leg is a prism, or a truncated cone, or an elongated cylinder, will come to his knowledge long after he has observed that the top of the table upon which he places things is rectangular. We do not, therefore, speak of the fact of recognising that a house is a prism or a cube. Indeed, the pure solid geometric forms *never exist* in the ordinary objects about us; these present, instead, a *combination of forms*. So, putting aside the difficulty of taking in at a glance the complex form of a house, the child recognises in it, not an *identity* of form, but an *analogy*.

He will, however, see the plane geometric forms perfectly represented in windows and doors, and in the faces of many solid objects in use at home. Thus the knowledge of the forms given him in the plane geometric insets will be for him a species of magic *key*, opening the external world, and making him feel that he knows its secrets.

I was walking one day upon the Pincian Hill with a boy from the elementary school. He had studied geometric design and understood the analysis of plane geometric figures. As we reached the highest terrace from which we could see the Piazza del Popolo with the city stretching away behind it, I stretched out my hand saying, "Look, all the works of man are a great mass of geometric figures;" and, indeed, rectangles, ovals, triangles, and semicircles, perforated, or ornamented, in a hundred different ways the grey rectangular façades of the various buildings. Such uniformity in such an expanse of buildings seemed to prove the *limitation* of human intelligence, while in an adjoining garden plot the shrubs and flowers spoke eloquently of the infinite variety of forms in nature.

The boy had never made these observations; he had studied the angles, the sides and the construction of outlined geometric figures, but without thinking beyond this, and feeling only annoyance at this arid work. At first he laughed at the idea of man's massing geometric figures together, then he became interested, looked long at the buildings before him, and an expression of lively and thoughtful interest came into his face. To the right of the Ponte Margherita was a factory building in the process of construction, and its steel framework delineated a series of rectangles. "What tedious work!" said the boy, alluding to the workmen. And, then, as we drew near the garden, and stood for a moment in silence admiring the grass and the flowers which sprang so freely from the earth, "It is beautiful!" he said. But that word "beautiful" referred to the inner awakening of his own soul.

This experience made me think that in the observation of the plane geometric forms, and in that of the plants which they saw growing in their own little gardens, there existed for the children precious sources of spiritual as well as intellectual education. For this reason, I have wished to make my work broad, leading the child, not only to observe the forms about him, but to distinguish the work of man from that of nature, and to appreciate the fruits of human labour.

(*a*) *Free Design.* I give the child a sheet of white paper and a pencil, telling him that he may draw whatever he wishes to. Such drawings have long been of interest to experimental psychologists. Their importance lies in the fact that they reveal the *capacity* of the child for observing, and also show his individual tendencies. Generally, the first drawings are unformed and confused, and the teacher should ask the child *what he wished to draw*, and should write it underneath the design that it may be a record. Little by little, the drawings become more intelligible, and verily reveal the progress which the child makes in the observation of the forms about him. Often the most minute details of an object have been observed and recorded in the crude sketch. And, since the child draws what he wishes, he reveals to us which are the objects that most strongly attract his attention.

(*b*) *Design Consisting of the Filling in of Outlined Figures.* These designs are most important as they constitute "the preparation for writing." They do for the colour sense what *free design* does for the sense of *form*. In other words, they reveal the capacity of the child *in the matter of observation of colours*, as the free design showed us the extent to which he was an observer of form in the objects surrounding him. I shall speak more fully of this work in the chapter on *writing*. The exercises consist in filling in with coloured pencil, certain outlines drawn in black. These outlines present the simple geometric figures and various objects with which the child is familiar in the schoolroom, the home, and the garden. The child must *select* his colour, and in doing so he shows us whether he has observed the colours of the things surrounding him.

Free Plastic Work

These exercises are analogous to those in free design and in the filling in of figures with coloured pencils. Here the child makes whatever he wishes with *clay*; that is, he models those objects which he remembers most distinctly and which have impressed him most deeply. We give the child a wooden tray containing a piece of clay, and then we await his work. We possess some very remarkable pieces of clay work done by our little ones. Some of them reproduce, with surprising minuteness of detail, objects which they have seen. And what is most surprising, these models often record not only the form, but even the *dimensions* of the objects which the child handled in school.

Many little ones model the objects which they have seen at home, especially kitchen furniture, water-jugs, pots, and pans. Sometimes, we are shown a simple cradle containing a baby brother or sister. At first it is necessary to place written descriptions upon these objects, as it is necessary to do with the free design. Later on, however, the models are easily recognisable, and the children learn to reproduce the geometric solids. These clay models are undoubtedly very valuable material for the teacher, and make clear many individual differences, thus helping her to understand her children more fully. In our method they are also valuable as psychological manifestations of development according to age. Such designs are precious guides also for the teacher in the matter of her intervention in the child's education. The children who, in this work reveal themselves as observers, will probably become spontaneous observers of all the world about them, and may be led toward such a goal by the indirect help of exercises tending to fix and to make more exact the various sensations and ideas.

These children will also be those who arrive most quickly at the act of *spontaneous writing*. Those whose clay work remains unformed and indefinite will probably need the direct revelation of the directress, who will need to call their attention in some material manner to the objects around them.

Geometric Analysis of Figures; Sides, Angles, Centre, Base

The geometric analysis of figures is not adapted to very young children. I have tried a means for the *introduction* of such analysis, limiting this work to the *rectangle* and making use of a game which includes the analysis without fixing the attention of the child upon it. This game presents the concept most clearly.

The *rectangle* of which I make use is the plane of one of the children's tables, and the game consists in laying the table for a meal. I have in each of the "Children's Houses" a collection of toy table-furnishings, such as may be found in any toy-store. Among these are dinner-plates, soup-plates, soup-tureen, saltcellars, glasses, decanters, little knives, forks, spoons, etc. I have them lay the table for six, putting *two places* on each of the longer sides, and one place on each of the shorter sides. One of the children takes the objects and places them as I indicate. I tell him to place the soup tureen in the *centre* of the table; this napkin in a *corner*. "Place this plate in the centre of the short *side*."

Then I have the child look at the table, and I say, "Something is lacking in this *corner*. We want another glass on this *side*. Now let us see if we have everything properly placed on the two longer sides. Is everything ready on the two shorter sides? Is there anything lacking in the four corners?"

I do not believe that we may proceed to any more complex analysis than this before the age of six years, for I believe that the child should one day take up one of the plane insets and *spontaneously* begin to count the sides and the angles. Certainly, if we taught them such ideas they would be able to learn them, but it would be a mere learning of formulae, and not applied experience.

Exercises in the Chromatic Sense

I have already indicated what colour exercises we follow. Here I wish to indicate more definitely the succession of these exercises and to describe them more fully.

Designs and Pictures. We have prepared a number of outline drawings which the children are to fill in with coloured pencil, and, later on, with a brush, preparing for themselves the water-colour tints which they will use. The first designs are of flowers, butterflies, trees and animals, and we then pass to simple landscapes containing grass, sky, houses, and human figures.

These designs help us in our study of the natural development of the child as an observer of his surroundings; that is, in regard to colour. The children *select the colours* and are left entirely free in their work. If, for example, they colour a chicken red, or a cow green, this shows that they have not yet become observers. But I have already spoken of this in the general discussion of the method. These designs also reveal the effect of the education of the chromatic sense. As the child selects delicate and harmonious tints, or strong and contrasting ones, we can judge of the progress he has made in the refinement of his colour sense.

The fact that the child must *remember* the colour of the objects represented in the design encourages him to observe those things which are about him. And then, too, he wishes to be able to fill in more difficult designs. Only those children who know how to keep the colour *within* the outline and to reproduce the *right colours* may proceed to the more ambitious work. These designs are very easy, and often very effective, sometimes displaying real artistic work. The directress of the school in

Mexico, who studied for a long time with me, sent me two designs; one representing a cliff in which the stones were coloured most harmoniously in light violet and shades of brown, trees in two shades of green, and the sky a soft blue. The other represented a horse with a chestnut coat and black mane and tail.

16

Methods for the Teaching of Reading and Writing

Spontaneous Development of Graphic Language. While I was directress of the Orthophrenic School at Rome, I had already began to experiment with various didactic means for the teaching of reading and writing. These experiments were practically original with me.

Itard and Séguin do not present any rational method through which writing may be learned. In the pages above quoted, it may be seen how Itard proceeded in the teaching of the alphabet and I give here what Séguin says concerning the teaching of writing.

"To have a child pass from design, to writing, which is its most immediate application, the teacher need only call D, a portion of a circle, resting its extremities upon a vertical; A, two obliques reunited at the summit and cut by a horizontal, etc., etc.

"We no longer need worry ourselves as to how the child shall learn to write: he designs, *then* writes. It need not be said that we should have the child draw the letters according to the laws of contrast and analogy. For instance, O beside I; B with P; T opposite L, etc."

According to Séguin, then, we do not need to *teach* writing. The child who draws, will write. But writing, for this author, means printed capitals! Nor does he, in any other place, explain whether his pupil shall write in any other way. He instead, gives much space to the description of *the design which prepares for,* and which *includes* writing. This method of design is full of difficulties and was only established by the combined attempts of Itard and Séguin.

"Chapter XL: Design. In design the first idea to be acquired is that of the plane destined to receive the design. The second is that of the trace or delineation. Within these two concepts lies all design, all linear creation.

"These two concepts are correlative, their relation generates the idea, or the capacity to produce the lines in this sense; that lines may only be called such when they follow a methodical and determined direction: the trace without direction is not a line; produced by chance, it has no name.

"The rational sign, on the contrary, has a name because it has a direction and since all writing or design is nothing other than a composite of the diverse directions followed by a line, we must, before approaching what is commonly called writing, *insist* upon these notions of plane and line. The ordinary child acquires these by instinct, but an insistence upon them is necessary in order to render the idiot careful and sensitive in their application. Through methodical design he will come into rational contact with all parts of the plane and will, guided by imitation, produce lines at first simple, but growing more complicated.

"The pupil may be taught: First, to trace the diverse species of lines. Second, to trace them in various directions and in different positions relative to the plane. Third, to reunite these lines to form figures varying from simple to complex. We must therefore, teach the pupil to distinguish straight lines from curves, vertical from horizontal, and from the various oblique lines; and must finally make clear the principal points of conjunction of two or more lines in forming a figure.

"This rational analysis of design, *from which writing will spring*, is so essential in all its parts, that a child who, before being confided to my care, already wrote many of the letters, has taken six days to learn to draw a perpendicular or a horizontal line; he spent fifteen days before imitating a curve and an oblique. Indeed the greater number of my pupils, are for a long time incapable of even imitating the movements of my hand upon the paper, before attempting to draw a line in a determined direction. The most imitative, or the least stupid ones, produce a sign diametrically opposite to that which I show them and all of them confound the points of conjunction of two lines no matter how evident this is. It is true that the thorough knowledge I have given them of lines and of configuration helps them to make the connection which must be established between the plane and the various marks with which they must cover the surface, but in the study rendered necessary by the deficiency of my pupils, the progression in the matter of the vertical, the horizontal, the oblique, and the curve must be determined by the consideration of the difficulty of comprehension and of execution which each offers to a torpid intelligence and to a weak unsteady hand.

"I do not speak here of merely having them perform a difficult thing, since I have them surmount a *series* of difficulties and for this reason I ask myself if some of these difficulties are not greater and some less, and if they do not grow one from the other, like theorems. Here are the ideas which have guided me in this respect.

"The vertical is a line which the eye and the hand follow directly, going up and down. The horizontal line is not natural to the eye, nor to the hand, which lowers itself and follows a curve (like the horizon from which it has taken its name), starting from the centre and going to the lateral extremity of the plane.

"The oblique line presupposes more complex comparative ideas, and the curve demands such firmness and so many differences in its relation to the plane that we would only lose time in taking up the study of these lines. The most simple line then, is the vertical, and this is how I have given my pupils an idea of it.

"The first geometric formula is this: only straight lines may be drawn from one given point to another.

"Starting from this axiom, which the hand alone can demonstrate, I have fixed two points upon the blackboard and have connected them by means of a vertical. My pupils try to do the same between the dots they have upon their paper, but with some the vertical descends to the right of the point and with others, to the left, to say nothing of those whose hand diverges in all directions. To arrest these various deviations which are often far more defects of the intelligence and of the vision, than of the hand, I have thought it wise to restrict the field of the plane, drawing two vertical lines to left and right of the points which the child is to join by means of a parallel line half way between the two enclosing lines. If these two lines are not enough, I place two rulers vertically upon the paper, which arrest the deviations of the hand absolutely. These material barriers are not, however, useful for very long. We first suppress the rulers and return to the two parallel lines, between which the idiot learns to draw the third line. We then take away one of the guiding lines, and leave, sometimes that on the right, sometimes that on the left, finally taking away this last line and at last, the dots, beginning by erasing the one at the top which indicates the starting point of the line and of the hand. The child thus learns to draw a vertical without material control, without points of comparison.

"The same method, the same difficulty, the same means of direction are used for the straight horizontal lines. If, by chance, these lines begin well, we must await until the child curves them, departing from the centre and proceeding to the extremity *as nature commands him*, and because of the reason which I have explained. If the two dots do not suffice to sustain the hand, we keep it from deviating by means of the parallel lines or of the rulers.

"Finally, have him trace a horizontal line, and by uniting with it a vertical ruler we form a right angles. The child will begin to understand, in this way, what the vertical and horizontal lines really are, and will see the relation of these two ideas as he traces a figure.

"In the sequence of the development of lines, it would seem that the study of the oblique should immediately follow that of the vertical and the horizontal, but this is not so! The oblique which partakes of the vertical in its inclination, and of the horizontal in its direction, and which partakes of both in its nature (since it is a straight line), presents perhaps, because of its relation to other lines, an idea too complex to be appreciated without preparation."

Thus Séguin goes on through many pages, to speak of the oblique in all directions, which he has his pupils trace between two parallels. He then tells of the four curves which he has them draw to right and left of a vertical and above and below a horizontal, and concludes: "So we find the solution of the problems for which we sought—the vertical line, the horizontal, the oblique, and the four curves, whose union forms the circle, contain all possible lines, *all writing*.

"Arrived at this point, Itard and I were for a long time at a standstill. The lines being known, the next step was to have the child trace regular figures, beginning of course, with the simplest. According to the general opinion, Itard had advised me to begin with the square and I had followed this advice *for three months*, without being able to make the child understand me."

After a long series of experiments, guided by his ideas of the genesis of geometric figures, Séguin became aware that the triangle is the figure most easily drawn.

"When three lines meet thus, they always form a triangle, while four lines may meet in a hundred different directions without remaining parallel and therefore without presenting a perfect square.

"From these experiments and many others, I have deduced the first principles of writing and of design for the idiot; principles whose application is *too simple* for me to discuss further."

Such was the proceeding used by my predecessors in the teaching of writing to deficients. As for reading, Itard proceeded thus: he drove nails into the wall and hung upon them, geometric figures of wood, such as triangles, squares, circles. He then drew the exact imprint of these upon the wall, after which he took the figures away and had the "boy of Aveyron" replace them upon the proper nails, guided by the design. From this design Itard conceived the idea of the plane geometric insets. He finally had large print letters made of wood and proceeded in the same way as with the geometric figures, that is, using the design upon the wall and arranging the nails in such a way that the child might place the letters upon them and then take them off again. Later, Séguin used the horizontal plane instead of the wall, drawing the letters on the bottom of a box and having the child superimpose solid letters. After twenty years, Séguin had not changed his method of procedure.

A criticism of the method used by Itard and Séguin for reading and writing seems to me superfluous. The method has two fundamental errors which make it inferior to the methods in use for normal children, namely: writing in printed capitals, and the preparation for writing through a study of rational geometry, which we now expect only from students in the secondary schools.

Séguin here confuses ideas in a most extraordinary way. He has suddenly jumped from the psychological observation of the child and from his relation to his environment, to the study of the origin of lines and their relation to the plane.

He says that the child *will readily design a vertical line*, but that the horizontal will soon become a curve, because "*nature commands it*" and this *command of nature* is represented by the fact that man sees the horizon as a curved line!

The example of Séguin serves to illustrate the necessity of a *special education* which shall fit man for *observation*, and shall direct *logical thought*.

The observation must be absolutely objective, in other words, stripped of preconceptions. Séguin has in this case the preconception that geometric design must prepare for writing, and that hinders him from discovering the truly natural proceeding necessary to such preparation. He has, besides, the preconception that the deviation of a line, as well as the inexactness with which the child traces it, are due to "*the mind and the eye, not to the hand*," and so he wearies himself *for weeks and months in explaining* the direction of lines and in guiding *the vision* of the idiot.

It seems as if Séguin felt that a good method must start from a superior point, geometry; the intelligence of the child is only considered worthy of attention in its relation to abstract things. And is not this a common defect?

Let us observe mediocre men; they pompously assume erudition and disdain simple things. Let us study the clear thought of those whom we consider men of genius. Newton is seated tranquilly in the open air; an apple falls from the tree, he observes it and asks, "Why?" Phenomena are never insignificant; the fruit which falls and universal gravitation may rest side by side in the mind of a genius.

If Newton had been a teacher of children he would have led the child to look upon the worlds on a starry night, but an erudite person might have felt it necessary first to prepare the child to understand the sublime calculus which is the key to astronomy—Galileo Galilei observed the oscillation of a lamp swung on high, and discovered the laws of the pendulum.

In the intellectual life *simplicity* consists in divesting one's mind of every preconception, and this leads to the discovery of new things, as, in the moral life, humility and material poverty guide us toward high spiritual conquests.

If we study the history of discoveries, we will find that they have come from *real objective observation* and *from logical thought*. These are simple things, but rarely found in one man.

Does it not seem strange, for instance, that after the discovery by Laveran of the malarial parasite which invades the red blood-corpuscles, we did not, in spite of the fact that we know the blood system to be a system of closed vessels, even so much as *suspect the possibility* that a stinging insect might inoculate us with the parasite? Instead, the theory that the evil emanated from low ground, that it was carried by the African winds, or that it was due to dampness, was given credence. Yet these were vague ideas, while the parasite was a definite biological specimen.

When the discovery of the malarial mosquito came to complete logically the discovery of Laveran, this seemed marvellous, stupefying. Yet we know in biology that the reproduction of molecular vegetable bodies is by scission with alternate sporation, and that of molecular animals is by scission with alternate conjunction. That is, after a certain period in which the primitive cell has divided and sub-divided into fresh cells, equal among themselves, there comes the formation of two diverse cells, one male and one female, which must unite to form a single cell capable of recommencing the cycle of reproduction by division. All this being known at the time of Laveran, and the malarial parasite being known to be a protozoon, it would have seemed logical to consider its segmentation in the stroma of the red corpuscle as the phase of scission and to await until the parasite gave place to the sexual forms, which must necessarily come in the phase succeeding scission. Instead, the division was looked upon as spore-formation, and neither Laveran, nor the numerous scientists who followed the research, knew how to give an explanation of the appearance of the sexual forms. Laveran expressed an idea, which was immediately received, that these two forms were degenerate forms of the malarial parasite, and therefore incapable of producing the changes determining the disease. Indeed, the malaria was apparently cured at the appearance of the two sexual forms of the parasite, the conjunction of the two cells being impossible in the human blood. The theory—then recent—of Morel upon human degeneration accompanied by deformity and weakness, inspired Laveran in his interpretation, and everybody found the idea of the illustrious pathologist a fortunate one, because it was inspired by the great concepts of the Morellian theory.

Had anyone, instead, limited himself to reasoning thus: the original form of the malarial insect is a protozoon; it reproduces itself by scission, under our eyes; when the scission is finished, we see two diverse cells, one a half-moon, the other threadlike. These are the feminine and masculine cells which must, by conjunction, alternate the scission,—such a reasoner would have opened the way to the discovery. But *so simple* a process of reasoning did not come. We might almost ask ourselves how great would be the world's progress if a special form of education prepared men for pure observation and logical thought.

A great deal of time and intellectual force are lost in the world, because the false seems great and the truth so small and insignificant.

I say all this to defend the necessity, which I feel we face, of preparing the coming generations by means of more rational methods. It is from these generations that the world awaits its progress. We have already learned to make use of our surroundings, but I believe that we have arrived at a time when the necessity presents itself for *utilising* human force, through a scientific education.

To return to Séguin's method of writing, it illustrates another truth, and that is the tortuous path we follow in our teaching. This, too, is allied to an instinct for complicating things, analogous to that which makes us so prone to appreciate complicated things. We have Séguin teaching *geometry* in order to teach a child to write; and making the child's mind exert itself to follow geometrical abstractions only to come down to the simple effort of drawing a printed D. After all, must the child not have to make another effort in order to *forget* the print, and *learn* the script!

And even we in these days still believe that in order to learn to write the child must first make vertical strokes. This conviction is very general. Yet it does not seem natural that to write the letters of the alphabet, which are all rounded, it should be necessary to begin with straight lines and acute angles.

In all good faith, we wonder that it should be difficult to do away with the angularity and stiffness with which the beginner traces the beautiful curve of the O.[1] Yet, through what effort on our part, and on his, was he forced to fill pages and pages with rigid lines and acute angles! To whom is due this time-honoured idea that the first sign to be traced must be a straight line? And why do we so avoid preparing for curves as well as angles?

Let us, for a moment, divest ourselves of such preconceptions and proceed in a more simple way. We may be able to relieve future generations of *all effort* in the matter of learning to write.

Is it necessary to begin writing with the making of vertical strokes? A moment of clear and logical thinking is enough to enable us to answer, no. The child makes too painful an effort in following such an exercise. The first steps should be the easiest, and the up and down stroke, is, on the contrary, one of the most difficult of all the pen movements. Only a professional penman could fill a whole page and preserve the regularity of such strokes, but a person who writes only moderately well would be able to complete a page of presentable writing. Indeed, the straight line is unique, expressing the shortest distance between two points, while *any deviation* from that direction signifies a line which is not straight. These infinite deviations are therefore easier than that *one* trace which is perfection.

If we should give to a number of adults the order to draw a straight line upon the blackboard, each person would draw a long line proceeding in a different direction, some beginning from one side, some from another, and almost all would succeed in making the line straight. Should we then ask that the line be drawn in a *particular direction*, starting from a determined point, the ability shown at first would greatly diminish, and we would see many more irregularities, or errors. Almost all the lines would be long—for the individual *must needs gather impetus* in order to succeed in making his line straight.

Should we ask that the lines be made short, and included within precise limits, the errors would increase, for we would thus impede the impetus which helps to conserve the definite direction. In the methods ordinarily used in teaching writing, we add, to such limitations, the further restriction that the instrument of writing must be held in a certain way, not as instinct prompts each individual.

Thus we approach in the most conscious and restricted way the first act of writing, which should be voluntary. In this first writing we still demand that the single strokes be kept parallel, making the child's task a difficult and barren one, since it has no purpose for the child, who does not understand the meaning of all this detail.

I had noticed in the note-books of the deficient children in France (and Voisin also mentions this phenomenon) that the pages of vertical strokes, although they began as such, ended in lines of C's. This goes to show that the deficient child, whose mind is less resistant than that of the normal child, exhausts, little by little, the initial effort of imitation, and the natural movement gradually comes to take the place of that which was forced or stimulated. So the straight lines are transformed into curves, more and more like the letter C. Such a phenomenon does not appear in the copy-books of normal children, for they resist, through effort, until the end of the page is reached, and, thus, as often happens, conceal the didactic error.

But let us observe the spontaneous drawings of normal children. When, for example, picking up a fallen twig, they trace figures in the sandy garden path, we never see short straight lines, but long and variously interlaced curves.

Séguin saw the same phenomenon when the horizontal lines he made his pupils draw became curves so quickly instead. And he attributed the phenomenon to the imitation of the horizon line!

That vertical strokes should prepare for alphabetical writing, seems incredibly illogical. The alphabet is made up of curves, therefore we must prepare for it by learning to make straight lines.

"But," says someone, "in many letters of the alphabet, the straight line does exist," True, but there is no reason why as a beginning of writing, we should select one of the details of a complete form. We may analyse the alphabetical signs in this way, discovering straight lines and curves, as by analysing discourse, we find grammatical rules. But we all *speak* independently of such rules, why then should we not write independently of such analysis, and without the separate execution of the parts constituting the letter?

It would be sad indeed if we could *speak* only *after* we had studied grammar! It would be much the same as demanding that before we *looked* at the stars in the firmament, we must study infinitesimal calculus; it is much the same thing to feel that before teaching an idiot to write, we must make him understand the abstract derivation of lines and the problems of geometry!

No less are we to be pitied if, in order to write, we must follow analytically the parts constituting the alphabetical signs. In fact the *effort* which we believe to be a necessary accompaniment to learning to write is a purely artificial effort, allied, not to writing, but to the *methods* by which it is taught.

Let us for a moment cast aside every dogma in this connection. Let us take no note of culture, or custom. We are not, here, interested in knowing how humanity began to write, nor what may have been the origin of writing itself. Let us put away the conviction, that long usage has given us, of the necessity of beginning writing by making vertical strokes; and let us try to be as clear and unprejudiced in spirit as the truth which, we are seeking.

"Let us observe an individual who is writing, and let us seek to analyse the acts he performs in writing," that is, the mechanical operations which enter into the execution of writing. This would be undertaking the *philosophical study of writing*, and it goes without saying that we should examine the individual who writes, not the *writing*; the *subject*, not the *object*. Many have begun with the object, examining the writing, and in this way many methods have been constructed.

But a method starting from the individual would be decidedly original—very different from other methods which preceded it. It would indeed signify a new era in writing, *based upon anthropology*.

In fact, when I undertook my experiments with normal children, if I had thought of giving a name to this new method of writing, I should have called it without knowing what the results would be, the *anthropological method*. Certainly, my studies in anthropology inspired the method, but experience has given me, as a surprise, another title which seems to me the natural one, "the method of *spontaneous* writing."

While teaching deficient children I happened to observe the following fact: An idiot girl of eleven years, who was possessed of normal strength and motor power in her hands, could not learn to sew, or even to take the first step, darning, which consists in passing the needle first over, then under the woof, now taking up, now leaving, a number of threads.

I set the child to weaving with the Froebel mats, in which a strip of paper is threaded transversely in and out among vertical strips of paper held fixed at top and bottom. I thus came to think of the analogy between the two exercises, and became much interested in my observation of the girl. When she had become skilled in the Froebel weaving, I led her back again to the sewing, and saw with pleasure that she was now able to follow the darning. From that time on, our sewing classes began with a regular course in the Froebel weaving.

I saw that the necessary movements of the hand in sewing *had been prepared without having the child sew*, and that we should really find the way to *teach* the child *how*, before *making him execute* a task. I saw especially that preparatory movements could be carried on, and reduced to a mechanism, by means of repeated exercises not in the work itself but in that which prepares for it. Pupils could then come to the real work, able to perform it without ever having directly set their hands to it before.

I thought that I might in this way prepare for writing, and the idea interested me tremendously. I marvelled at its simplicity, and was annoyed that *I had not thought before* of the method which was suggested to me by my observation of the girl who could not sew.

In fact, seeing that I had already taught the children to touch the contours of the plane geometric insets, I had now only to teach them to touch with their fingers the *forms of the letters of the alphabet*.

I had a beautiful alphabet manufactured, the letters being in flowing script, the low letters 8 centimetres high, and the taller ones in proportion. These letters were in wood, 1/2 centimetre in thickness, and were painted, the consonants in blue enamel, the vowels in red. The under side of these letter-forms, instead of being painted, were covered with bronze that they might be more durable. We had only one copy of this wooden alphabet; but there were a number of cards upon which the letters were painted in the same colours and dimensions as the wooden ones. These painted letters were arranged upon the cards in groups, according to contrast, or analogy of form.

Corresponding to each letter of the alphabet, we had a picture representing some object the name of which began, with the letter. Above this, the letter was painted in large script, and near it, the same letter, much smaller and in its printed form. These pictures served to fix the memory of the sound of the letter, and the small printed letter united to the one in script, was to form the passage to the reading of books. These pictures do not, indeed, represent a new idea, but they completed an arrangement which did not exist before. Such an alphabet was undoubtedly most expensive and when made by hand the cost was fifty dollars.

The interesting part of my experiment was, that after I had shown the children how to place the movable wooden letters upon those painted in groups upon the cards, I had them *touch them repeatedly in the fashion of flowing writing.*

I multiplied these exercises in various ways, and the children thus learned to make *the movements necessary to reproduce the form of the graphic signs without writing.*

I was struck by an idea which had never before entered my mind—that in writing we make *two diverse* forms of movement, for, besides the movement by which the form is reproduced, there is also that of *manipulating the instrument of writing.* And, indeed, when the deficient children had become expert in touching all the letters according to form, *they did not yet know how to hold a pencil.* To hold and to manipulate a little stick securely, corresponds to the *acquisition of a special muscular mechanism which is independent of the writing movement;* it must in fact go along with the motions necessary to produce all of the various letter forms. It is, then, *a distinct mechanism,* which must exist together with the motor memory of the single graphic signs. When I provoked in the deficients the movements characteristic of writing by having them touch the letters with their fingers, I exercised mechanically the psycho-motor paths, and fixed the muscular memory of each letter. There remained the preparation of the muscular mechanism necessary in holding and managing the instrument of writing, and this I provoked by adding two periods to the one already described. In the second period, the child touched the letter, not only with the index finger of his right hand, but with two, the index and the middle finger. In the third period, he touched the letters with a little wooden stick, held as a pen in writing. In substance I was making him repeat the same movements, now with, and now without, holding the instrument.

I have said that the child was to follow the *visual* image of the outlined letter. It is true that his finger had already been trained through touching the contours of the geometric figures, but this was not always a sufficient preparation. Indeed, even we grown people, when we trace a design through glass or tissue paper, cannot follow perfectly the line which we see and along which we should draw our pencil. The design should furnish some sort of control, some mechanical guide, for the pencil, in order to follow with *exactness* the trace, *sensible in reality only to the eye.*

The deficients, therefore, did not always follow the design exactly with either the finger or the stick. The didactic material did not offer *any control* in the work, or rather it offered only the uncertain control of the child's glance, which could, to be sure, see if the finger continued upon the sign, or not. I now thought that in order to have the pupil follow the movements more exactly, and to guide the execution more directly, I should need to prepare letter forms so indented, as to represent a *furrow* within which the wooden stick might run. I made the designs for this material, but the work being too expensive I was not able to carry out my plan.

After having experimented largely with this method, I spoke of it very fully to the teachers in my classes in didactic methods at the State Orthophrenic School. These lectures were printed, and I give below the words which, though they were placed in the hands of more than 200 elementary teachers, did not draw from them a single helpful idea. Professor Ferreri[2] in an article speaks with amazement of this fact.[3]

"At this point we present the cards bearing the vowels

painted in red. The child sees irregular figures painted in red. We give him the vowels in wood, painted red, and have him superimpose these upon the letters painted on the card. We have him touch the wooden vowels in the fashion of writing, and give him the name of each letter. The vowels are arranged on the cards according to analogy of form:

o	*e*	*a*
i		*u*

"We then say to the child, for example, 'Find o. Put it in its place.' Then, 'What letter is this?' We here discover that many children make mistakes in the letters if they only look at the letter.

"They could however tell the letter by touching it. Most interesting observations may be made, revealing various individual types: visual, motor.

"We have the child touch the letters drawn upon the cards,—using first the index finger only, then the index with the middle finger,—then with a small wooden stick held as a pen. The letter must be traced in the fashion of writing.

"The consonants are painted in blue, and are arranged upon the cards according to analogy of form. To these cards are annexed a movable alphabet in blue wood, the letters of which are to be placed upon the consonants as they were upon the vowels. In addition to these materials there is another series of cards, where, besides the consonant, are painted one or two figures the names of which begin with that particular letter. Near the script letter, is a smaller printed letter painted in the same colour.

"The teacher, naming the consonant according to the phonetic method, indicates the letter, and then the card, pronouncing the names of the objects painted there, and emphasizing the first letter, as, for example, '*p-pear*: give me the consonant *p*—put it in its place, touch it,' etc. *In all this we study the linguistic defects of the child.*

"Tracing the letter, in the fashion of writing, begins the muscular education which prepares for writing. One of our little girls taught by this method has reproduced all the letters with the pen, though she does not as yet recognise them all. She has made them about eight centimetres high, and with surprising regularity. This child also does well in hand work. The child who looks, recognises, and touches the letters in the manner of writing, prepares himself simultaneously for reading and writing.

"Touching the letters and looking at them at the same time, fixes the image more quickly through the co-operation of the senses. Later, the two facts separate; looking becomes reading; touching becomes writing. According to the type of the individual, some learn to read first, others to write."

I had thus, about the year 1899, initiated my method for reading and writing upon the fundamental lines it still follows. It was with great surprise that I noted the *facility* with which a deficient child, to whom I one day gave a piece of chalk, traced upon the blackboard, in a firm hand, the letters of the entire alphabet, writing for the first time.

This had arrived much more quickly than I had supposed. As I have said, some of the children wrote the letters *with a pen and yet could not recognise one of them*. I have noticed, also, in normal children, that the muscular sense is most easily developed in infancy, and this makes writing exceedingly easy for children. It is not so with reading, which requires a much longer course of instruction, and which calls for a superior intellectual development, since it treats of the *interpretation of signs*, and of the *modulation of accents of the voice*, in order that the word may be understood. And all this is a purely mental task, while in writing, the child, under dictation, *materially translates* sounds into signs, and *moves*, a thing which is always easy and pleasant for him. Writing develops in the little child with *facility* and *spontaneity*, analogous to the development of spoken language—which is a motor translation of audible sounds. Reading, on the contrary, makes part of an abstract intellectual culture, which is the interpretation of ideas from graphic symbols, and is only acquired later on.

My first experiments with normal children were begun in

the first half of the month of November, 1907.

In the two "Children's Houses" in San Lorenzo, I had, from the date of their respective inaugurations (January 6 in one and March 7 in the other), used only the games of practical life, and of the education of the senses. I had not presented exercises for writing, because, like everybody else, I held the prejudice that it was necessary to begin as late as possible the teaching of reading and writing, and certainly to avoid it before the age of six.

But the children seemed to demand some *conclusion* of the exercises, which had already developed them intellectually in a most surprising way. They knew how to dress and undress, and to bathe, themselves; they knew how to sweep the floors, dust the furniture, put the room in order, to open and close boxes, to manage the keys in the various locks; they could replace the objects in the cupboards in perfect order, could care for the plants; they knew how to observe things, and how to see objects with their hands. A number of them came to us and frankly demanded to be taught to read and write. Even in the face of our refusal several children came to school and proudly showed us that they knew how to make an O on the blackboard.

Finally, many of the mothers came to beg us as a favour to teach the children to write, saying, "Here in the 'Children's Houses' the children are awakened, and learn so many things easily that if you only teach reading and writing they will soon learn, and will then be spared the great fatigue this always means in the elementary school." This faith of the mothers, that their little ones would, from us, be *able to learn to read and write without fatigue*, made a great impression upon me. Thinking upon the results I had obtained in the school for deficients, I decided during the August vacation to make a trial upon the reopening of the school in September. Upon second thought I decided that it would be better to take up the interrupted work in September, and not to approach reading and writing until October, when the elementary schools opened. This presented the added advantage of permitting us to compare the progress of the children of the first elementary with that made by ours, who would have begun the same branch of instruction at the same time.

In September, therefore, I began a search for someone who could manufacture didactic materials, but found no one willing to undertake it. I wished to have a splendid alphabet made, like the one used with the deficients. Giving this up, I was willing to content myself with the ordinary enamelled letters used upon shop windows, but I could find them in script form nowhere. My disappointments were many.

So passed the whole mouth of October. The children in the first elementary had already filled pages of vertical strokes, and mine were still waiting. I then decided to cut out large paper letters, and to have one of my teachers colour these roughly on one side with a blue tint. As for the touching of the letters, I thought of cutting the letters of the alphabet out of sandpaper, and of gluing them upon smooth cards, thus making objects much like those used in the primitive exercises for the tactile sense.

Only after I had made these simple things, did I become aware of the superiority of this alphabet to that magnificent one I had used for my deficients, and in the pursuit of which I had wasted two months! If I had been rich, I would have had that beautiful but barren alphabet of the past! We wish the old things because we cannot understand the new, and we are always seeking after that gorgeousness which belongs to things already on the decline, without recognising in the humble simplicity of new ideas the germ which shall develop in the future.

I finally understood that a paper alphabet could easily be multiplied, and could be used by many children at one time, not only for the recognition of letters, but for the composition of words. I saw that in the sandpaper alphabet I had found the looked-for guide for the fingers which touched the letter. This was furnished in such a way that no longer the sight alone, but the touch, lent itself directly to teaching the movement of writing with exactness of control.

In the afternoon after school, the two teachers and I, with

great enthusiasm, set about cutting out letters from writing-paper, and others from sandpaper. The first, we painted blue, the second, we mounted on cards, and, while we worked, there unfolded before my mind a clear vision of the method in all its completeness, so simple that it made me smile to think I had not seen it before.

The story of our first attempts is very interesting. One day one of the teachers was ill, and I sent as a substitute a pupil of mine, Signorina Anna Fedeli, a professor of pedagogy in a Normal school. When I went to see her at the close of the day, she showed me two modifications of the alphabet which she had made. One consisted in placing behind each letter, a transverse strip of white paper, so that the child might recognise the direction of the letter, which he often turned about and upside down. The other consisted in the making of a cardboard case where each letter might be put away in its own compartment, instead of being kept in a confused mass as at first. I still keep this rude case made from an old pasteboard box, which Signorina Fedeli had found in the court and roughly sewed with white thread.

She showed it to me laughing, and excusing herself for the miserable work, but I was most enthusiastic about it. I saw at once that the letters in the case were a precious aid to the teaching. Indeed, it offered to the eye of the child the possibility of comparing all of the letters, and of selecting those he needed. In this way the didactic material described below had its origin.

I need only add that at Christmas time, less than a month and a half later, while the children in the first elementary were laboriously working to forget their wearisome pothooks and to prepare for making the curves of O and the other vowels, two of my little ones of four years old, wrote, each one in the name of his companions, a letter of good wishes and thanks to Signor Edoardo Talamo. These were written upon note paper without blot or erasure and the writing was adjudged equal to that which is obtained in the third elementary grade.

NOTES

1. It will, of course, be understood that this is a criticism of the system in use in Italian schools. A. E. G.
2. G. Ferreri—Per l'insegnamento della scrittura (Sistema della Dott M. Montessori) Bollettino dell' Associazione Romana per la cura medico—pedigogica dei fanciulli anormali e deficienti poveri, anno 1, n. 4, ottobre 1907. Roma Tipografia delle Terme Diocleziane.
3. Riassunto delle lezion di didattica, della dott. Montessori anno 1900, Stab. lit. Romano, via Frattina 62, Disp. 6a, pag. 46: "*Lettura e Scrittura simultanee.*"

17

Description of the Method and Didactic Material Used

FIRST PERIOD: EXERCISE TENDING TO DEVELOP THE MUSCULAR MECHANISM NECESSARY IN HOLDING AND USING THE INSTRUMENT IN WRITING

Design Preparatory to Writing.—Didactic Material. Small wooden tables; metal insets, outline drawings, coloured pencils. I have among my materials two little wooden tables, the tops of which form an inclined plane sloping toward a narrow cornice, which prevents objects placed upon the table from slipping off. The top of each table is just large enough to hold four of the square frames, into which the metal plane geometric insets are fitted, and is so painted as to represent three of these brown frames, each containing a square centre of the same dark blue as the centres of the metal insets.

The metal insets are in dimension and form a reproduction of the series of plane geometric insets in wood already described.

Exercises. Placed side by side upon the teacher's desk, or upon one of the little tables belonging to the children, these two little tables may have the appearance of being one long table containing eight figures. The child may select one or more figures, taking at the same time the frame of the inset. The analogy between these metal insets and the plane geometric insets of wood is complete. But in this case, the child can freely use the pieces, where before, he arranged them in the wooden frame. He first takes the metal frame, places it upon a sheet of white paper, and with a coloured pencil *draws around the contour of the empty centre*. Then, he takes away the frame, and upon the paper there remains a geometric figure.

This is the first time that the child has reproduced through design, a geometric figure. Until now, he has only placed the geometric insets above the figures delineated on the three series of cards. He now places upon the figure, which he himself has drawn, the metal inset, just as he placed the wooden inset upon the cards. His next act is to follow the contour of this inset with a pencil of a different colour. Lifting the metal piece, he sees the figure reproduced upon the paper, in two colours.

Here, for the first time is born the abstract concept of the geometric figure, for, from two metal pieces so different in form as the frame and the inset, there has resulted the same design, which is a *line* expressing a determined figure. This fact strikes the attention of the child. He often marvels to find the same figure reproduced by means of two pieces so different, and looks for a long time with evident pleasure at the duplicate design—almost as if it were *actually produced* by the objects which serve to guide his hand.

Besides all this, the child learns *to trace lines* determining figures. There will come a day in which, with still greater surprise and pleasure, he will trace graphic signs determining words.

After this, he begins the work which directly prepares for the formation of the muscular mechanism relative to the holding and manipulation of the instrument of writing. With a coloured pencil of his own selection, held as the pen is held in writing, he *fills in* the figure which he has outlined. We teach him not to pass outside the contour, and in doing so we attract his attention to this contour, and thus *fix* the idea that a line may determine a figure.

The exercise of filling in one figure alone, causes the child to perform repeatedly the movement of manipulation which would be necessary to fill ten copy-book pages with vertical strokes. And yet, the child feels no weariness, because, although he makes exactly the muscular co-ordination which is necessary to the work, he does so freely and in any way that he wishes, while his eyes are fixed upon a large and brightly coloured figure. At first, the children fill pages and pages of paper with these big squares, triangles, ovals, trapezoids; colouring them red, orange, green, blue, light blue, and pink.

Gradually they limit themselves to the use of the dark blue and brown, both in drawing the figure and in filling it in, thus reproducing the appearance of the metal piece itself. Many of the children, quite of their own accord, make a little orange-coloured circle in the centre of the figure, in this way representing the little brass button by which the metal piece is to be held. They take great pleasure in feeling that they have reproduced exactly, like true artists, the objects which they see before them on the little shelf.

Observing the successive drawings of a child, there is revealed to us a duplicate form of progression:

First. Little by little, the lines tend less and less to go outside the enclosing line until, at last, they are perfectly contained within it, and both the centre and the frame are filled in with close and uniform strokes.

Second. The strokes with which the child fills in the figures, from being at first short and confused, become gradually *longer, and more nearly parallel*, until in many cases the figures are filled in by means of perfectly regular up and down strokes, extending from one side of the figure to the other. In such a case, it is evident that the child is *master of the pencil*. The muscular mechanism, necessary to the management of the instrument of writing, *is established*. We may, therefore, by examining such designs, arrive at a clear idea of the maturity of the child in the matter of *holding the pencil or pen in hand*. To vary these exercises, we use the *outline drawings* already described. Through these designs, the manipulation of the pencil is perfected, for they oblige the child to make lines of various lengths, and make him more and more secure in his use of the pencil.

If we could count the lines made by a child in the filling in of these figures, and could transform them into the signs used in writing, they would fill many, many copy-books! Indeed, the security which our children attain is likened to that of children in our ordinary third elementary grade. When for the first time they take a pen or a pencil in hand, they know how to manage it almost as well as a person who has written for a long time.

I do not believe that any means can be found which will so successfully and, in so short a space of time, establish this mastery. And with it all, the child is happy and diverted. My old method for the deficients, that of following with a small stick the contours of raised letters, was, when compared with this, barren and miserable!

Even when the children *know how to write* they continue these exercises, which furnish an unlimited progression, since the designs may be varied and complicated. The children follow in each design essentially the same movements, and acquire a varied collection of pictures which grow more and more perfect, and of which they are very proud. For I not only *provoke*, but perfect, the writing through the exercises which we call preparatory. The control of the pen is rendered more and more secure, not by repeated exercises in the writing, but by means of these filled-in designs. In this way, my children *perfect themselves in writing, without actually writing.*

SECOND PERIOD: EXERCISES TENDING TO ESTABLISH THE VISUAL-MUSCULAR IMAGE OF THE ALPHABETICAL SIGNS, AND TO ESTABLISH THE MUSCULAR MEMORY OF THE MOVEMENTS NECESSARY TO WRITING

Didactic Material. Cards upon which the single letters of the alphabet are mounted in sandpaper; larger cards containing groups of the same letters.

The cards upon which the sandpaper letters are mounted are adapted in size and shape to each letter. The vowels are in light-coloured sandpaper and are mounted upon dark cards, the consonants and the groups of letters are in black sandpaper mounted upon white cards. The grouping is so arranged as to call attention to contrasted, or analogous forms.

The letters are cut in clear script form, the shaded parts being made broader. We have chosen to reproduce the vertical script in use in the elementary schools.

Exercises. In teaching the letters of the alphabet, we begin with the *vowels* and proceed to the consonants, pronouncing the *sound*, not the name. In the case of the consonants, we immediately unite the sound with one of the vowel sounds, repeating the syllable according to the usual phonetic method.

The teaching proceeds according to the three periods already illustrated.

First. Association of the visual and muscular-tactile sensation with the letter sound.

The directress presents to the child two of the cards upon which vowels are mounted (or two of the consonants, as the case may be). Let us suppose that we present the letters i and o, saying, "This is i! This is o!" As soon as we have given the sound of a letter, we have the child trace it, taking care to show him *how* to trace it, and if necessary guiding the index finger of his right hand over the sandpaper letter *in the sense of writing*.

"Knowing how to trace" will consist in *knowing the direction* in which a given graphic sign must be followed.

The child learns quickly, and his finger, already expert in the tactile exercise, *is led,* by the slight roughness of the fine sandpaper, over the exact track of the letter. *He may then repeat indefinitely* the movements necessary to produce the letters of the alphabet, without the fear of the mistakes of which a child writing with a pencil for the first time is so conscious. If he deviates, the smoothness of the card immediately warns him of his error.

The children, as soon as they have become at all expert in this tracing of the letters, take great pleasure in repeating it *with closed eyes,* letting the sandpaper lead them in following the form which they do not see. Thus the perception will be established by the direct muscular-tactile sensation of the letter. In other words, it is no longer the visual image of the letter, but the *tactile sensation,* which guides the hand of the child in these movements, which thus become fixed in the muscular memory.

There develop, contemporaneously, three sensations when

the directress *shows the letter* to the child and has him trace it; the visual sensation, the tactile sensation, and the muscular sensation. In this way the *image of the graphic sign* is fixed *in a much shorter space of time* than when it was, according to ordinary methods, acquired only through the visual image. It will be found that the *muscular memory* is in the young child the most tenacious and, at the same time, the most ready. Indeed, he sometimes recognises the letters by touching them, when he cannot do so by looking at them. These images are, besides all this, contemporaneously associated with the alphabetical sound.

Second. Perception. *The child should know how to compare and to recognise the figures, when he hears the sounds corresponding to them.*

The directress asks the child, for example, "Give me o!—Give me i!" If the child does not recognise the letters by looking at them, she invites him to trace them, but if he still does not recognise them, the lesson is ended, and may be resumed another day. I have already spoken of the necessity of *not revealing* the error, and of not insisting in the teaching when the child does not respond readily.

Third. Language. *Allowing the letters to lie for some instants upon the table, the directress asks the child, "What is this?" and he should respond, o, i.*

In teaching the consonants, the directress pronounces only the *sound*, and as soon as she has done so unites with it a vowel, pronouncing the syllable thus formed and alternating this little exercise by the use of different vowels. She must always be careful to emphasize the sound of the consonant, repeating it by itself, as, for example, *m, m, m, ma, me, mi,m, m.* When the child *repeats* the sound he isolates it, and then accompanies it with the vowel.

It is not necessary to teach all the vowels before passing to the consonants, and as soon as the child knows one consonant he may begin to compose words. Questions of this sort, however, are left to the judgment of the educator.

I do not find it practical *to follow a special rule* in the teaching of the consonants. Often the curiosity of the child concerning a letter leads us to teach that desired consonant; a name pronounced may awaken in him a desire to know what consonants are necessary to compose it, and this *will*, or *willingness*, of the pupil is a much more *efficacious* means than any rule concerning the *progression* of the letters.

When the child pronounces *the sounds* of the consonants, he experiences an evident pleasure. It is a great novelty for him, this series of sounds, so varied and yet so distinct, *presenting* such enigmatic signs as the letters of the alphabet. There is mystery about all this, which provokes most decided interest. One day I was on the terrace while the children were having their free games; I had with me a little boy of two years and a half left with me, for a moment, by his mother. Scattered about upon a number of chairs, were the alphabets which we use in the school. These had become mixed, and I was putting the letters back into their respective compartments. Having finished my work, I placed the boxes upon two of the little chairs near me. The little boy watched me. Finally, he drew near to the box, and took one of the letters in his hand. It chanced to be an f. At that moment the children, who were running in single file, passed us, and, seeing the letter, called out in chorus the corresponding sound and passed on. The child paid no attention to them, but put back the f and took up an r. The children running by again, looked at him laughing, and then began to cry out "r, r, r! r, r, r!" Little by little the baby understood that, when he took a letter in hand, the children, who were passing, cried out a sound. This amused him so much that I wished to observe how long he would persist in this game without becoming tired. He kept it up for *three-quarters of an hour*! The children had become interested in the child, and grouped themselves about him, pronouncing the sounds in chorus, and laughing at his pleased surprise. At last, after he had several times held up f, and had received from his public the same sound, he took the letter again, showing it to me, and saying, "f, f, f!" He had learned this from out the great confusion of sounds which he had heard; the long letter which had first arrested the attention of the running children, had made a great impression upon him.

It is not necessary to show how the separate pronunciation of the alphabetical sounds *reveals* the condition of the child's speech. Defects, which are almost all related to the *incomplete* development of the language itself, manifest themselves, and the directress may take note of them one by one. In this way she will be possessed of a record of the child's progress, which will help her in her individual teaching, and will reveal much concerning the development of the language in this particular child.

In the matter of *correcting linguistic defects*, we will find it helpful to follow the physiological rules relating to the child's development, and to modify the difficulties in the presentation of our lesson. When, however, the child's speech is sufficiently developed, and when he *pronounces all the sounds*, it does not matter which of the letters we select in our lessons.

Many of the defects which have become permanent in adults are due to *functional errors in the development* of the language during the period of infancy. If, for the attention which we pay to the correction of linguistic defects in children in the upper grades, we would substitute *a direction of the development of the language* while the child is still young, our results would be much more practical and valuable. In fact, many of the defects in pronunciation arise from the use of a *dialect*, and these it is almost impossible to correct after the period of childhood. They may, however, be most easily removed through the use of educational methods especially adapted to the perfecting of the language in little children.

We do not speak here of actual linguistic *defects* related to anatomical or physiological weaknesses, or to pathological facts which alter the function of the nervous system. I speak at present only of those irregularities which are due to a repetition of incorrect sounds, or to the imitation of imperfect pronunciation. Such defects may show themselves in the pronunciation of any one of the consonant sounds, and I can conceive of no more practical means for a methodical correction of speech defects than this exercise in pronunciation, which is a necessary part in learning the graphic language through my method. But such important questions deserve a chapter to themselves.

Turning directly to the method used in teaching writing, I may call attention to the fact that it is contained in the two periods already described. Such exercises have made it possible for the child to learn, and to fix, the muscular mechanism necessary to the proper holding of the pen, and to the making of the graphic signs. If he has exercised himself for a sufficiently long time in these exercises, he will be *potentially* ready to write all the letters of the alphabet and all of the simple syllables, without ever having taken chalk or pencil in his hand.

We have, in addition to this, begun the teaching of *reading* at the same time that we have been teaching *writing*. When we present a letter to the child and enunciate its sound, he fixes the image of this letter by means of the visual sense, and also by means of the muscular-tactile sense. He associates the sound with its relative sign; that is, he relates the sound to the graphic sign. But *when he sees and recognises, he reads; and when he traces, he writes*. Thus his mind receives as one, two acts, which, later on, as he develops, will separate, coming to constitute the two diverse processes of *reading and writing*. By teaching these two acts contemporaneously, or, better, by their *fusion*, we place the child *before a new form of language* without determining which of the acts constituting it should be most prevalent.

We do not trouble ourselves as to whether the child in the development of this process, first learns to read or to write, or if the one or the other will be the easier. We must rid ourselves of all preconceptions, and must *await from experience* the answer to these questions. We may expect that individual differences will show themselves in the prevalence of one or the other act in the development of different children. This makes possible the most interesting psychological study of the individual, and should broaden the work of this method, which is based upon the free expansion of individuality.

THIRD PERIOD: EXERCISES FOR THE COMPOSITION OF WORDS

Didactic Material. This consists chiefly of alphabets. The letters of the alphabet used here are identical in form and dimension with the sandpaper ones already described, but these are cut out of cardboard and are not mounted. In this way each letter represents an object which can be easily handled by the child and placed wherever he wishes it. There are several examples of each letter, and I have designed cases in which the alphabets

(a) Training the Sense of Touch. Learning the difference between rough and smooth by running fingers alternately over sandpaper and smooth cardboard; distinguishing different shapes by fitting geometric insets into place; distinguishing textures. (b) Learning to Write and Read by Touch. The child at the left is tracing sandpaper letters and learning to know them by touch. The boy and girl are making words out of cardboard letters.

may be kept. These cases or boxes are very shallow, and are divided and subdivided into many compartments, in each one of which I have placed a group of four copies of the same letter. The compartments are not equal in size, but are measured according to the dimensions of the letters themselves. At the bottom of each compartment is glued a letter which is not to be taken out. This letter is made of black cardboard and relieves the child of the fatigue of hunting about for the right compartment when he is replacing the letters in the case after he has used them. The vowels are cut from blue cardboard, and the consonants from red.

(a) Children Touching Letters. The child on the left has acquired lightness and delicacy of touch by very thorough preparatory exercises. The one on the right has not had so much training. (b) Making Words with Cardboard Script.

In addition to these alphabets we have a set of the capital letters mounted in sandpaper upon cardboard, and another, in which they are cut from cardboard. The numbers are treated in the same way.

Exercises. As soon as the child knows some of the vowels and the consonants we place before him the big box containing all the vowels and the consonants which he knows. The directress pronounces very clearly a word; for example, "mama," brings out the sound of the m very distinctly, repeating the sounds a number of times. Almost always the little one with an impulsive movement seizes an m and places it upon the table. The directress repeats "ma—ma." The child selects the a and places it near the m. He then composes the other syllable very easily. But the reading of the word which he has composed is not so easy. Indeed, he generally succeeds in reading it only after a *certain effort*. In this case I help the child, urging him to read, and reading the word with him once or twice, always pronouncing very distinctly, *mama, mama*. But once he has understood the mechanism of the game, the child goes forward by himself, and becomes intensely interested. We may pronounce any word, taking care only that the child understands separately the letters of which it is composed. He composes the new word, placing, one after the other, the signs corresponding to the sounds.

It is most interesting indeed to watch the child at this work. Intensely attentive, he sits watching the box, moving his lips almost imperceptibly, and taking one by one the necessary letters, rarely committing an error in spelling. The movement of the lips reveals the fact that he *repeats to himself an infinite number of times* the words whose sounds he is translating into signs. Although the child is able to compose any word which is clearly pronounced, we generally dictate to him only those words which are well-known, since we wish his composition to result in an idea. When these familiar words are used, he spontaneously rereads many times the word he has composed, repeating its sounds in a thoughtful, contemplative way.

The importance of these exercises is very complex. The child analyses, perfects, fixes his own spoken language,—placing an object in correspondence to every sound which he utters. The composition of the word furnishes him with substantial proof of the necessity for clear and forceful enunciation.

The exercise, thus followed, associates the sound which is heard with the graphic sign which represents it, and lays a most solid foundation for accurate and perfect spelling.

In addition to this, the composition of the words is in itself an exercise of intelligence. The word which is pronounced presents to the child a problem which he must solve, and he will do so by remembering the signs, selecting them from among others, and arranging them in the proper order. He will have the *proof* of the exact solution of his problem when he *rereads* the word—this word which he has composed, and which represents for all those who know how to read it, *an idea*.

When the child hears others read the word he has composed, he wears an expression of satisfaction and pride, and is possessed by a species of joyous wonder. He is impressed by this correspondence, carried on between himself and others by means of symbols. The written language represents for him the highest attainment reached by his own intelligence, and is at the same time, the reward of a great achievement.

When the pupil has finished the composition and the reading of the word we have him, according to the habits of order which we try to establish in connection with all our work, *"put away"* all the letters, each one in its own compartment. In composition, pure and simple, therefore, the child unites the two exercises of comparison and of selection of the graphic signs; the first, when from the entire box of letters before him he takes those necessary; the second, when he seeks the compartment in which each letter must be replaced. There are, then, three exercises united in this one effort, all three uniting to *fix the image of the graphic sign* corresponding to the sounds of the word. The work of learning is in this case facilitated in three ways, and the ideas are acquired in a third of the time which would have been necessary with the old methods. We shall soon see that the child, on hearing the word, or on thinking of a word which he already knows, *will see*, with his mind's eye, all the letters, necessary to compose the word, arrange themselves. He will reproduce this vision with a facility most surprising to us. One day a little boy four years old, running alone about the terrace, was heard to repeat many times, "To make Zaira, I must have z-a-i-r-a." Another time, Professor Di Donato, in a visit to the "Children's House," pronounced his own name for a four-year-old child. The child was composing the name, using small letters and making it all one word, and had begun, thus—*diton*. The professor at once pronounced the word more distinctly; di *do* nato, whereupon the child, without scattering the letters, picked up the syllable *to* and placed it to one side, putting *do* in the empty space. He then placed an *a* after the *n*, and, taking up the *to* which he had put aside, completed the word with it. This made it evident that the child, when the word was pronounced more clearly, understood that the syllable *to* did not belong at that place in the word, realised that it belonged at the end of the word, and therefore placed it aside until he should need it. This was most surprising in a child of four years, and amazed all of those present. It can be explained by the clear and, at the same time, complex vision of the signs which the child must have, if he is to form a word which he hears spoken. This extraordinary act was largely due to the orderly mentality which the child had acquired through repeated spontaneous exercises tending to develop his intelligence.

These three periods contain the entire method for the acquisition of written language. The significance of such a method is clear. The psycho-physiological acts which unite to establish reading and writing are prepared separately and carefully. The muscular movements peculiar to the making of the signs or letters are prepared apart, and the same is true of the manipulation of the instrument of writing. The composition of the words, also, is reduced to a psychic mechanism of association between images heard and seen. There comes a moment in which the child, without thinking of it, fills in the geometric figures with an up and down stroke, which is free and regular; a moment in which he touches the letters with closed eyes, and in which he reproduces their form, moving his finger through the air; a moment in which the composition of words has become a psychic impulse, which makes the child, even when alone, repeat to himself "To make Zaira I must have z-a-i-r-a."

Now this child, it is true, *has never written*, but he has mastered all the acts necessary to writing. The child who, when taking dictation, not only knows how to compose the word, but instantly embraces in his thought its composition as a whole, will be able to write, since he knows how to make, with his eyes closed, the movements necessary to produce these letters, and since he manages almost unconsciously the instrument of writing.

More than this, the freedom with which the child has acquired this mechanical dexterity makes it possible for the impulse or spirit to act at any time through the medium of his mechanical ability. He should, sooner or later, come into his full power by way of a spontaneous explosion into writing. This is, indeed, the marvellous reaction which has come from my experiment with normal children. In one of the "Children's Houses," directed by Signorina Bettini, I had been especially careful in the way in which writing was taught, and we have had from this school most beautiful specimens of writing, and for this reason, perhaps I cannot do better than to describe the development of the work in this school.

One beautiful December day when the sun shone and the air was like spring, I went up on the roof with the children. They were playing freely about, and a number of them were gathered about me. I was sitting near a chimney, and said to a little five-year-old boy who sat beside me, "Draw me a picture of this chimney," giving him as I spoke a piece of chalk. He got down obediently and made a rough sketch of the chimney on the tiles which formed the floor of this roof terrace. As is my custom with little children, I encouraged him, praising his work. The child looked at me, smiled, remained for a moment as if on the point of bursting into some joyous act, and then cried out, "I can write! I can write!" and kneeling down again he wrote on the pavement the word "hand." Then, full of enthusiasm, he wrote also "chimney," "roof." As he wrote, he continued to cry out, "I can write! I know how to write!" His cries of joy brought the other children, who formed a circle about him, looking down at his work in stupefied amazement. Two or three of them said to me, trembling with excitement, "Give me the chalk. I can write too." And indeed they began to write various words: *mama, hand, John, chimney, Ada.*

Not one of them had ever taken chalk or any other instrument in hand for the purpose of writing. It was the *first time* that they had ever written, and they traced an entire word, as a child, when speaking for the first time, speaks the entire word.

The first word spoken by a baby causes the mother ineffable joy. The child has chosen perhaps the word "mother," seeming to render thus a tribute to maternity. The first word written by my little ones aroused within themselves an indescribable emotion of joy. Not being able to adjust in their minds the connection between the preparation and the act, they were possessed by the illusion that, having now grown to the proper size, they knew how to write. In other words, writing seemed to them only one among the many gifts of nature.

They believe that, as they grow bigger and stronger, there will come some beautiful day when they *shall know how to write.* And, indeed, this is what it is in reality. The child who speaks, first prepares himself unconsciously, perfecting the psycho-muscular mechanism which leads to the articulation of the word. In the case of writing, the child does almost the same thing, but the direct pedagogical help and the possibility of preparing the movements for writing in an almost material way, causes the ability to write to develop much more rapidly and more perfectly than the ability to speak correctly.

In spite of the ease with which this is accomplished, the preparation is not partial, but complete. The child possesses *all* the movements necessary for writing. And written language develops not gradually, but in an explosive way; that is, the child can write *any word*. Such was our first experience in the development of the written language in our children. Those first days we were a prey to deep emotions. It seemed as if we walked in a dream, and as if we assisted at some miraculous achievement.

The child who wrote a word for the first time was full of excited joy. He might be compared to the hen who has just laid an egg. Indeed, no one could escape from the noisy manifestations of the little one. He would call everyone to see, and if there were some who did not go, he ran to take hold of their clothes forcing them to come and see. We all had to go and stand about the written word to admire the marvel, and to unite our exclamations of surprise with the joyous cries of the fortunate author. Usually, this first word was written on the floor, and, then, the child knelt down before it in order to be nearer to his work and to contemplate it more closely.

After the first word, the children, with a species of frenzied joy, continued to write everywhere. I saw children crowding about one another at the blackboard, and behind the little ones who were standing on the floor another line would form consisting of children mounted upon chairs, so that they might write above the heads of the little ones. In a fury at being thwarted, other children, in order to find a little place where they might write, overturned the chairs upon which their companions were mounted. Others ran toward the window shutters or the door, covering them with writing. In these first days we walked upon a carpet of written signs. Daily accounts showed us that the same thing was going on at home, and some of the mothers, in order to save their pavements, and even the crust of their loaves upon which they found words written, made their children presents of *paper* and *pencil*. One of these children brought to me one day a little note-book entirely filled with writing, and the mother told me that the child had written all day long and all evening, and had gone to sleep in his bed with the paper and pencil in his hand.

This impulsive activity which we could not, in those first days control, made me think upon the wisdom of Nature, who develops the spoken language little by little, letting it go hand in hand with the gradual formation of ideas. Think of what the result would have been had Nature acted imprudently as I had done! Suppose Nature had first allowed the human being to gather, by means of the senses, a rich and varied material, and to acquire a store of ideas, and had then completely prepared in him the means for articulate language, saying finally to the child, mute until that hour, "Go—Speak!" The result would have been a species of sudden madness, under the influence of which the child, feeling no restraints, would have burst into an exhausting torrent of the most strange and difficult words.

I believe, however, that there exists between the two extremes a happy medium which is the true and practical way. We should lead the child more gradually to the conquest of written language, yet we should still have it come as a *spontaneous fact*, and his work should from the first be almost perfect.

Experience has shown us how to control this phenomenon, and how to lead the child more *calmly* to this new power. The fact that the children *see* their companions writing, leads them, through imitation, to write *as soon as* they can. In this way, when the child writes he does not have the entire alphabet at his disposal, and the number of words which he can write is limited. He is not even capable of making all of the words possible through a combination of the letters which he does know. He still has the great joy of the *first written word*, but this is no longer the source of *an overwhelming surprise*, since he sees just such wonderful things happening each day, and knows that sooner or later the same gift will come to all. This tends to create a calm and ordered environment, still full of beautiful and wonderful surprises.

Making a visit to the "Children's House," even during the opening weeks, one makes fresh discoveries. Here, for instance, are two little children, who, though they fairly radiate pride and joy, are writing tranquilly. Yet, these children, until yesterday, had never thought of writing!

The directress tells me that one of them began to write yesterday morning at eleven o'clock, the other, at three in the afternoon. We have come to accept the phenomenon with calmness, and tacitly recognise it as a *natural form of the child's development*.

The wisdom of the teacher shall decide when it is necessary to encourage a child to write. This can only be when he is already perfect in the three periods of the preparatory exercise, and yet does not write of his own accord. There is danger that in retarding the act of writing, the child may plunge finally into a tumultuous effort, due to the fact that he knows the entire alphabet and has no natural check.

The signs by which the teacher may almost precisely diagnose the child's maturity in this respect are: the *regularity* of the *parallel* lines which fill in the geometric figures; the recognition with closed eyes of the sandpaper letters; the security and readiness shown in the composition of words. Before intervening by means of a direct invitation to write, it is best to wait at least a week in the hope that the child may write spontaneously. When he has begun to write spontaneously the teacher may intervene to *guide* the progress of the writing. The first help which she may give is that of *ruling* the blackboard, so that the child may be led to maintain regularity and proper dimensions in his writing.

The second, is that of inducing the child, whose writing is not firm, to *repeat the tracing* of the sandpaper letters. She should do this instead of *directly* correcting his actual writing, for the child does not perfect himself by repeating the act of writing, but by repeating the acts preparatory to writing. I remember a little beginner who, wishing to make his blackboard writing perfect, brought all of the sandpaper letters with him, and before writing touched two or three times *all of the letters needed in the words he wished to write*. If a letter did not seem to him to be perfect he erased it and *retouched* the letter upon the card before rewriting.

Our children, even after they have been writing for a year, continue to repeat the three preparatory exercises. They thus learn both to write, and to perfect their writing, without really going through the actual act. With our children, actual writing is a test; it springs from an inner impulse, and from the pleasure of explaining a superior activity; it is not an exercise. As the soul of the mystic perfects itself through prayer, even so in our little ones, that highest expression of civilisation, written language, is acquired and improved through exercises which are akin to, but which are not, writing.

There is educational value in this idea of preparing oneself before trying, and of perfecting oneself before going on. To go forward correcting his own mistakes, boldly attempting things which he does imperfectly, and of which he is as yet unworthy dulls the sensitiveness of the child's spirit toward his own errors. My method of writing contains an educative concept; teaching the child that prudence which makes him avoid errors, that dignity which makes him look ahead, and which guides him to perfection, and that humility which unites him closely to those sources of good through which alone he can make a spiritual conquest, putting far from him the illusion that the immediate success is ample justification for continuing in the way he has chosen.

The fact that all the children, those who are just beginning the three exercises and those who have been writing for months, daily repeat the same exercise, unites them and makes it easy for them to meet upon an apparently equal plane. Here there are no *distinctions* of beginners, and experts. All of the children fill in the figures with coloured pencils, touch the sandpaper letters and compose words with the movable alphabets; the little ones beside the big ones who help them. He who prepares himself, and he who perfects himself, both follow the same path. It is the same way in life, for, deeper than any social distinction, there lies an equality, a common meeting point, where all men are brothers, or, as in the spiritual life, aspirants and saints again and again pass through the same experiences.

Writing is very quickly learned, because we begin to teach it only to those children who show a desire for it by spontaneous attention to the lesson given by the directress to other children, or by watching the exercises in which the others are occupied. Some individuals *learn* without ever having received any lessons, solely through listening to the lessons given to others.

In general, all children of four are intensely interested in writing, and some of our children have begun to write at the age of three and a half. We find the children particularly enthusiastic about tracing the sandpaper letters.

During the first period of my experiments, when the children were shown the alphabet *for the first time,* I one day asked Signorina Bettini to bring out to the terrace where the children were at play, all of the various letters which she herself had made. As soon as the children saw them they gathered about us, their fingers outstretched in their eagerness to touch the letters. Those who secured cards were unable to touch them properly because of the other children, who crowded about trying to reach the cards in our laps. I remember with what an impulsive movement the possessors of the cards held them on high like banners, and began to march, followed by all the other children who clapped their hands and cried out joyously. The procession passed before us, and all, big and little, laughed merrily, while the mothers, attracted by the noise, leaned from the windows to watch the sight.

The average time that elapses between the first trial of the preparatory exercises and the first written word is, for children of four years, from a month to a month and a half. With children of five years, the period is much shorter, being about a month. But one of our pupils learned to use in writing all the letters of the alphabet in twenty days. Children of four years, after they have been in school for two months and a half, can write any word from dictation, and can pass to writing with ink in a notebook. Our little ones are generally experts after three months' time, and those who have written for six months may be compared to the children in the third elementary. Indeed, writing is one of the easiest and most delightful of all the conquests made by the child.

If adults learned as easily as children under six years of age, it would be an easy matter to do away with illiteracy. We would probably find two grave hinderances to the attainment of such a brilliant success: the torpor of the muscular sense, and those permanent defects of spoken language, which would be sure to translate themselves into the written language. I have not made experiments along this line, but I believe that one school year would be sufficient to lead an illiterate person, not only to write, but to express his thoughts in written language.

So much for the time necessary for learning. As to the execution, our children *write well* from the moment in which they begin. The *form* of the letters, beautifully rounded and flowing, is surprising in its similarity to the form of the sandpaper models. The beauty of our writing is rarely equalled by any scholars in the elementary schools, *who have not had special exercises in penmanship*. I have made a close study of penmanship, and I know how difficult it would be to teach pupils of twelve or thirteen years to write an entire word without lifting the pen, except for the few letters which require this. The up and down strokes with which they have filled their copy-book make flowing writing almost impossible to them.

Our little pupils, on the other hand, spontaneously, and with a marvellous security, write entire words without lifting the pen, maintaining perfectly the slant of the letters, and making the distance between each letter equal. This has caused more than one visitor to exclaim, "If I had not seen it I should never have believed it." Indeed, penmanship is a superior form of teaching and is necessary to correct defects already acquired and fixed. It is a long work, for the child, *seeing* the model, must follow the *movements* necessary to reproduce it, while there is no direct correspondence between the visual sensation and the movements which he must make. Too often, penmanship is taught at an age when all the defects have become established, and when the physiological period in which the *muscular memory* is ready, has been passed.

We directly prepare the child, not only for writing, but also for *penmanship*, paying great attention to the *beauty of form* (having the children touch the letters in script form) and to the flowing quality of the letters. (The exercises in filling-in prepare for this.)

READING

Didactic Material. The Didactic Material for the lessons in reading consists in slips of paper or cards upon which are written in clear, large script, words and phrases. In addition to these cards we have a great variety of toys.

Experience has taught me to distinguish clearly between *writing and reading*, and has shown me that the two acts *are not absolutely contemporaneous*. Contrary to the usually accepted idea, writing *precedes reading*. I do not consider as *reading* the test which the child makes *when he verifies* the word that he has written. He is translating signs into sounds, as he first translated sounds into signs. In this verification he already knows the word and has repeated it to himself while writing it. What I understand by reading is the *interpretation* of an idea from the written signs. The child who has not heard the word pronounced, and who recognises it when he sees it composed upon the table with the cardboard letters, and who can tell what it means; this child *reads*. The word which he reads has the same relation to written language that the word which he hears bears to articulate language. Both serve to *receive the language* transmitted to us *by others*. So, until the child reads a transmission of ideas from the written word, *he does not read*.

We may say, if we like, that writing as described is a fact in which the psycho-motor mechanism prevails, while in reading, there enters a work which is purely intellectual. But it is evident how our method for writing prepares for reading, making the difficulties almost imperceptible. Indeed, writing prepares the child to interpret mechanically the union of the letter sounds of which the written word is composed. When a child in our school knows how to write, *he knows how to read the sounds* of which the word is composed. It should be noticed, however, that when the child composes the words with the movable alphabet, or when he writes, he has *time to think* about the signs which he must select to form the word. The writing of a word requires a great deal more time than that necessary for reading the same word.

The child who *knows how to write,* when placed before a word which he must interpret by reading, is silent for a long time, and generally reads the component sounds with the same slowness with which he would have written them. But *the sense of the word* becomes evident only when it is pronounced clearly and with the phonetic accent. Now, in order to place the phonetic accent the child must recognise the word; that is, he must recognise the idea which the word represents. The intervention of a superior work of the intellect is necessary if he is to read. Because of all this, I proceed in the following way with the exercises in reading, and, as will be evident, I do away entirely with the old-time primer.

I prepare a number of little cards made from ordinary writing-paper. On each of these I write in large clear script some well-known word, one which has already been pronounced many times by the children, and which represents an object actually present or well known to them. If the word refers to an object which is before them, I place this object under the eyes of the child, in order to facilitate his interpretation of the word. I will say, in this connection, the objects used in these writing games are for the most part toys of which we have a great many in the "Children's Houses." Among these toys, are the furnishings of a doll's house, balls, dolls, trees, flocks of sheep, or various animals, tin soldiers, railways, and an infinite variety of simple figures.

If writing serves to correct, or better, to direct and perfect the mechanism of the articulate language of the child, reading serves to help the development of ideas, and relates them to the development of the language. Indeed, writing aids the physiological language and reading aids the social language.

We begin, then, as I have indicated, with the nomenclature, that is, with the reading of names of objects which are well known or present.

There is no question of beginning with words that are *easy or difficult*, for the *child already knows how to read any word*; that is, he knows how to read *the sounds which compose it*. I allow the little one to translate the written word slowly into sounds, and if the interpretation is exact, I limit myself to saying, "Faster." The child reads more quickly the second time, but still often without understanding. I then repeat, "Faster, faster." He reads faster each time, repeating the same accumulation of sounds, and finally the word bursts upon his consciousness. Then he looks upon it as if he recognised a friend, and assumes that air of satisfaction which so often radiates our little ones. This completes the exercise for reading. It is a lesson which goes very rapidly, since it is only presented to a child who is already prepared through writing. Truly, we have buried the tedious and stupid A B C primer side by side with the useless copy-books!

When the child has read the word, he places the explanatory card under the object whose name it bears, and the exercise is finished.

One of our most interesting discoveries was made in the effort to devise a game through which the children might, without effort, learn to read words. We spread out upon one of the large tables a great variety of toys. Each one of them had a corresponding card upon which the name of the toy was written. We folded these little cards and mixed them up in a basket, and the children who knew how to read were allowed to take turns in drawing these cards from the basket. Each child had to carry his card back to his desk, unfold it quietly, and read it mentally, not showing it to those about him. He then had to fold it up again, so that the secret which it contained should remain unknown. Taking the folded card in his hand, he went to the table. He had then to pronounce clearly the name of a toy and present the card to the directress in order that she might verify the word he had spoken. The little card thus became current coin with which he might acquire the toy he had named. For, if he pronounced the word clearly and indicated the correct object, the directress allowed him to take the toy, and to play with it as long as he wished.

When each child had had a turn, the directress called the first child and let him draw a card from another basket. This card he read as soon as he had drawn it. It contained the name of one of his companions who did not yet know how to read, and for that reason could not have a toy. The child who had read the name then offered to his little friend the toy with which he had been playing. We taught the children to present these toys in a gracious and polite way, accompanying the act with a bow. In this way we did away with every idea of class distinction, and inspired the sentiment of kindness toward those who did not possess the same blessings as ourselves.This reading game proceeded in a marvellous way. The contentment of these poor children in possessing even for a little while such beautiful toys can be easily imagined.

But what was my amazement, when the children, having learned to understand the written cards, *refused* to take the toys! They explained that they did not wish to waste time in playing, and, with a species of insatiable desire, preferred to draw out and read the cards one after another!

I watched them, seeking to understand the secret of these souls, of whose greatness I had been so ignorant! As I stood in meditation among the eager children, the discovery that it was knowledge they loved, and not the silly *game*, filled me with wonder and made me think of the greatness of the human soul!

We therefore put away the toys, and set about making *hundreds* of written slips, containing names of children, cities, and objects; and also of colours and qualities known through the sense exercises. We placed these slips in open boxes, which we left where the children could make free use of them. I expected that childish inconstancy would at least show itself in a tendency to pass from one box to another; but no, each child finished emptying the box under his hand before passing to another, being verily *insatiable* in the desire to read.

Coming into the school one day, I found that the directress had allowed the children to take the tables and chairs out upon the terrace, and was having school in the open air. A number of little ones were playing in the sun, while others were seated in a circle about the tables containing the sandpaper letters and the movable alphabet.

A little apart sat the directress, holding upon her lap a long narrow box full of written slips, and all along the edge of her box were little hands, fishing for the beloved cards. "You may not believe me," said the directress, "but it is more than an hour since we began this, and they are not satisfied yet!" We tried the experiment of bringing balls, and dolls to the children, but without result; such futilities had no power beside the joys of *knowledge*.

Seeing these surprising results, I had already thought of testing the children with print, and had suggested that the directress *print* the word under the written word upon a number of slips. But the children forestalled us! There was in the hall a calendar upon which many of the words were printed in clear type, while others were done in Gothic characters. In their mania for reading the children began to look at this calendar, and, to my inexpressible amazement, read not only the print, but the Gothic script.

There therefore remained nothing but the presentation of a book, and I did not feel that any of those available were suited to our method.

The mothers soon had proofs of the progress of their children; finding in the pockets of some of them little slips of paper upon which were written rough notes of marketing done; bread, salt, etc. Our children were making lists of the marketing they did for their mothers! Other mothers told us that their children no longer ran through the streets, but stopped to read the signs over the shops.

A four-year-old boy, educated in a private house by the same method, surprised us in the following way. The child's father was a Deputy, and received many letters. He knew that his son had for two months been taught by means of exercises apt to facilitate the learning of reading and writing, but he had paid slight attention to it, and, indeed, put little faith in the method. One day, as he sat reading, with the boy playing near, a servant entered, and placed upon the table a large number of letters that had just arrived. The little boy turned his attention to these, and holding up each letter read aloud the address. To his father this seemed a veritable miracle.

As to the average time required for learning to read and write, experience would seem to show that, starting from the moment in which the child writes, the passage from such an inferior stage of the graphic language to the superior state of reading averages a fortnight. *Security* in reading is, however, arrived at much more slowly than perfection in writing. In the greater majority of cases the child who writes beautifully, still reads rather poorly.

Not all children of the same age are at the same point in this matter of reading and writing. We not only do not force a child, but we do not even *invite* him, or in any way attempt to coax him to do that which he does not wish to do. So it sometimes happens that certain children, *not having spontaneously presented themselves* for these lessons, are left in peace, and do not know how to read or write.

If the old-time method, which tyrannized over the will of the child and destroyed his spontaneity, does not believe in making a knowledge of written language *obligatory* before the age of six, much less do we!

I am not ready to decide, without a wider experience, whether the period when the spoken language is fully developed is, in every case, the proper time for beginning to develop the written language.

In any case, almost all of the normal children treated with our method begin to write at four years, and at five know how to read and write, at least as well as children who have finished the first elementary. They could enter the second elementary a year in advance of the time when they are admitted to first.

Games for the Reading of Phrases. As soon as my friends saw that the children could read print, they made me gifts of beautifully illustrated books. Looking through these books of simple fairy lore, I felt sure that the children would not be able to understand them. The teachers, feeling entirely satisfied as to the ability of their pupils, tried to show me I was wrong, having different children read to me, and saying that they read much more perfectly than the children who had finished the second elementary.

I did not, however, allow myself to be deceived, and made two trials. I first had the teacher tell one of the stories to the children while I observed to what extent they were spontaneously interested in it. The attention of the children wandered after a few words. I had *forbidden* the teacher to recall to order those who did not listen, and thus, little by little, a hum arose in the schoolroom, due to the fact that each child, not caring to listen had returned to his usual *occupation*.

It was evident that the children, who seemed to read these books with such pleasure, *did not take pleasure in the sense*, but enjoyed the mechanical ability they had acquired, which consisted in translating the graphic signs into the sounds of a word they recognised. And, indeed, the children did not display the same *constancy* in the reading of books which they showed toward the written slips, since in the books they met with so many unfamiliar words.

My second test, was to have one of the children read the book to me. I did not interrupt with any of those explanatory remarks by means of which a teacher tries to help the child follow the thread of the story he is reading, saying for example: "Stop a minute. Do you understand? What have you read? You told me how the little boy went to drive in a big carriage, didn't you? Pay attention to what the book says, etc."

I gave the book to a little boy, sat down beside him in a friendly fashion, and when he had read I asked him simply and seriously as one would speak to a friend, "Did you understand what you were reading?" He replied: "No." But the expression of his face seemed to ask an explanation of my demand. In fact, the idea that *through the reading of a series of words the complex thoughts of others might be communicated to us*, was to be for my children one of the beautiful conquests of the future, a new source of surprise and joy.

The *book* has recourse to *logical language*, not to the mechanism of the language. Before the child can understand and enjoy a book, the *logical language* must be established in him. Between knowing how to read the *words*, and how to read the *sense*, of a book there lies the same distance that exists between knowing how to pronounce a word and how to make a speech. I, therefore, stopped the reading from books and waited.

One day, during a free conversation period, *four* children arose at the same time and with expressions of joy on their faces ran to the blackboard and wrote phrases upon the order of the following:

"Oh, how glad we are that our garden has begun to bloom." It was a great surprise for me, and I was deeply moved. These children had arrived spontaneously at the art of *composition*, just as they had spontaneously written their first word.

The mechanical preparation was the same, and the phenomenon developed logically. Logical articulate language had, when the time was ripe, provoked the corresponding explosion in written language.

I understood that the time had come when we might proceed to *the reading of phrases*. I had recourse to the means used by the children; that is, I wrote upon the blackboard, "Do you love me?" The children read it slowly aloud, were silent for a moment as if thinking, then cried out, "Yes! Yes!" I continued to write; "Then make the silence, and watch me." They read this aloud, almost shouting, but had barely finished when a solemn silence began to establish itself, interrupted only by the sounds of the chairs as the children took positions in which they could sit quietly. Thus began between me and them a communication by means of written language, a thing which interested the children intensely. Little by little, they *discovered* the great quality of writing—that it transmits thought. Whenever I began to write, they fairly *trembled* in their eagerness to understand what was my meaning without hearing me speak a word.

Indeed, *graphic* language does not need spoken words. It can only be understood in all its greatness when it is completely isolated from spoken language.

This introduction to reading was followed by the following game, which is greatly enjoyed by the children. Upon a number of cards I wrote long sentences describing certain actions which the children were to carry out; for example, "Close the window blinds; open the front door; then wait a moment, and arrange things as they were at first." "Very politely ask eight of your companions to leave their chairs, and to form in double file in the centre of the room, then have them march forward and back on tiptoe, making no noise." "Ask three of your oldest companions who sing nicely, if they will please come into the centre of the room. Arrange them in a nice row, and sing with them a song that you have selected," etc., etc. As soon as I finished writing, the children seized the cards, and taking them to their seats read them spontaneously with great intensity of attention, and all *amid the most complete silence.*

I asked then, "Do you understand?" "Yes! Yes!" "Then do what the card tells you," said I, and was delighted to see the children rapidly and accurately follow the chosen action. A great activity, a movement of a new sort, was born in the room. There were those who closed the blinds, and then reopened them; others who made their companions run on tiptoe, or sing; others wrote upon the blackboard, or took certain objects from the cupboards. Surprise and curiosity produced a general silence, and the lesson developed amid the most intense interest. It seemed as if some magic force had gone forth from me stimulating an activity hitherto unknown. This magic was graphic language, the greatest conquest of civilisation.

And how deeply the children understood the importance of it! When I went out, they gathered about me with expressions of gratitude and affection, saying, "Thank you! Thank you! Thank you for the lesson!"

This has become one of the favourite games: We first establish *profound silence*, then present a basket containing folded slips, upon each one of which is written a long phrase describing an action. All those children who know how to read may draw a slip, and read it *mentally* once or twice until they are certain they understand it. They then give the slip back to the directress and set about carrying out the action. Since many of these actions call for the help of the other children who do not know how to read, and since many of them call for the handling and use of the materials, a general activity develops amid marvellous order, while the silence is only interrupted by the sound of little feet running lightly, and by the voices of the children who sing. This is an unexpected revelation of the perfection of spontaneous discipline.

Experience has shown us that *composition* must *precede logical* reading, as writing preceded the reading of the word. It has also shown that reading, if it is to teach the child to *receive an idea,* should be *mental* and not *vocal.*

Reading aloud implies the exercise of two mechanical forms of the language—articulate and graphic—and is, therefore, a complex task. Who does not know that a grown person who is to read a paper in public prepares for this by making himself master of the content? Reading aloud is one of the most difficult intellectual actions. The child, therefore, who *begins* to read by interpreting thought *should read mentally.* The written language must isolate itself from the articulate, when it rises to the interpretation of logical thought. Indeed, it represents the language which *transmits thought at a distance,* while the senses and the muscular mechanism are silent. It is a spiritualised language, which puts into communication all men who know how to read.

Education having reached such a point in the "Children's Houses," the entire elementary school must, as a logical consequence, be changed. How to reform the lower grades in the elementary schools, eventually carrying them on according to our methods, is a great question which cannot be discussed here. I can only say that the *first elementary* would be completely done away with by our infant education, which includes it.

The elementary classes in the future should begin with children such as ours who know how to read and write; children who know how to take care of themselves; how to dress and undress, and to wash themselves; children who are familiar with the rules of good conduct and courtesy, and who are thoroughly disciplined in the highest sense of the term, having developed, and become masters of themselves, through liberty; children who possess, besides a perfect mastery of the articulate language, the ability to read written language in an elementary way, and who begin to enter upon the conquest of logical language.

These children pronounce clearly, write in a firm hand, and are full of grace in their movements. They are the earnest of a humanity grown in the cult of beauty—the infancy of an all-conquering humanity, since they are intelligent and patient observers of their environment, and possess in the form of intellectual liberty the power of spontaneous reasoning.

For such children, we should found an elementary school worthy to receive them and to guide them further along the path of life and of civilisation, a school loyal to the same educational principles of respect for the freedom of the child and for his spontaneous manifestations—principles which shall form the personality of these little men.

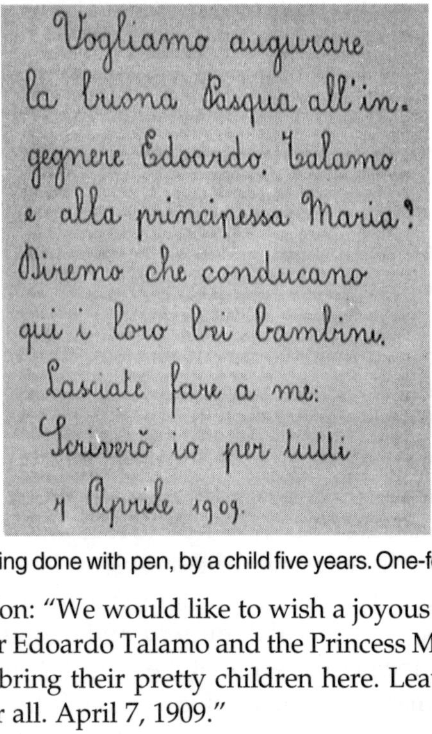
Vogliamo augurare
la buona Pasqua all'in.
gegnere Edoardo Talamo
e alla principessa Maria?
Diremo che conducano
qui i loro bei bambini.
Lasciate fare a me:
Scriverò io per tutti
7 Aprile 1909.

Example of writing done with pen, by a child five years. One-fourth reduction.

Translation: "We would like to wish a joyous Easter to the civil engineer Edoardo Talamo and the Princess Maria. We will ask them to bring their pretty children here. Leave it to me: I will write for all. April 7, 1909."

18

Language in Childhood

Graphic language, comprising dictation and reading, contains articulate language in its complete mechanism (auditory channels, central channels, motor channels), and, in the manner of development called forth by my method, is based essentially on articulate language.

Graphic language, therefore, may be considered from two points of view:

(*a*) That of the conquest of a new language of eminent social importance which adds itself to the articulate language of natural man; and this is the cultural significance which is commonly given to graphic language, which is therefore taught in the schools without any consideration of its relation to spoken language, but solely with the intention of offering to the social being a necessary instrument in his relations with his fellows.

(*b*) That of the relation between graphic and articulate language and, in this relation, of an eventual possibility of utilising the written language to perfect the spoken: a new consideration upon which I wish to insist and which gives to graphic language a *physiological importance.*

Moreover, as spoken language is at the same time a *natural function* of man and an instrument which he utilises for social ends, so written language may be considered in itself, in its *formation*, as an organic *ensemble* of new mechanisms which are established in the nervous system, and as an instrument which may be utilised for social ends.

In short, it is a question of giving to written language not only a physiological importance, but also a *period of development* independent of the high functions which it is destined to perform later.

It seems to me that graphic language bristles with difficulties in its beginning, not only because it has heretofore been taught by irrational methods, but because we have tried to make it perform, as soon as it has been acquired, the high function of teaching *the written language* which has been fixed by centuries of perfecting in a civilised people.

Think how irrational have been the methods we have used! We have analysed the graphic signs rather than the physiological acts necessary to produce the alphabetical signs; and this without considering that *any graphic sign* is difficult to achieve, because the visual representation of the signs have no hereditary connection with the motor representations necessary for producing them; as, for example, the auditory representations of the word have with the motor mechanism of the articulate language. It is, therefore, always a difficult thing to provoke a stimulative motor action unless we have already established the movement before the visual representation of the sign is made. It is a difficult thing to arouse an activity that shall produce a motion unless that motion shall have been previously established by practice and by the power of habit.

Thus, for example, the analysis of writing into *little straight lines and curves* has brought us to present to the child a sign without significance, which therefore does not interest him, and whose representation is incapable of determining a spontaneous motor impulse. The artificial act constituted, therefore, an *effort* of the will which resulted for the child in rapid exhaustion exhibited in the form of boredom and suffering. To this effort was added the effort of constituting *synchronously* the muscular associations co-ordinating the movements necessary to the holding and manipulating the instrument of writing.

All sorts of *depressing* feelings accompanied such efforts and conduced to the production of imperfect and erroneous signs which the teachers had to correct, discouraging the child still more with the constant criticism of the error and of the imperfection of the signs traced. Thus, while the child was urged to make an effort, the teacher depressed rather than revived his psychical forces.

Although such a mistaken course was followed, the graphic language, so painfully learned, was nevertheless to be *immediately* utilised for social ends; and, still imperfect and immature, was made to do service in the *syntactical construction of the language*, and in the ideal expression of the superior psychic centres. One must remember that in nature the spoken language is formed gradually; and it is already established in *words* when the superior psychic centres use these words in what Kussmaul calls *dictorium*, in the syntactical grammatical formation of language which is necessary to the expression of complex ideas; that is, in the language of the *logical mind*.

In short the mechanism of language is a necessary antecedent of the higher psychic activities which are to *utilise it*.

There are, therefore, two periods in the development of language: a lower one which prepares the nervous channel and the central mechanisms which are to put the sensory channels in relation with the motor channels; and a higher one determined by the higher psychic activities which are *exteriorized* by means of the preformed mechanisms of language.

Thus for example in the scheme which Kussmaul gives on the mechanism of articulate language we must first of all distinguish a sort of cerebral diastaltic arc (representing the pure mechanism of the word), which is established in the first formation of the spoken language. Let E be the ear, and T the motor organs of speech, taken as a whole and here represented by the tongue, A the auditory centre of speech, and M the motor centre.

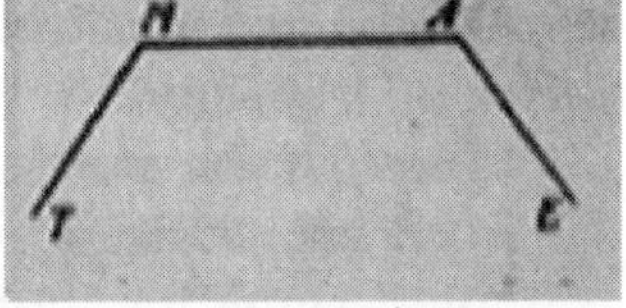

The channels EA and MT are peripheral channels, the former centripetal and the latter centrifugal, and the channel AM is the inter-central channel of association.

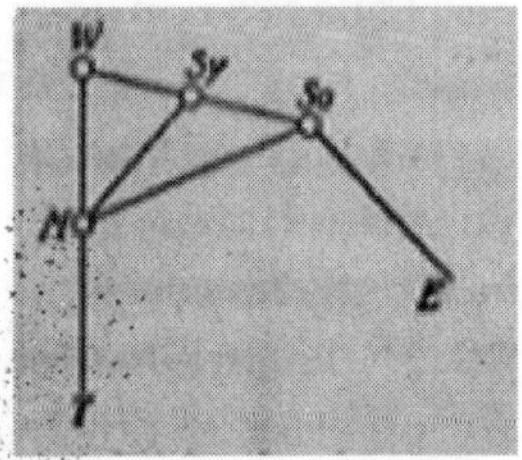

The centre A in which reside the auditive images of words may be again subdivided into three, as in the following scheme, viz.: Sound (So), syllables (Sy), and words (W).

That partial centres for sounds and syllables can really be formed, the pathology of language seems to establish, for in some forms of centro-sensory dysphasia, the patients can pronounce only sounds, or at most sounds and syllables.

Small children, too, are, at the beginning, particularly sensitive to simple sounds of language, with which indeed, and especially with *s*, their mothers caress them and attract their attention; while later the child is sensitive to syllables, with which also the mother caresses him, saying: *"ba, ba, punf, tuf!"*

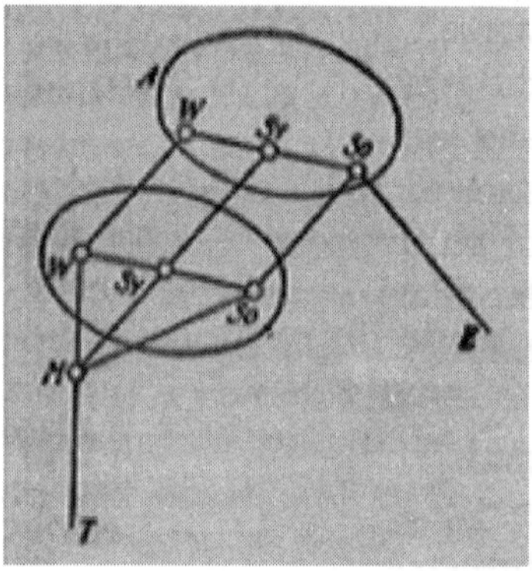

Finally it is the simple word, dissyllabic in most cases, which attracts the child's attention.

But for the motor centres also the same thing may be repeated; the child utters at the beginning simple or double sounds, as for example *bl, gl, ch,* an expression which the mother greets with joy; then distinctly syllabic sounds begin to manifest themselves in the child: *ga, ba*; and, finally, the dissyllabic word, usually labial: *mama.*

We say that the spoken language begins with the child when the word pronounced by him signifies an *idea;* when for example, seeing his mother and recognising her he says "*mamma;*" and seeing a dog says, "*tettè;*" and wishing to eat says: "*pappa.*"

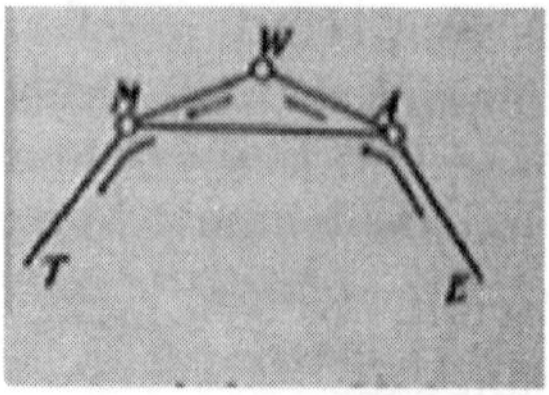

Thus we consider *language begun* when it is established in relation to perception; while the language itself is still, in its psycho-motor mechanism, perfectly rudimentary.

That is, when above the diastaltic arc where the mechanical formation of the language is still unconscious, the recognition of the word takes place, that is, the word is perceived and associated with the object which it represents, language is considered to have begun.

On this level, *later*, language continues the process of perfecting in proportion as the hearing perceives better the component sounds of the words and the psycho-motor channels become more permeable to articulation.

This is the first stage of spoken language, which has its own beginning and its own development, leading, through the perceptions, to the *perfecting* of the primordial mechanism of the language itself; and at this stage precisely is established what we call *articulate language*, which will later be the means which the adult will have at his disposal to express his own thoughts, and which the adult will have great difficulty in perfecting or correcting when it has once been established: in fact a high stage of culture sometimes accompanies an imperfect articulate language which prevents the æsthetic expression of one's thought.

The development of articulate language takes place in the period between the age of two and the age of seven: the age of *perceptions* in which the attention of the child is spontaneously turned towards external objects, and the memory is particularly tenacious. It is the age also of *motility* in which all the psycho-motor channels are becoming permeable and the muscular mechanisms establish themselves. In this period of life by the mysterious bond between the auditory channel and the motor channel of the spoken language it would seem that the auditory perceptions have the direct power of *provoking* the complicated movements of articulate speech which develop instinctively after such stimuli as if awaking from the slumber of heredity. It is well known that it is only at this age that it is possible to acquire all the characteristic modulations of a language which it would be vain to attempt to establish later. The mother tongue alone is well pronounced because it was established in the period of childhood; and the adult who learns to speak a new language must bring to it the imperfections characteristic of the foreigner's speech: only children who under the age of seven years learn several languages at the same time can receive and reproduce all the characteristic mannerisms of accent and pronunciation.

Thus also the *defects* acquired in childhood such as dialectic defects or those established by bad habits, become indelible in the adult.

What develops later, the *superior* language, the *dictorium,* no longer has its origin in the mechanism of language but in the intellectual development which makes use of the mechanical language. As the articulate language develops by the exercise of its mechanism and is enriched by perception, the *dictorium* develops with syntax and is enriched by *intellectual culture.* Going back to the scheme of language we see that above the arc which defines the lower language, is established the *dictorium, D,*—from which now come the motor impulses of speech—which is established as *spoken language* fit to manifest the ideation of the intelligent man; this language will be enriched little by little by intellectual culture and perfected by the grammatical study of syntax.

Hitherto, as a result of a preconception, it has been believed that written language should enter only into the development of the *dictorium,* as the suitable means for the acquisition of culture and of permitting grammatical analysis and construction of the language. Since "spoken words have wings" it has been admitted that intellectual culture could only proceed by the aid of a language which was stable, objective, and capable of being analysed, such as the graphic language.

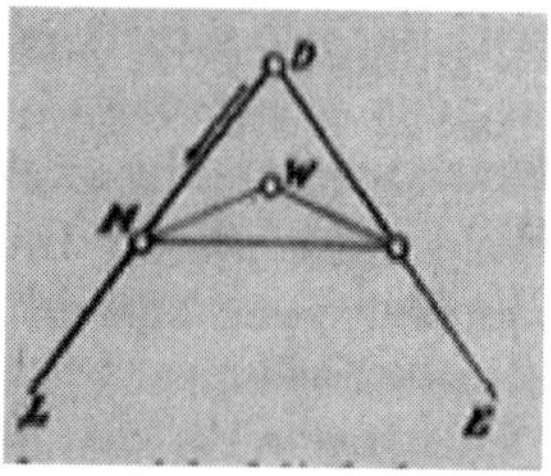

But why, when we acknowledge the graphic language as a precious, nay indispensable, instrument of intellectual education, for the reason that it *fixes the ideas* of men and permits of their analysis and of their assimilation in books, where they remain indelibly written as an ineffaceable memory of words which are therefore always present and by which we can analyse the syntactical structure of the language, why shall we not acknowledge that it is *useful* in the more humble task of *fixing* the *words* which represent perception and of analysing their component sounds?

Compelled by a pedagogical prejudice we are unable to separate the idea of a graphic language from that of a function which heretofore we have made it exclusively perform; and it seems to us that by teaching such a language to children still in the age of simple perceptions and of motility we are committing a serious psychological and pedagogical error.

But let us rid ourselves of this prejudice and consider the graphic language in itself, reconstructing its psycho-physiological mechanism. It is far more simple than the psycho-physiological mechanism of the articulate language, and is far more directly accessible to education.

Writing especially is surprisingly simple. For let us consider *dictated* writing: we have a perfect parallel with spoken language since a *motor* action must correspond with *heard* speech. Here there does not exist, to be sure, the mysterious hereditary relations between the heard speech and the articulate speech; but the movements of writing are far simpler than those necessary to the spoken word, and are performed by large muscles, all external, *upon which we can directly act*, rendering the motor channels permeable, and establishing psycho-muscular mechanisms.

This indeed is what is done by my method, which *prepares the movements directly*; so that the psycho-motor impulse of the heard speech *finds the motor channels already established*, and is manifested in the act of writing, like an explosion.

The real difficulty is in the *interpretation of the graphic signs*; but we must remember that we are in the *age of perceptions*, where the sensations and the memory as well as the primitive associations are involved precisely in the characteristic progress of natural development. Moreover our children are already prepared by various exercises of the senses, and by methodical construction of ideas and mental associations to perceive the graphic signs; something like a patrimony of perceptive ideas offers material to the language in the process of development.

The child who recognises a triangle and calls it a triangle can recognise a letter *s* and denominate it by the sound *s*. This is obvious.

Let us not talk of premature teaching; ridding ourselves of prejudices, let us appeal to experience which shows that in reality children proceed without effort, nay rather with evident manifestations of pleasure to the recognition of graphic signs presented as objects.

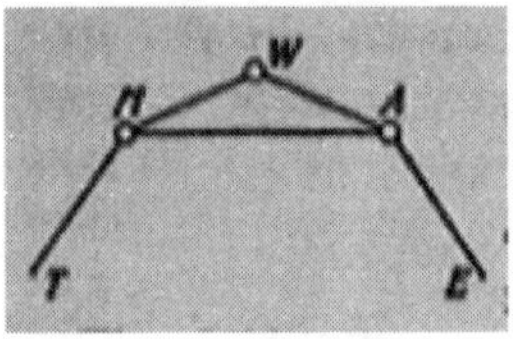

And with this premise let us consider the relations between the mechanisms of the two languages.

The child of three or four has already long begun his articulate language according to our scheme. But he finds himself in the period in which the *mechanism of articulate language is being perfected*; a period contemporary with that in which he is acquiring a content of language along with the patrimony of perception.

The child has perhaps not heard perfectly in all their component parts the words which he pronounces, and, if he has heard them perfectly, they may have been pronounced badly, and consequently have left an erroneous auditory perception. It would be well that the child, by exercising the motor channels of articulate language should establish exactly the movements necessary to a perfect articulation, *before* the age of easy motor adaptations is passed, and, by the fixation of erroneous mechanisms, the defects become incorrigible.

To this end the *analysis of speech* is necessary. As when we wish to perfect the language we first start children at composition and then pass to grammatical study; and when we wish to perfect the style we first teach to write grammatically and then come to the analysis of style—so when we wish to perfect the *speech* it is first necessary that the speech *exist*, and then it is proper to proceed to its analysis. When, therefore, the child *speaks*, but before the completion of the development of speech which renders it fixed in mechanisms already established, the speech should be analysed with a view to perfecting it.

Now, as grammar and rhetoric are not possible with the spoken language but demand recourse to the written language which keeps ever before the eye the discourse to be analysed, so it is with speech.

The analysis of the transient is impossible.

The language must be materialised and made stable. Hence the necessity of the written word or the word represented by graphic signs.

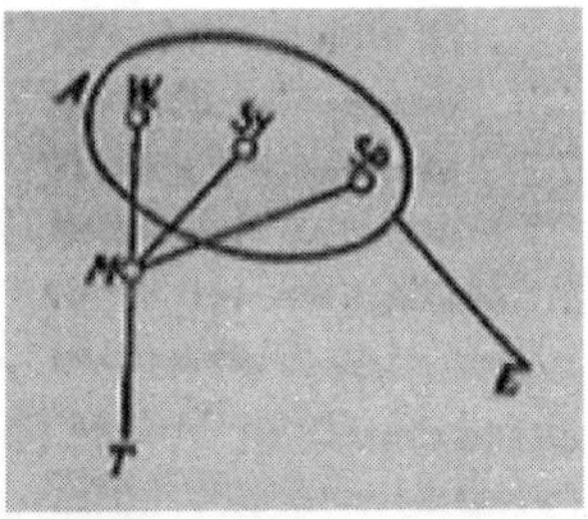

In the third stage of my method for writing, that is, composition of speech, is included the *analysis of the word* not only into signs, but into the component sounds; the signs representing its translation. The child, that is, *divides* the heard word which he perceives integrally as a *word*, knowing also its meanings, into sounds and syllables.

Let me call attention to the following diagram which represents the interrelation of the two mechanisms for writing and for articulate speech.

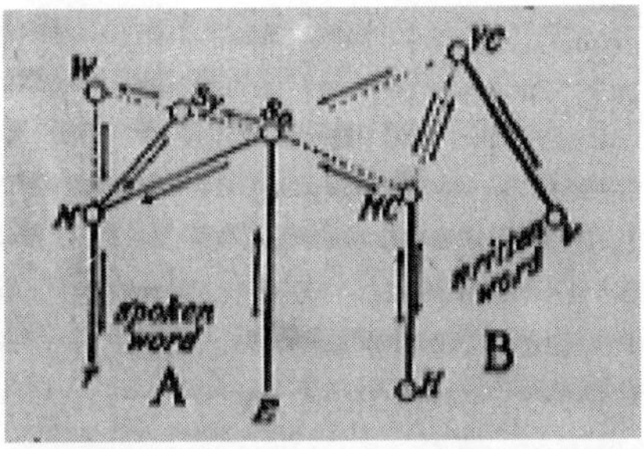

The peripheric channels are indicated by heavy lines; the central channels of association by dotted lines; and those referring to association in relation to the development of the heard speech by light lines.

E ear; *So* auditory centre of sounds; *Sy* auditory centre of syllables; *W* auditory centre of word; *M* motor centre of the articulate speech; *T* external organs of articulate speech (tongue); *H* external organs of writing (hand); *MC* motor centre of writing;

VC visual centre of graphic signs; *V* organ of vision.

Whereas in the development of spoken language the sound composing the word might be imperfectly perceived, here in the teaching of the graphic sign corresponding to the sound (which teaching consists in presenting to the child a sandpaper letter, naming it *distinctly* and making the child *see* it and *touch* it), not only is the perception of the heard sound *clearly* fixed—separately and clearly—but this perception is associated with two others: the centro-motor perception and the centro-visual perception of the written sign.

The triangle *VC, MC, So* represents the association of three sensations in relation with the analysis of speech.

When the letter is presented to the child and he is made to touch and see it, while it is being named, the centripetal channels *ESo; H, MC, So; V, VC, So* are acting and when the child is made to name the letter, alone or accompanied by a vowel, the external stimulus acts in *V* and passes through the channels *V, VC, So, M, T*; and *V, CV, So, Sy, M, T*.

When these channels of association have been established by presenting visual stimuli in the graphic sign, the corresponding movements of articulate language can be provoked and studied one by one in their defects; while, by maintaining the visual stimulus of the graphic sign which provokes articulation and accompanying it by the auditory stimulus of the corresponding *sound* uttered by the teacher, their articulation can be perfected; this articulation is by innate conditions connected with the heard speech; that is, in the course of the pronunciation provoked by the visual stimulus, and during the repetition of the relative movements of the organs of language, the auditory stimulus which is introduced into the exercise contributes to the perfecting of the pronunciation of the isolated or syllabic sounds composing the spoken word.

When later the child writes under dictation, translating into signs the sounds of speech, he analyses the heard speech into its sounds, translating them into graphic movements through channels already rendered permeable by the corresponding muscular sensations.

DEFECTS OF LANGUAGE DUE TO LACK OF EDUCATION

Defects and imperfections of language are in part due to organic causes, consisting in malformations or in pathological alterations of the nervous system; but in part they are connected with functional defects acquired in the period of the formation of language and consist in an erratic pronunciation of the component sounds of the spoken word. Such errors are acquired by the child who hears words imperfectly pronounced, or *hears bad speech*, The dialectic accent enters into this category; but there also enter vicious habits which make the natural defects of the articulate language of childhood persist in the child, or which provoke in him by imitation the defects of language peculiar to the persons who surrounded him in his childhood.

The normal defects of child language are due to the fact that the complicated muscular agencies of the organs of articulate language do not yet function well and are consequently incapable of reproducing the *sound* which was the sensory stimulus of a certain innate movement. The association of the movements necessary to the articulation of the spoken words is established little by little. The result is a language made of words with sounds which are imperfect and often lacking (whence incomplete words). Such defects are grouped under the name *blæsitas* and are especially due to the fact that the child is not yet capable of directing the movements of his tongue. They comprise chiefly: *sigmatism* or imperfect pronunciation of *s*; *rhotacism* or imperfect pronunciation of *r*; *lambdacism* or imperfect pronunciation of *l*; *gammacism* or imperfect pronunciation, of *g*; *iotacism*, defective pronunciation of the gutturals; *mogilalia*, imperfect pronunciation of the labials, and according to some authors, as Preyer, mogilalia is made to include also the suppression of the first sound of a word.

Some defects of pronunciation which concern the utterance of the vowel sound as well as that of the consonant are due to the fact that the child *reproduces perfectly* sounds imperfectly heard.

In the first case, then, it is a matter of functional insufficiencies of the peripheral motor organ and hence of the nervous channels, and the cause lies in the individual; whereas in the second case the error is caused by the auditory stimulus and the cause lies outside.

These defects often persist, however attenuated, in the boy and the adult: and produce finally an erroneous language to which will later be added in writing orthographical errors, such for example as dialectic orthographical errors.

If one considers the charm of human speech one is bound to acknowledge the inferiority of one who does not possess a correct spoken language; and an æsthetic conception in education cannot be imagined unless special care be devoted to perfecting articulate language. Although the Greeks had transmitted to Rome the art of educating in language, this practice was not resumed by Humanism which cared more for the æsthetics of the environment and the revival of artistic works than for the perfecting of the man.

To-day we are just beginning to introduce the practice of correcting by pedagogical methods the serious defects of language, such as stammering; but the idea of *linguistic gymnastics* tending to its perfection has not yet penetrated into our schools as a *universal method*, and as a detail of the great work of the æsthetic perfecting of man.

Some teachers of deaf mutes and intelligent devotees of orthophony are trying nowadays with small practical success to introduce into the elementary schools the correction of the various forms of *blæsitas*, as a result of statistical studies which have demonstrated the wide diffusion of such defects among the pupils. The exercises consist essentially in *silence* cures which procure calm and repose for the organs of language, and in patient *repetition* of the *separate* vowel and consonant *sounds*; to these exercises is added also respiratory gymnastics. This is not the place to describe in detail the methods of these exercises which are long and patient and quite out of harmony with the teachings of the school. But in my methods are to be found all exercises for the corrections of language:

(*a*) *Exercises of Silence*, which prepare the nervous channels of language to receive new stimuli perfectly;

(*b*) *Lessons* which consist first of the distinct pronunciation by the teacher of *few words* (especially of *nouns* which must be associated with a concrete idea); by this means clear and perfect *auditory stimuli* of language are started, stimuli which are *repeated* by the teacher when the child has conceived the idea of the object represented by the word (recognition of the object); finally of the provocation of articulate language on the part of the child who must repeat *that word alone* aloud, pronouncing its separate sounds;

(*c*) *Exercises in Graphic Language*, which analyse the sounds of speech and cause them to be repeated separately in several ways: that is, when the child learns the separate letters of the alphabet and when he composes or writes words, repeating their sounds which he translates separately into composed or written speech;

(*d*) *Gymnastic Exercises*, which comprise, as we have seen, both *respiratory exercises* and those of *articulation*.

I believe that in the schools of the future the conception will disappear which is beginning to-day of "*correcting in the elementary schools*" the defects of language; and will be replaced by the more rational one of *avoiding them by caring for the development of language* in the "Children's Houses"; that is, in the very age in which language is being established in the child.

19

Teaching of Numeration; Introduction to Arithmetic

Children of three years already know how to count as far as two or three when they enter our schools. They therefore *very easily* learn numeration, which consists *in counting objects*. A dozen different ways may serve toward this end, and daily life presents many opportunities; when the mother says, for instance, "There are two buttons missing from your apron," or "We need three more plates at table."

One of the first means used by me, is that of counting with money. I obtain *new* money, and if it were possible I should have good reproductions made in cardboard. I have seen such money used in a school for deficients in London.

The *making of change* is a form of numeration so attractive as to hold the attention of the child. I present the one, two, and four centime pieces and the children, in this way learn to count to *ten*.

No form of instruction is more *practical* than that tending to make children familiar with the coins in common use, and no exercise is more useful than that of making change. It is so closely related to daily life that it interests all children intensely.

Having taught numeration in this empiric mode, I pass to more methodical exercises, having as didactic material one of the sets of blocks already used in the education of the senses; namely, the series of ten rods heretofore used for the teaching of length. The shortest of these rods corresponds to a decimetre, the longest to a metre, while the intervening rods are divided into sections a decimetre in length. The sections are painted alternately red and blue.

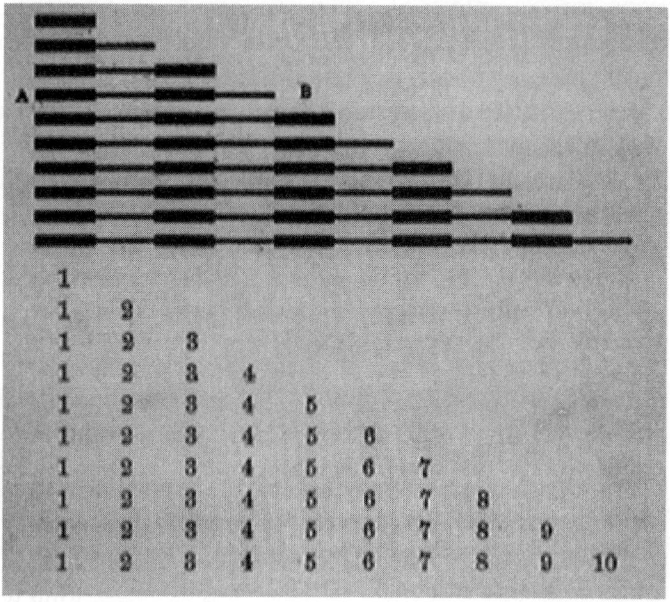

Some day, when a child has arranged the rods, placing them in order of length, we have him count the red and blue signs, beginning with the smallest piece; that is, *one*; one, two; one, two, three, etc., always going back to one in the counting of each rod, and starting from the side A. We then have him name the single rods from the shortest to the longest, according to the total number of the sections which each contains, touching the rods at the sides B, on which side the stair ascends. This results in the same numeration as when we counted the longest rod—1, 2, 3, 4, 5, 6, 7, 8, 9, 10. Wishing to know the number of rods, we count them from the side A and the same numeration results; 1, 2, 3, 4, 5, 6, 7, 8, 9, 10. This correspondence of the three sides of the triangle causes the child to verify his knowledge and as the exercise interests him he repeats it many times.

We now unite to the exercises in *numeration* the earlier, sensory exercises in which the child recognised the long and short rods. Having mixed the rods upon a carpet, the directress selects one, and showing it to the child, has him count the sections; for example, 5. She then asks him to give her the one next in length. He selects it *by his eye*, and the directress has him *verify* his choice by *placing the two pieces side by side and by counting their sections*. Such exercises may be repeated in great variety and through them the child learns to assign a *particular name to each one of the pieces in the long stair*. We may now call them piece number one; piece number two, etc., and finally, for brevity, may speak of them in the lessons as one, two, three, etc.

THE NUMBERS AS REPRESENTED BY THE GRAPHIC SIGNS

At this point, if the child already knows how to write, we may present the figures cut in sandpaper and mounted upon cards. In presenting these, the method is the same used in teaching the letters. "This is one." "This is two." "Give me one." "Give me two." "What *number* is this?" The child traces the number with his finger as he did the letters.

Exercises with Numbers. Association of the graphic sign with the quantity.

I have designed two trays each divided into five little compartments. At the back of each compartment may be placed a card bearing a figure. The figures in the first tray should be 0, 1, 2, 3, 4, and in the second, 5, 6, 7, 8, 9.

The exercise is obvious; it consists in placing within the compartments a number of objects corresponding to the figure indicated upon the card at the back of the compartment. We give the children various objects in order to vary the lesson, but chiefly make use of large wooden pegs so shaped that they will not roll off the desk. We place a number of these before the child whose part is to arrange them in their places, one peg corresponding to the card marked one, etc. When he has finished he takes his tray to the directress that she may verify his work.

The Lesson on Zero. We wait until the child, pointing to the compartment containing the card marked zero, asks, "And what must I put in here?" We then reply, "Nothing; zero is nothing." But often this is not enough. It is necessary to make the child *feel* what we mean by *nothing*. To this end we make use of little games which vastly entertain the children. I stand among them, and turning to one of them who has already used this material, I say, "Come, dear, come to me *zero* times." The child almost always comes to me, and then runs back to his place. "But, my boy, you came *one* time, and I told you to come *zero* times." Then he begins to wonder. "But what must I do, then?" "Nothing; zero is nothing." "But how shall I do nothing?" "Don't do anything. You must sit still. You must not come at all, not any times. Zero times. No times at all." I repeat these exercises until the children understand, and they are then, immensely amused at remaining quiet when I call to them to come to me zero times, or to throw me zero kisses. They themselves often cry out, "Zero is nothing! Zero is nothing!"

EXERCISES FOR THE MEMORY OF NUMBERS

When the children recognise the written figure, and when this figure signifies to them the numerical value, I give them the following exercise:

I cut the figures from old calendars and mount them upon slips of paper which are then folded and dropped into a box. The children draw out the slips, carry them still folded, to their seats, where they look at them and refold them, *conserving the secret*. Then, one by one, or in groups, these children (who are naturally the oldest ones in the class) go to the large table of the directress where groups of various small objects have been placed. Each one selects *the quantity* of objects corresponding to the number he has drawn. The number, meanwhile, has been left *at the child's place*, a slip of paper mysteriously folded. The child, therefore, must *remember* his number not only during the movements which he makes in coming and going, but while he collects his pieces, counting them one by one. The directress may here make interesting individual observations upon the number memory.

When the child has gathered up his objects he arranges them upon his own table, in columns of two, and if the number is uneven, he places the odd piece at the bottom and between the last two objects. The arrangement of the pieces is therefore as follows:—

```
O  O  O  O  O  O  O  O  O  O
X XX XX XX XX XX XX XX XX XX
         X  XX XX XX XX XX XX XX
                  X  XX XX XX XX XX
                           X  XX XX XX
                                    X  XX
```

The crosses represent the objects, while the circle stands for the folded slip containing the figure. Having arranged his objects, the child awaits the verification. The directress comes, opens the slip, reads the number, and counts the pieces.

When we first played this game it often happened that the children took *more objects* than were called for upon the card, and this was not always because they did not remember the number, but arose from a mania for having the greatest number of objects. A little of that instinctive greediness, which is common to primitive and uncultured man. The directress seeks to explain to the children that it is useless to have all those things upon the desk, and that the point of the game lies in taking the exact number of objects called for.

Little by little they enter into this idea, but not so easily as one might suppose. It is a real effort of self-denial which holds the child within the set limit, and makes him take, for example, only two of the objects placed at his disposal, while he sees others taking more. I therefore consider this game more an exercise of will power than of numeration. The child who has the *zero*, should not move from his place when he sees all his companions rising and taking freely of the objects which are inaccessible to him. Many times zero falls to the lot of a child who knows how to count perfectly, and who would experience great pleasure in accumulating and arranging a fine group of objects in the proper order upon his table, and in awaiting with security the teacher's verification.

It is most interesting to study the expressions upon the faces of those who possess zero. The individual differences which result are almost a revelation of the "character" of each one. Some remain impassive, assuming a bold front in order to hide the pain of the disappointment; others show this disappointment by involuntary gestures. Still others cannot hide the smile which is called forth by the singular situation in which they find themselves, and which will make their friends curious. There are little ones who follow every movement of their companions with a look of desire, almost of envy, while others show instant acceptance of the situation. No less interesting are the expressions with which they confess to the holding of the zero, when asked during the verification, "and you, you haven't taken anything?" "I have zero." "It is zero." These are the usual words, but the expressive face, the tone of the voice, show widely varying sentiments. Rare, indeed, are those who seem to give with pleasure the explanation of an extraordinary fact. The greater number either look unhappy or merely resigned.

We therefore give lessons upon the meaning of the game, saying, "It is hard to keep the zero secret. Fold the paper tightly and don't let it slip away. It is the most difficult of all." Indeed, after awhile, the very difficulty of remaining quiet appeals to the children, and when they open the slip marked zero it can be seen that they are content to keep the secret.

ADDITION AND SUBTRACTION FROM ONE TO TWENTY: MULTIPLICATION AND DIVISION

The didactic material which we use for the teaching of the first arithmetical operations is the same already used for numeration; that is, the rods graduated as to length which, arranged on the scale of the metre, contain the first idea of the decimal system.

The rods, as I have said, have come to be called by the numbers which they represent; one, two, three, etc. They are arranged in order of length, which is also in order of numeration.

The first exercise consists in trying to put the shorter pieces together in such a way as to form tens. The most simple way of doing this is to take successively the shortest rods, from one up, and place them at the end of the corresponding long rods from nine down. This may be accompanied by the commands, "Take one and add it to nine; take two and add it to eight; take three and add it to seven; take four and add it to six." In this way we make four rods equal to ten. There remains the five, but, turning this upon its head (in the long sense), it passes from one end of the ten to the other, and thus makes clear the fact that two times five makes ten.

These exercises are repeated and little by little the child is taught the more technical language; nine plus one equals ten, eight plus two equals ten, seven plus three equals ten, six plus four equals ten, and for the five, which remains, two times five equals ten. At last, if he can write, we teach the signs *plus* and *equals* and *times*. Then this is what we see in the neat note-books of our little ones:

$$9 + 1 = 10$$
$$8 + 2 = 10 \qquad 5 \times 2 = 10$$
$$7 + 3 = 10$$
$$6 + 4 = 10$$

When all this is well learned and has been put upon the paper with great pleasure by the children, we call their attention to the work which is done when the pieces grouped together to form tens are taken apart, and put back in their original positions. From the ten last formed we take away four and six remains; from the next we take away three and seven remains; from the next, two and eight remains; from the last, we take away one and nine remains. Speaking of this properly we say, ten less four equals six; ten less three equals seven; ten less two equals eight; ten less one equals nine.

In regard to the remaining five, it is the half of ten, and by cutting the long rod in two, that is dividing ten by two, we would have five; ten divided by two equals five. The written record of all this reads:

$$10 - 4 = 6$$
$$10 - 3 = 7 \qquad 10 \div 2 = 5$$
$$10 - 2 = 8$$
$$10 - 1 = 9$$

Once the children have mastered this exercise they multiply it spontaneously. Can we make three in two ways? We place the one after the two and then write, in order that we may remember what we have done, 2 + 1 = 3. Can we make two rods equal to number four? 3 + 1 = 4, and 4 – 3 = 1; 4 - 1 = 3. Rod number two in its relation to rod number four is treated as was five in relation to ten; that is, we turn it over and show that it is contained in four exactly two times: 4 ÷ 2 = 2; 2 × 2 = 4. Another problem: let us see with how many rods we can play this same game. We can do it with three and six; and with four and eight; that is,

2 × 2 = 4	3 × 2 = 6	4 × 2 = 8	5 × 2 = 10
10 ÷ 2 = 5	8 ÷ 2 = 4	6 ÷ 2 = 3	4 ÷ 2 = 2

At this point we find that the cubes with which we played the number memory games are of help:

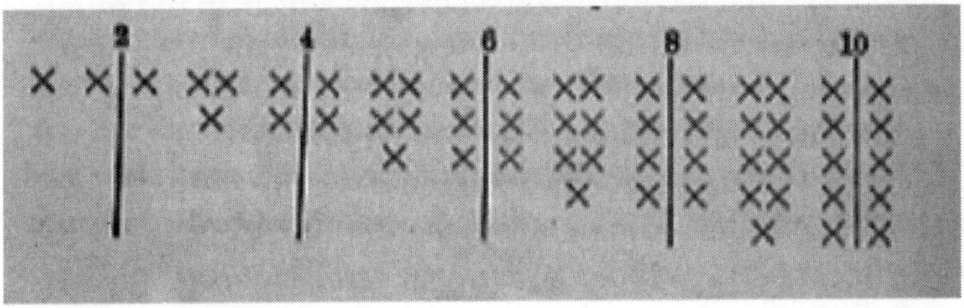

From this arrangement, one sees at once which are the numbers which can be divided by two—all those which have not an odd cube at the bottom. These are the even numbers, because they can be arranged in pairs, two by two; and the division by two is easy, all that is necessary being to separate the two lines of twos that stand one under the other. Counting the cubes of each file we have the quotient. To recompose the primitive number we need only reassemble the two files thus 2 × 3 = 6. All this is not difficult for children of five years.

The repetition soon becomes monotonous, but the exercises may be most easily changed, taking again the set of long rods, and instead of placing rod number one after nine, place it after ten. In the same way, place two after nine, and three after eight. In this way we make rods of a greater length than ten; lengths which we must learn to name eleven, twelve, thirteen, etc., as far as twenty. The little cubes, too, may be used to fix these higher numbers.

Having learned the operations through ten, we proceed with no difficulty to twenty. The one difficulty lies in the *decimal numbers* which require certain lessons.

LESSONS ON DECIMALS: ARITHMETICAL CALCULATIONS BEYOND TEN

The necessary didactic material consists of a number of square cards upon which the figure ten is printed in large type, and of other rectangular cards, half the size of the square, and containing the single numbers from one to nine. We place the numbers in a line; 1, 2, 3, 4, 5, 6, 7, 8, 9, 10. Then, having no more numbers, we must begin over again and take the 1 again. This 1 is like that section in the set of rods which, in rod number 10, extends beyond nine. Counting along *the stair* as far as nine, there remains this one section which, as there are no more numbers, we again designate as 1; but this is a higher 1 than the first, and to distinguish it from the first we put near it a zero, a sign which means nothing. Here then is 10. Covering the zero with the separate rectangular number cards in the order of their succession we see formed: 11, 12, 13, 14, 15, 16, 17, 18, 19. These numbers are composed by adding to rod number 10, first rod number 1, then 2, then 3, etc., until we finally add rod number 9 to rod number 10, thus obtaining a very long rod, which, when its alternating red and blue sections are counted, gives us nineteen.

The directress may then show to the child the cards, giving the number 16, and he may place rod 6 after rod 10. She then takes away the card bearing 6, and places over the zero the card bearing the figure 8, whereupon the child takes away rod 6 and replaces it with rod 8, thus making 18. Each of these acts may

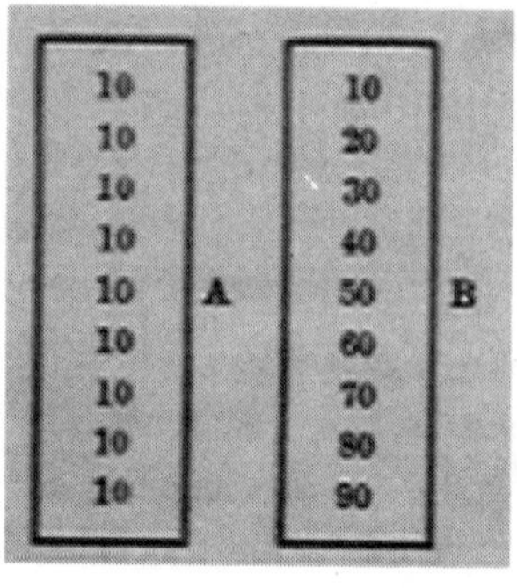

be recorded thus: 10 + 6 = 16; 10 + 8 = 18, etc. We proceed in the same way to subtraction.

When the number itself begins to have a clear meaning to the child, the combinations are made upon one long card, arranging the rectangular cards bearing the nine figures upon the two columns of numbers shown in the figures A and B.

Upon the card A we superimpose upon the zero of the second 10, the rectangular card bearing the 1: and under this the one bearing two, etc. Thus while the one of the ten remains the same the numbers to the right proceed from zero to nine, thus:

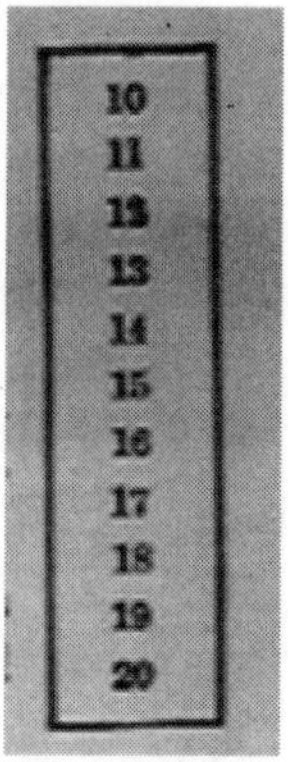

In card B the applications are more complex. The cards are superimposed in numerical progression by tens.

Almost all our children count to 100, a number which was given to them in response to the curiosity they showed in regard to learning it.

I do not believe that this phase of the teaching needs further illustrations. Each teacher may multiply the practical exercises in the arithmetical operations, using simple objects which the children can readily handle and divide.

20

Sequence of Exercises

In the practical application of the method it is helpful to know the sequence, or the various series, of exercises which must be presented to the child successively.

In the first edition of my book there was clearly indicated a progression for each exercise; but in the "Children's Houses" we began contemporaneously with the most varied exercises; and it develops that there exist *grades* in the presentation of the material in its entirety. These grades have, since the first publication of the book, become clearly defined through experience in the "Children's Houses."

SEQUENCE AND GRADES IN THE PRESENTATION OF MATERIAL AND IN THE EXERCISES

First Grade

As soon as the child comes to the school he may be given the following exercises:

Moving the seats, in silence (practical life).

Lacing, buttoning, hooking, etc.

The cylinders (sense exercises).

Among these the most useful exercise is that of the cylinders (solid insets). The child here begins to *fix his attention*. He makes his first comparison, his first selection, in which he exercises judgment. Therefore he exercises his intelligence.

Among these exercises with the solid insets, there exists the following progression from easy to difficult:

(a) The cylinders in which the pieces are of the same height and of decreasing diameter.

(b) The cylinders decreasing in all dimensions.

(c) Those decreasing only in height.

Second Grade

Exercises of Practical Life. To rise and be seated in silence. To walk on the line.

Sense Exercises. Material dealing with dimensions. The Long Stair. The prisms, or Big Stair. The cubes. Here the child makes exercises in the recognition of dimensions as he did in the cylinders but under a very different aspect. The objects are much larger. The differences much more evident than they were in the preceding exercises, but here, *only the eye of the child* recognises the differences and controls the errors. In the preceding exercises, the errors were mechanically revealed to the child by the didactic material itself. The impossibility of placing the objects in order in the block in any other than their respective spaces gives this control. Finally, while in the preceding exercises the child makes much more simple movements (being seated he places little objects in order with his hands), in these new exercises he accomplishes movements which are decidedly more complex and difficult and makes small muscular efforts. He does this by moving from the table to the carpet, rises, kneels, carries heavy objects.

We notice that the child continues to be confused between the two last pieces in the growing scale, being for a long time unconscious of such an error after he has learned to put the other pieces in correct order. Indeed the difference between these pieces being throughout the varying dimensions the same for all, the relative difference diminishes with the increasing size of the pieces themselves. For example, the little cube which has a base of 2 centimetres is double the size, as to base, of the smallest cube which has a base of 1 centimetre, while the largest cube having a base of 10 centimetres, differs by barely 1/10 from the base of the cube next it in the series (the one of 9 centimetres base).

Thus it would seem that, theoretically, in such exercises we should begin with the smallest piece. We can, indeed, do this with the material through which size and length are taught. But we cannot do so with the cubes, which must be arranged as a little "tower." This column of blocks must always have as its base the largest cube.

The children, attracted above all by the tower, begin very early to play with it. Thus we often see very little children playing with the tower, happy in believing that they have constructed it, when they have inadvertently used the next to the largest cube as the base. But when the child, repeating the exercise, *corrects himself of his own accord*, in a permanent fashion, we may be certain that *his eye* has become trained to perceive even the slightest differences between the pieces.

In the three systems of blocks through which dimensions are taught that of length has pieces differing from each other by 10 centimetres, while in the other two sets, the pieces differ only 1 centimetre. Theoretically it would seem that the long rods *should be the first to attract the attention* and to exclude errors. This, however, is not the case. The children are attracted by this set of blocks, but they commit the greatest number of errors in using it, and only after they have for a long time eliminated every error in constructing the other two sets, do they succeed in arranging the Long Stair perfectly. This may then be considered as the most difficult among the series through which dimensions are taught.

Arrived at this point in his education, the child is capable of fixing his attention, with interest, upon the thermic and tactile stimuli.

The progression in the sense development is not, therefore, in actual practice identical with the theoretical progression which psychometry indicates in the study of its subjects. Nor does it follow the progression which physiology and anatomy indicate in the description of the relations of the sense organs.

In fact, the tactile sense is the *primitive* sense; the organ of touch is the most *simple* and the most widely diffused. But it is easy to explain how the most simple sensations, the least complex organs, are not the first through which to attract the *attention* in a didactic presentation of sense stimuli.

Therefore, when the *education of the attention has been begun*, we may present to the child the rough and smooth surfaces (following certain thermic exercises described elsewhere in the book).

These exercises, if presented at the proper time, *interest* the children *immensely*. It is to be remembered that these games are of the *greatest importance* in the method, because upon them, in union with the exercises for the movement of the hand, which we introduce later, we base the acquisition of writing.

Together with the two series of sense exercises described above, we may begin what we call the "pairing of the colours," that is, the recognition of the identity of two colours. This is the first exercise of the chromatic sense.

Here, also, it is only the *eye* of the child that intervenes in the judgment, as it was with the exercises in dimension. This first colour exercise is easy, but the child must already have acquired a certain grade of education of the attention through preceding exercises, if he is to repeat this one with interest.

Meanwhile, the child has heard music; has walked on the line, while the directress played a rhythmic march. Little by little he has learned to accompany the music spontaneously with certain movements. This of course necessitates the repetition of the same music. (To acquire the sense of rhythm *the repetition of the same exercise is necessary*, as in all forms of education dealing with spontaneous activity.)

The exercises in silence are also repeated.

Third Grade

Exercises of Practical Life. The children wash themselves, dress and undress themselves, dust the tables, learn to handle various objects, etc.

Sense Exercises. We now introduce the child to the recognition of gradations of stimuli (tactile gradations, chromatic, etc.), allowing him to exercise himself freely.

We begin to present the stimuli for the sense of hearing (sounds, noises), and also the baric stimuli (the little tablets differing in weight).

Contemporaneously with the gradations we may present the *plane geometric insets*. Here begins the education of the movement of the hand in following the contours of the insets, an exercise which, together with the other and contemporaneous one of the recognition of tactile stimuli in gradation, *prepares for writing*.

The series of cards bearing the geometric forms, we give after the child recognises perfectly the same forms in the wooden insets. These cards serve to prepare for the *abstract signs* of which writing consists. The child learns to recognise a delineated form, and after all the preceding exercises have formed within him an ordered and intelligent personality, they may be considered the bridge by which he passes from the sense exercises to writing, from the *preparation*, to the actual *entrance into instruction*.

Fourth Grade

Exercises of Practical Life. The children set and clear the table for luncheon. They learn to put a room in order. They are now taught the most minute care of their persons in the making of the toilet. (How to brush their teeth, to clean their nails, etc.)

They have learned, through the rhythmic exercises on the line, to walk with perfect freedom and balance.

They know how to control and direct their own movements (how to make the silence,—how to move various objects without dropping or breaking them and without making a noise).

Sense Exercises. In this stage we repeat all the sense exercises. In addition we introduce the recognition of musical notes by the help of the series of duplicate bells.

Exercises Related to Writing/Design. The child passes to the *plane geometric insets in metal*. He has already co-ordinated the movements necessary to follow the contours. Here he no longer *follows them with his finger*, but with a pencil, leaving the double sign upon a sheet of paper. Then he fills in the figures with coloured pencils, holding the pencil as he will later hold the pen in writing.

Contemporaneously the child is taught to *recognise* and *touch* some of the letters of the alphabet made in sandpaper.

Exercises in Arithmetic. At this point, repeating the sense exercises, we present the Long Stair with a different aim from that with which it has been used up to the present time. We have the child *count* the different pieces, according to the blue and red sections, beginning with the rod consisting of one section and continuing through that composed of ten sections. We continue such exercises and give other more complicated ones.

In Design we pass from the outlines of the geometric insets to such outlined figures as the practice of four years has established and which will be published as models in design.

These have an educational importance, and represent in their content and in their gradations one of the most carefully studied details of the method.

They serve as a means for the continuation of the sense education and help the child to observe his surroundings. They thus add to his intellectual refinement, and, as regards writing, they prepare for the high and low strokes. After such practice it will be *easy for the child to make high or low letters,* and this will do away with the *ruled note-books*such as are used in Italy in the various elementary classes.

In the *acquiring* of the use of *written language* we go as far as the knowledge of the letters of the alphabet, and of composition with the movable alphabet.

In Arithmetic, as far as a knowledge of the figures. The child places the corresponding figures beside the number of blue and red sections on each rod of the Long Stair.

The children now take the exercise with the wooden pegs.

Also the games which consist in placing under the figures, on the table, a corresponding number of coloured counters. These are arranged in columns of twos, thus making the question of odd and even numbers clear. (This arrangement is taken from Séguin.)

Fifth Grade

We continue the preceding exercises. We begin more

complicated rhythmic exercises.

In design we begin:

(*a*) The use of water colours.

(*b*) Free drawing from nature (flowers, etc.).

Composition of words and phrases with the movable alphabet.

(*a*) Spontaneous writing of words and phrases.

(*b*) Reading from slips prepared by the directress.

We continue the arithmetical operations which we began with the Long Stair.

The children at this stage present most interesting differences of development. They fairly *run* toward instruction, and order their *intellectual growth* in a way that is remarkable.

This joyous growth is what we so rejoice in, as we watch in these children, humanity, growing in the spirit according to its own deep laws. And only he who experiments can say how great may be the harvest from the sowing of such seed.

21

General Review of Discipline

The accumulated experience we have had since the publication of the Italian version has repeatedly proved to us that in our classes of little children, numbering forty and even fifty, the discipline is much better than in ordinary schools. For this reason I have thought that an analysis of the discipline obtained by our method—which is based upon liberty,—would interest my American readers.

Whoever visits a well kept school (such as, for instance, the one in Rome directed by my pupil Anna Maccheroni) is struck by the discipline of the children. There are forty little beings—from three to seven years old, each one intent on his own work; one is going through one of the exercises for the senses, one is doing an arithmetical exercise; one is handling the letters, one is drawing, one is fastening and unfastening the pieces of cloth on one of our little wooden frames, still another is dusting. Some are seated at the tables, some on rugs on the floor. There are muffled sounds of objects lightly moved about, of children tiptoeing. Once in a while comes a cry of joy only partly repressed, "Teacher! Teacher!" an eager call, "Look! see what I've done." But as a rule, there is entire absorption in the work in hand.

The teacher moves quietly about, goes to any child who calls her, supervising operations in such a way that anyone who needs her finds her at his elbow, and whoever does not need her is not reminded of her existence. Sometimes, hours go by without a word. They seem "little men," as they were called by some visitors to the "Children's House"; or, as another suggested, "judges in deliberation."

In the midst of such intense interest in work it never happens that quarrels arise over the possession of an object. If one accomplishes something especially fine, his achievement is a source of admiration and joy to others: no heart suffers from another's wealth, but the triumph of one is a delight to all. Very often he finds ready imitators. They all seem happy and satisfied to do what they can, without feeling jealous of the deeds of others. The little fellow of three works peaceably beside the boy of seven, just as he is satisfied with his own height and does not envy the older boy's stature. Everything is growing in the most profound peace.

If the teacher wishes the whole assembly to do something, for instance, leave the work which interests them so much, all she needs to do is to speak a word in a low tone, or make a gesture, and they are all attention, they look toward her with eagerness, anxious to know how to obey. Many visitors have seen the teacher write orders on the blackboard, which were obeyed joyously by the children. Not only the teachers, but anyone who asks the pupils to do something is astonished to see them obey in the minutest detail and with obliging cheerfulness. Often a visitor wishes to hear how a child, now painting, can sing. The child leaves his painting to be obliging, but the instant his courteous action is completed, he returns to his interrupted work. Sometimes the smaller children finish their work before they obey.

A very surprising result of this discipline came to our notice during the examinations of the teachers who had followed my course of lectures. These examinations were practical, and, accordingly, groups of children were put at the disposition of the teachers being examined, who, according to the subject drawn by lot, took the children through a given exercise. While the children were waiting their turn, they were allowed to do just as they pleased. *They worked incessantly*, and returned to their undertakings as soon as the interruption caused by the examination was over. Every once in a while, one of them came to show us a drawing made during the interval. Miss George of Chicago was present many times when this happened, and

Madame Pujols, who founded the first "Children's House" in Paris, was astonished at the patience, the perseverance, and the inexhaustible amiability of the children.

One might think that such children had been severely repressed were it not for their lack of timidity, for their bright eyes, for their happy, free aspect, for the cordiality of their invitations to look at their work, for the way in which they take visitors about and explain matters to them. These things make us feel that we are in the presence of the masters of the house; and the fervour with which they throw their arms around the teacher's knees, with which they pull her down to kiss her face, shows that their little hearts are free to expand as they will.

Anyone who has watched them setting the table must have passed from one surprise to another. Little four-year-old waiters take the knives and forks and spoons and distribute them to the different places; they carry trays holding as many as five water-glasses, and finally they go from table to table, carrying big tureens full of hot soup. Not a mistake is made, not a glass is broken, not a drop of soup is spilled. All during the meal unobtrusive little waiters watch the table assiduously; not a child

Montessori Children at Dinner
The tables are set in the grounds of the school of the Franciscan Nuns, in Rome.

empties his soup-plate without being offered more; if he is ready for the next course a waiter briskly carries off his soup-plate. Not a child is forced to ask for more soup, or to announce that he has finished.

School at Tarrytown, N. Y.
The two girls at the left are constructing the big stair and the tower. The boy in the center has constructed the long stair, and is placing the figures beside the corresponding rods. The child to the right is tracing sandpaper letters.

Remembering the usual condition of four-year-old children, who cry, who break whatever they touch, who need to be waited on, everyone is deeply moved by the sight I have just described, which evidently results from the development of energies latent in the depths of the human soul. I have often seen the spectators at this banquet of little ones, moved to tears.

But such discipline could never be obtained by commands, by sermonizings, in short, through any of the disciplinary devices universally known. Not only were the actions of those children set in an orderly condition, but their very lives were deepened and enlarged. In fact, such discipline is on the same plane with school-exercises extraordinary for the age of the children; and it certainly does not depend upon the teacher but upon a sort of miracle, occurring in the inner life of each child.

If we try to think of parallels in the life of adults, we are reminded of the phenomenon of conversion, of the superhuman heightening of the strength of martyrs and apostles, of the constancy of missionaries, of the obedience of monks. Nothing else in the world, except such things, is on a spiritual height equal to the discipline of the "Children's Houses."

To obtain such discipline it is quite useless to count on reprimands or spoken exhortations. Such means might perhaps at the beginning have an appearance of efficacy: but very soon, the instant that real discipline appears, all of this falls miserably to the earth, an illusion confronted with reality—"night gives way to day."

The first dawning of real discipline comes through work. At a given moment it happens that a child becomes keenly interested in a piece of work, showing it by the expression of his face, by his intense attention, by his perseverance in the same exercise. That child has set foot upon the road leading to discipline. Whatever be his undertaking—an exercise for the senses, an exercise in buttoning up or lacing together, or washing dishes—it is all one and the same.

On our side, we can have some influence upon the permanence of this phenomenon, by means of repeated "Lessons of Silence." The perfect immobility, the attention alert to catch the sound of the names whispered from a distance, then the carefully co-ordinated movements executed so as not to strike against chair or table, so as barely to touch the floor with the feet—all this is a most efficacious preparation for the task of setting in order the whole personality, the motor forces and the psychical.

Once the habit of work is formed, we must supervise it with scrupulous accuracy, graduating the exercises as experience has taught us. In our effort to establish discipline, we must rigorously apply the principles of the method. It is not to be obtained by words; no man learns self-discipline "through hearing another man speak." The phenomenon of discipline needs as preparation a series of complete actions, such as are presupposed in the genuine application of a really educative method. Discipline is reached always by indirect means. The end is obtained, not by attacking the mistake and fighting it, but by developing activity in spontaneous work.

This work cannot be arbitrarily offered, and it is precisely here that our method enters; it must be work which the human being instinctively desires to do, work towards which the latent tendencies of life naturally turn, or towards which the individual step by step ascends.

Such is the work which sets the personality in order and opens wide before it infinite possibilities of growth. Take, for instance, the lack of control shown by a baby; it is fundamentally a lack of muscular discipline. The child is in a constant state of disorderly movement: he throws himself down, he makes queer gestures, he cries. What underlies all this is a latent tendency to seek that co-ordination of movement which will be established later. The baby is a man not yet sure of the movements of the various muscles of the body; not yet master of the organs of speech. He will eventually establish these various movements, but for the present he is abandoned to a period of experimentation full of mistakes, and of fatiguing efforts towards a desirable end latent in his instinct, but not clear in his consciousness. To say to the baby, "Stand still as I do," brings no light into his darkness; commands cannot aid in the process of bringing order into the complex psycho-muscular system of an individual in process of evolution. We are confused at this point by the example of the adult who through a wicked impulse *prefers* disorder, and who may (granted that he can) obey a sharp admonishment which turns his will in another direction, towards that order which he recognises and which it is within his capacity to achieve. In the case of the little child it is a question of aiding the natural evolution of voluntary action. Hence it is necessary to teach all the co-ordinated movements, analysing them as much as possible and developing them bit by bit.

Thus, for instance, it is necessary to teach the child the various degrees of immobility leading to silence; the movements connected with rising from a chair and sitting down, with walking, with tiptoeing, with following a line drawn on the floor keeping an upright equilibrium. The child is taught to move objects about, to set them down more or less carefully, and finally the complex movements connected with dressing and undressing himself (analysed on the lacing and buttoning frames at school), and for even each of these exercises, the different parts of the movement must be analysed. Perfect immobility and the successive perfectioning of action, is what takes the place of the customary command, "Be quiet! Be still!" It is not astonishing but very natural that the child by means of such exercises should acquire self-discipline, so far as regards the lack of muscular discipline natural to his age. In short, he responds to nature because he is in action; but these actions being directed towards an end, have no longer the appearance of disorder but of work. This is discipline which represents an end to be attained by means of a number of conquests. The child disciplined in this way, is no longer the child he was at first, who knows how to *be* good passively; but he is an individual who has made himself better, who has overcome the usual limits of his age, who has made a great step forward, who has conquered his future in his present.

He has therefore enlarged his dominion. He will not need to have someone always at hand, to tell him vainly (confusing two opposing conceptions), "Be quiet! Be good!" The goodness he has conquered cannot be summed up by inertia: his goodness is now all made up of action. As a matter of fact, good people are those who advance towards the good—that good which is made up of their own self-development and of external acts of order and usefulness.

In our efforts with the child, external acts are the means which stimulate internal development, and they again appear as its manifestation, the two elements being inextricably intertwined. Work develops the child spiritually; but the child with a fuller spiritual development works better, and his improved work delights him,—hence he continues to develop spiritually. Discipline is, therefore, not a fact but a path, a path in following which the child grasps the abstract conception of goodness with an exactitude which is fairly scientific.

But beyond everything else he savours the supreme delights of that spiritual *order* which is attained indirectly through conquests directed towards determinate ends. In that long preparation, the child experiences joys, spiritual awakenings and pleasures which form his inner treasure-house—the treasure-house in which he is steadily storing up the sweetness and strength which will be the sources of righteousness.

In short, the child has not only learned to move about and to perform useful acts; he has acquired a special grace of action which makes his gestures more correct and attractive, and which beautifies his hands and indeed his entire body now so balanced and so sure of itself; a grace which refines the expression of his face and of his serenely brilliant eyes, and which shows us that the flame of spiritual life has been lighted in another human being.

It is obviously true that co-ordinated actions, developed spontaneously little by little (that is, chosen and carried out in the exercises by the child himself), must call for less effort than the disorderly actions performed by the child who is left to his own devices. True rest for muscles, intended by nature for action, is in orderly action; just as true rest for the lungs is the normal rhythm of respiration taken in pure air. To take action away from the muscles is to force them away from their natural motor impulse, and hence, besides tiring them, means forcing them into a state of degeneration; just as the lungs forced into immobility, would die instantly and the whole organism with them.

It is therefore necessary to keep clearly in mind the fact that rest for whatever naturally acts, lies in some specified form of action, corresponding to its nature.

To act in obedience to the hidden precepts of nature—that is rest; and in this special case, since man is meant to be an intelligent creature, the more intelligent his acts are the more he finds repose in them. When a child acts only in a disorderly, disconnected manner, his nervous force is under a great strain; while on the other hand his nervous energy is positively increased and multiplied by intelligent actions which give him real satisfaction, and a feeling of pride that he has overcome himself, that he finds himself in a world beyond the frontiers formerly set up as insurmountable, surrounded by the silent respect of the one who has guided him without making his presence felt.

This "multiplication of nervous energy" represents a process which can be physiologically analysed, and which comes from the development of the organs by rational exercise, from better circulation of the blood, from the quickened activity of all the tissues—all factors favourable to the development of the body and guaranteeing physical health. The spirit aids the body in its growth; the heart, the nerves and the muscles are helpful in their evolution by the activity of the spirit, since the upward path for soul and body is one and the same.

By analogy, it can be said of the intellectual development of the child, that the mind of infancy, although characteristically disorderly, is also "a means searching for its end," which goes through exhausting experiments, left, as it frequently is, to its own resources, and too often really persecuted. Once in our public park in Rome, the Pincian Gardens, I saw a baby of about a year and a half, a beautiful smiling child, who was working away trying to fill a little pail by shoveling gravel into it. Beside him was a smartly dressed nurse evidently very fond of him, the sort of nurse who would consider that she gave the child the most affectionate and intelligent care. It was time to go home and the nurse was patiently exhorting the baby to leave his work and let her put him into the baby-carriage. Seeing that her exhortations made no impression on the little fellow's firmness, she herself filled the pail with gravel and set pail and baby into the carriage with the fixed conviction that she had given him what he wanted.

I was struck by the loud cries of the child and by the expression of protest against violence and injustice which wrote itself on his little face. What an accumulation of wrongs weighed down that nascent intelligence! The little boy did not wish to have the pail full of gravel; he wished to go through the motions necessary to fill it, thus satisfying a need of his vigorous organism. The child's unconscious aim was his own self-development; not the external fact of a pail full of little stones. The vivid attractions of the external world were only empty apparitions; the need of his life was a reality. As a matter of fact, if he had filled his pail he would probably have emptied it out again in order to keep on filling it up until his inner self was satisfied. It was the feeling of working towards this satisfaction which, a few moments before, had made his face so rosy and smiling; spiritual joy, exercise, and sunshine, were the three rays of light ministering to his splendid life.

This commonplace episode in the life of that child, is a detail of what happens to all children, even the best and most cherished. They are not understood, because the adult judges them by his own measure: he thinks that the child's wish is to obtain some tangible object, and lovingly helps him to do this: whereas the child as a rule has for his unconscious desire, his own self-development. Hence he despises everything already attained, and yearns for that which is still to be sought for. For instance, he prefers the action of dressing himself to the state of being dressed, even finely dressed. He prefers the act of washing himself to the satisfaction of being clean: he prefers to make a little house for himself, rather than merely to own it. His own self-development is his true and almost his only pleasure. The self-development of the little baby up to the end of his first year consists to a large degree in taking in nutrition; but afterwards it consists in aiding the orderly establishment of the psycho-physiological functions of his organism.

That beautiful baby in the Pincian Gardens is the symbol of this: he wished to co-ordinate his voluntary actions; to exercise his muscles by lifting; to train his eye to estimate distances; to exercise his intelligence in the reasoning connected with his undertaking; to stimulate his will-power by deciding his own actions; whilst she who loved him, believing that his aim was to possess some pebbles, made him wretched.

A similar error is that which we repeat so frequently when we fancy that the desire of the student is to possess a piece of information. We aid him to grasp intellectually this detached piece of knowledge, and, preventing by this means his self-development, we make him wretched. It is generally believed in schools that the way to attain, satisfaction is "to learn something." But by leaving the children in our schools in liberty we have been able with great clearness to follow them in their natural method of spontaneous self-development.

To have learned something is for the child only a point of departure. When he has learned the meaning of an exercise, then he begins to enjoy repeating it, and he does repeat it an infinite number of times, with the most evident satisfaction. He enjoys executing that act because by means of it he is developing his psychic activities.

There results from the observation of this fact a criticism of what is done to-day in many schools. Often, for instance when the pupils are questioned, the teacher says to someone who is eager to answer, "No, not you, because you know it" and puts her question specially to the pupils who she thinks are uncertain of the answer. Those who do not know are made to speak, those who do know to be silent. This happens because of the general habit of considering the act of knowing something as final.

And yet how many times it happens to us in ordinary life to *repeat* the very thing we know best, the thing we care most for, the thing to which some living force in us responds. We love to sing musical phrases very familiar, hence enjoyed and become a part of the fabric of our lives. We love to repeat stories of things which please us, which we know very well, even though we are quite aware that we are saying nothing new. No matter how many times we repeat the Lord's Prayer, it is always new. No two persons could be more convinced of mutual love than sweethearts and yet they are the very ones who repeat endlessly that they love each other.

But in order to repeat in this manner, there must first exist the idea to be repeated. A mental grasp of the idea, is indispensable to the beginning of *repetition*. The exercise which develops life, consists *in the repetition, not in the mere grasp of the idea*. When a child has attained this stage, of repeating an exercise, he is on the way to self-development, and the external sign of this condition is his self-discipline.

This phenomenon does not always occur. The same exercises are not repeated by children of all ages. In fact, repetition corresponds to a *need*. Here steps in the experimental method of education. It is necessary to offer those exercises which correspond to the need of development felt by an organism, and if the child's age has carried him past a certain need, it is never possible to obtain, in its fulness, a development which missed its proper moment. Hence children grow up, often fatally and irrevocably, imperfectly developed.

Another very interesting observation is that which relates to the length of time needed for the execution of actions. Children, who are undertaking something for the first time are extremely slow. Their life is governed in this respect by laws especially different from ours. Little children accomplish slowly and perseveringly, various complicated operations agreeable to them, such as dressing, undressing, cleaning the room, washing themselves, setting the table, eating, etc. In all this they are extremely patient, overcoming all the difficulties presented by an organism still in process of formation. But we, on the other hand, noticing that they are "tiring themselves out" or "wasting time" in accomplishing something which we would do in a moment and without the least effort, put ourselves in the child's place and do it ourselves. Always with the same erroneous idea, that the end to be obtained is the completion of the action, we dress and wash the child, we snatch out of his hands objects which he loves to handle, we pour the soup into his bowl, we feed him, we set the table for him. And after such services, we consider him with that injustice always practised by those who domineer over others even with benevolent intentions, to be incapable and inept. We often speak of him as "impatient" simply because we are not patient enough to allow his actions to follow laws of time differing from our own; we call him "tyrannical" exactly because we employ tyranny towards him. This stain, this false imputation, this calumny on childhood has become an integral part of the theories concerning childhood, in reality so patient and gentle.

The child, like every strong creature fighting for the right to live, rebels against whatever offends that occult impulse within him which is the voice of nature, and which he ought to obey; and he shows by violent actions, by screaming and weeping that he has been overborne and forced away from his mission in life. He shows himself to be a rebel, a revolutionist, an iconoclast, against those who do not understand him and who, fancying that they are helping him, are really pushing him backward in the highway of life. Thus even the adult who loves him, rivets about his neck another calumny, confusing his defence of his molested life with a form of innate naughtiness characteristic of little children.

What would become of us if we fell into the midst of a population of jugglers, or of lightning-change impersonators of the variety-hall? What should we do if, as we continued to act in our usual way, we saw ourselves assailed by these sleight-of-hand performers, hustled into our clothes, fed so rapidly that we could scarcely swallow, if everything we tried to do was snatched from our hands and completed in a twinkling and we ourselves reduced to impotence and to a humiliating inertia? Not knowing how else to express our confusion we would defend ourselves with blows and yells from these madmen, and they having only the best will in the world to serve us, would call us haughty, rebellious, and incapable of doing anything. We, who know our own *milieu*, would say to those people, "Come into our countries and you will see the splendid civilisation we have established, you will see our wonderful achievements." These jugglers would admire us infinitely, hardly able to believe their eyes, as they observed our world, so full of beauty and activity, so well regulated, so peaceful, so kindly, but all so much slower than theirs.

Something of this sort occurs between children and adults.

It is exactly in the repetition of the exercises that the education of the senses consists; their aim is not that the child shall *know* colours, forms and the different qualities of objects, but that he refine his senses through an exercise of attention, of comparison, of judgment. These exercises are true intellectual gymnastics. Such gymnastics, reasonably directed by means of various devices, aid in the formation of the intellect, just as physical exercises fortify the general health and quicken the growth of the body. The child who trains his various senses separately, by means of external stimuli, concentrates his attention and develops, piece by piece, his mental activities, just as with separately prepared movements he trains his muscular activities. These mental gymnastics are not merely psycho-sensory, but they prepare the way for spontaneous association of ideas, for ratiocination developing out of definite knowledge, for a harmoniously balanced intellect. They are the powder-trains that bring about those mental explosions which delight the child so intensely when he makes discoveries in the world about him, when he, at the same time, ponders over and glories in the new things which are revealed to him in the outside world, and in the exquisite emotions of his own growing consciousness; and finally when there spring up within him, almost by a process of spontaneous ripening, like the internal phenomena of growth, the external products of learning—writing and reading.

I happened once to see a two-year-old child, son of a medical colleague of mine, who, fairly fleeing away from his mother who had brought him to me, threw himself on the litter of things covering his father's desk, the rectangular writing-pad, the round cover of the ink-well. I was touched to see the intelligent little creature trying his best to go through the exercises which our children repeat with such endless pleasure till they have fully committed them to memory. The father and the mother pulled the child away, reproving him, and explaining that there was no use trying to keep that child from handling his father's desk-furniture, "The child is restless and naughty." How often we see all children reproved because, though they are told not to, they will "take hold of everything." Now, it is precisely by means of guiding and developing this natural instinct "to take hold of everything," and to recognise the relations of geometrical figures, that we prepare our little four-year-old men for the joy and triumph they experience later over the phenomenon of spontaneous writing.

The child who throws himself on the writing-pad, the cover to the ink-well, and such objects, always struggling in vain to attain his desire, always hindered and thwarted by people stronger than he, always excited and weeping over the failure of his desperate efforts, *is wasting* nervous force. His parents are mistaken if they think that such a child ever gets any real rest, just as they are mistaken when they call "naughty" the little man longing for the foundations of his intellectual edifice. The children in our schools are the ones who are really at rest, ardently and blessedly free to take out and put back in their right places or grooves, the geometric figures offered to their instinct for higher self-development; and they, rejoicing in the most entire spiritual calm, have no notion that their eyes and hands are initiating them into the mysteries of a new language.

The majority of our children become calm as they go through such exercises, because their nervous system is at rest. Then we say that such children are quiet and good; external discipline, so eagerly sought after in ordinary schools is more than achieved.

However, as a calm man and a self-disciplined man are not one and the same, so here the fact which manifests itself externally by the calm of the children is in reality a phenomenon merely physical and partial compared to the real *self-discipline* which is being developed in them.

Often (and this is another misconception) we think all we need to do, to obtain a voluntary action from a child, is to order him to do it. We pretend that this phenomenon of a forced voluntary action exists, and we call this pretext, "the obedience of the child." We find little children specially disobedient, or rather their resistance, by the time they are four or five years old, has become so great that we are in despair and are almost tempted to give up trying to make them obey. We force ourselves to praise to little children "the virtue of obedience" a virtue which, according to our accepted prejudices, should belong specially to infancy, should be the "infantile virtue" yet we fail to learn anything from the fact that we are led to emphasize it so strongly because we can only with the greatest difficulty make children practise it.

It is a very common mistake, this of trying to obtain by means of prayers, or orders, or violence, what is difficult, or impossible to get. Thus, for instance, we ask little children to be obedient, and little children in their turn ask for the moon.

We need only reflect that this "obedience" which we treat so lightly, occurs later, as a natural tendency in older children, and then as an instinct in the adult to realise that it springs spontaneously into being, and that it is one of the strongest instincts of humanity. We find that society rests on a foundation of marvellous obedience, and that civilisation goes forward on a road made by obedience. Human organisations are often founded on an abuse of obedience, associations of criminals have obedience as their key-stone.

How many times social problems centre about the necessity of rousing man from a state of "obedience" which has led him to be exploited and brutalised!

Obedience naturally is *sacrifice*. We are so accustomed to an infinity of obedience in the world, to a condition of self-sacrifice, to a readiness for renunciation, that we call matrimony the "blessed condition," although it is made up of obedience and self-sacrifice. The soldier, whose lot in life is to obey if it kills him is envied by the common people, while we consider anyone who tries to escape from obedience as a malefactor or a madman. Besides, how many people have had the deeply spiritual experience of an ardent desire to obey something or some person leading them along the path of life—more than this, a desire to sacrifice something for the sake of this obedience.

It is therefore entirely natural that, loving the child, we should point out to him that obedience is the law of life, and there is nothing surprising in the anxiety felt by nearly everyone who is confronted with the characteristic disobedience of little children. But obedience can only be reached through a complex formation of the psychic personality. To obey, it is necessary not only to wish to obey, but also to know how to. Since, when a command to do a certain thing is given, we presuppose a corresponding active or inhibitive power of the child, it is plain that obedience must follow the formation of the will and of the mind. To prepare, in detail, this formation by means of detached exercises is therefore indirectly, to urge the child towards obedience. The method which is the subject of this book contains in every part an exercise for the will-power, when the child completes co-ordinated actions directed towards a given end, when he achieves something he set out to do, when he repeats patiently his exercises, he is training his positive will-power. Similarly, in a very complicated series of exercises he is establishing through activity his powers of inhibition; for instance in the "lesson of silence," which calls for a long continued inhibition of many actions, while the child is waiting to be called and later for a rigorous self-control when he is called and would like to answer joyously and run to his teacher, but instead is perfectly silent, moves very carefully, taking the greatest pains not to knock against chair or table or to make a noise.

Other inhibitive exercises are the arithmetical ones, when the child having drawn a number by lot, must take from the great mass of objects before him, apparently entirely at his disposition, only the quantity corresponding to the number in his hand, whereas (as experience has proved) he would *like* to take the greatest number possible. Furthermore if he chances to draw the zero he sits patiently with empty hands. Still another training for the inhibitive will-power is in "the lesson of zero" when the child, called upon to come up zero times and give zero kisses, stands quiet, conquering with a visible effort the instinct which would lead him to "obey" the call. The child at our school dinners who carries the big tureen full of hot soup, isolates himself from every external stimulant which might disturb him, resists his childish impulse to run and jump, does not yield to the temptation to brush away the fly on his face, and is entirely concentrated on the great responsibility of not dropping or tipping the tureen. A little thing of four and a half, every time he set the tureen down on a table so that the little guests might help themselves, gave a hop and a skip, then took up the tureen again to carry it to another table, repressing himself to a sober walk. In spite of his desire to play he never left his task before he had passed soup to the twenty tables, and he never forgot the vigilance necessary to control his actions.

Will-power, like all other activities is invigorated and developed through methodical exercises, and all our exercises for will-power are also mental and practical. To the casual onlooker the child seems to be learning exactitude and grace of action, to be refining his senses, to be learning how to read and write; but much more profoundly he is learning how to become his own master, how to be a man of prompt and resolute will.

We often hear it said that a child's will should be "broken" that the best education for the will of the child is to learn to give it up to the will of adults. Leaving out of the question the injustice which is at the root of every act of tyranny, this idea is irrational because the child cannot give up what he does not possess. We prevent him in this way from forming his own will-power, and we commit the greatest and most blameworthy mistake. He never has time or opportunity to test himself, to estimate his own force and his own limitations because he is always interrupted and subjected to our tyranny, and languishes in injustice because he is always being bitterly reproached for not having what adults are perpetually destroying.

There springs up as a consequence of this, childish timidity, which is a moral malady acquired by a will which could not develop; and which with the usual calumny with which the tyrant consciously or not, covers up his own mistakes, we consider as an inherent trait of childhood. The children in our schools are never timid. One of their most fascinating qualities is the frankness with which they treat people, with which they go on working in the presence of others, and showing their work frankly, calling for sympathy. That moral monstrosity, a repressed and timid child, who is at his ease nowhere except alone with his playmates, or with street urchins, because his will-power was allowed to grow only in the shade, disappears in our schools. He presents an example of thoughtless barbarism, which resembles the artificial compression of the bodies of those children intended for "court dwarfs," museum monstrosities or buffoons. Yet this is the treatment under which nearly all the children of our time are growing up spiritually.

As a matter of fact in all the pedagogical congresses one hears that the great peril of our time is the lack of individual character in the scholars; yet these alarmists do not point out that this condition is due to the way in which education is managed, to scholastic slavery, which has for its specialty the repression of will-power and of force of character. The remedy is simply to enfranchise human development.

Besides the exercises it offers for developing will-power, the other factor in obedience is the capacity to perform the act it becomes necessary to obey. One of the most interesting observations made by my pupil Anna Maccheroni (at first in the school in Milan and then in that in the Via Guisti in Rome), relates to the connection between obedience in a child and his "knowing how." Obedience appears in the child as a latent instinct as soon as his personality begins to take form. For instance, a child begins to try a certain exercise and suddenly some time he goes through it perfectly; he is delighted, stares at it, and wishes to do it over again, but for some time the exercise is not a success. Then comes a time when he can do it nearly every time he tries voluntarily but makes mistakes if someone else asks him to do it. The external command does not as yet produce the voluntary act. When, however, the exercise always succeeds, with absolute certainty, then an order from someone else brings about on the child's part, orderly adequate action; that is, the child *is able* each time to execute the command received. That these facts (with variations in individual cases) are laws of psychical development is apparent from everyone's experience with children in school or at home.

One often hears a child say, "I did do such and such a thing but now I can't!" and a teacher disappointed by the incompetence of a pupil will say, "Yet that child was doing it all right—and now he can't!"

Finally there is the period of complete development in which the capacity to perform some operation is permanently acquired. There are, therefore, three periods: a first, subconscious one, when in the confused mind of the child, order produces itself by a mysterious inner impulse from out the midst of disorder, producing as an external result a completed act, which, however, being outside the field of consciousness, cannot be reproduced at will; a second, conscious period, when there is some action on the part of the will which is present during the process of the development and establishing of the acts; and a third period when the will can direct and cause the acts, thus answering the command from someone else.

Now, obedience follows a similar sequence. When in the first period of spiritual disorder, the child does not obey it is exactly as if he were psychically deaf, and out of hearing of commands. In the second period he would like to obey, he looks as though he understood the command and would like to respond to it, but cannot,—or at least does not always succeed in doing it, is not "quick to mind" and shows no pleasure when he does. In the third period he obeys at once, with enthusiasm, and as he becomes more and more perfect in the exercises he is proud that he knows how to obey. This is the period in which he runs joyously to obey, and leaves at the most imperceptible request whatever is interesting him so that he may quit the solitude of his own life and enter, with the act of obedience into the spiritual existence of another.

To this order, established in a consciousness formerly chaotic, are due all the phenomena of discipline and of mental development, which open out like a new Creation. From minds thus set in order, when "night is separated from day" come sudden emotions and mental feats which recall the Biblical story of Creation. The child has in his mind not only what he has laboriously acquired, but the free gifts which flow from spiritual life, the first flowers of affection, of gentleness, of spontaneous love for righteousness which perfume the souls of such children and give promise of the "fruits of the spirit" of St. Paul—"The fruit of the Spirit is love, joy, peace, long-suffering gentleness, goodness, faith, meekness."

They are virtuous because they exercise patience in repeating their exercises, long-suffering in yielding to the commands and desires of others, good in rejoicing in the well-being of others without jealousy or rivalry; they live, doing good in joyousness of heart and in peace, and they are eminently, marvellously industrious. But they are not proud of such righteousness because they were not conscious of acquiring it as a moral superiority. They have set their feet in the path leading to righteousness, simply because it was the only way to attain true self-development and learning; and they enjoy with simple hearts the fruits of peace that are to be gathered along that path.

These are the first outlines of an experiment which shows a form of indirect discipline in which there is substituted for the critical and sermonizing teacher a rational organisation of work and of liberty for the child. It involves a conception of life more usual in religious fields than in those of academic pedagogy, inasmuch as it has recourse to the spiritual energies of mankind, but it is founded on work and on liberty which are the two paths to all civic progress.

22

Conclusions and Impressions

In the "Children's Houses," the old-time teacher, who wore herself out maintaining discipline of immobility, and who wasted her breath in loud and continual discourse, has disappeared.

For this teacher we have substituted the *didactic material*, which contains within itself the control of errors and which makes auto-education possible to each child. The teacher has thus become a *director* of the spontaneous work of the children. She is not a *passive* force, a *silent* presence.

The children are occupied each one in a different way, and the directress, watching them, can make psychological observations which, if collected in an orderly way and according to scientific standards, should do much toward the reconstruction of child psychology and the development of experimental psychology. I believe that I have by my method established the conditions necessary to the development of scientific pedagogy; and whoever adopts this method opens, in doing so, a laboratory of experimental pedagogy.

From such work, we must await the positive solution of all those pedagogical problems of which we talk to-day. For through such work there has already come the solution of some of these very questions: that of the liberty of the pupils; auto-education; the establishment of harmony between the work and activities of home life and school tasks, making both work together for the education of the child.

The problem of religious education, the importance of which we do not fully realise, should also be solved by positive pedagogy. If religion is born with civilisation, its roots must lie deep in human nature. We have had most beautiful proof of an instinctive love of knowledge in the child, who has too often been misjudged in that he has been considered addicted to meaningless play, and games void of thought. The child who left the game in his eagerness for knowledge, has revealed himself as a true son of that humanity which has been throughout centuries the creator of scientific and civil progress. We have belittled the son of man by giving him foolish and degrading toys, a world of idleness where he is suffocated by a badly conceived discipline. Now, in his liberty, the child should show us, as well, whether man is by nature a religious creature.

To deny, *a priori*, the religions sentiment in man, and to deprive humanity of the education of this sentiment, is to commit a pedagogical error similar to that of denying, *a priori*, to the child, the love of learning for learning's sake. This ignorant assumption led us to dominate the scholar, to subject him to a species of slavery, in order to render him apparently disciplined.

The fact that we assume that religions education is only adapted to the adult, may be akin to another profound error existing in education to-day, namely, that of overlooking the education of the senses at the very period when this education is possible. The life of the adult is practically an application of the senses to the gathering of sensations from the environment. A lack of preparation for this, often results in inadequacy in practical life, in that lack of poise which causes so many individuals to waste their energies in purposeless effort. Not to form a parallel between the education of the senses as a guide to practical life, and religious education as a guide to the moral life, but for the sake of illustration, let me call attention to how often we find inefficiency, instability, among irreligious persons, and how much precious individual power is miserably wasted.

How many men have had this experience! And when that spiritual awakening comes late, as it sometimes does, through the softening power of sorrow, the mind is unable to establish an equilibrium, because it has grown too much accustomed to a life deprived of spirituality. We see equally piteous cases of religious fanaticism, or we look upon intimate dramatic struggles between the heart, ever seeking its own safe and quiet port, and the mind that constantly draws it back to the sea of conflicting ideas and emotions, where peace is unknown. These are all psychological phenomena of the highest importance; they present, perhaps, the gravest of all our human problems. We Europeans are still filled with prejudices and hedged about with preconceptions in regard to these matters. We are very slaves of thought. We believe that liberty of conscience and of thought consists in denying certain sentimental beliefs, while liberty never can exist where one struggles to stifle some other thing, but only where unlimited expansion is granted; where life is left free and untrammelled. He who really does not believe, does not fear that which he does not believe, and does not combat that which for him does not exist. If he believes and fights, he then becomes an enemy to liberty.

In America, the great positive scientist, William James, who expounds the physiological theory of emotions, is also the man who illustrates the psychological importance of religious "conscience." We cannot know the future of the progress of thought: here, for example, in the "Children's Houses" the triumph of *discipline* through the conquest of liberty and independence marks the foundation of the progress which the future will see in the matter of pedagogical methods. To me it offers the greatest hope for human redemption through education.

Perhaps, in the same way, through the conquest of liberty of thought and of conscience, we are making our way toward a great religious triumph. Experience will show, and the psychological observations made along this line in the "Children's Houses" will undoubtedly be of the greatest interest.

This book of methods compiled by one person alone, must be followed by many others. It is my hope that, starting from the *individual study of the child* educated with our method, other educators will set forth the results of their experiments. These are the pedagogical books which await us in the future.

From the practical side of the school, we have with our

methods the advantage of being able to teach in one room, children of very different ages. In our "Children's Houses" we have little ones of two years and a half, who cannot as yet make use of the most simple of the sense exercises, and children of five and a half who because of their development might easily pass into the third elementary. Each one of them perfects himself through his own powers, and goes forward guided by that inner force which distinguishes him as an individual.

One great advantage of such a method is that it will make instruction in the rural schools easier, and will be of great advantage in the schools in the small provincial towns where there are few children, yet where all the various grades are represented. Such schools are not able to employ more than one teacher. Our experience shows that one directress may guide a group of children varying in development from little ones of three years old to the third elementary. Another great advantage lies in the extreme facility with which written language may be taught, making it possible to combat illiteracy and to cultivate the national tongue.

As to the teacher, she may remain for a whole day among children in the most varying stages of development, just as the mother remains in the house with children of all ages, without becoming tired.

The children work by themselves, and, in doing so, make a conquest of active discipline, and independence in all the acts of daily life, just as through daily conquests they progress in intellectual development. Directed by an intelligent teacher, who watches over their physical development as well as over their intellectual and moral progress, children are able with our methods to arrive at a splendid physical development, and, in addition to this, there unfolds within them, in all its perfection, the soul, which distinguishes the human being.

We have been mistaken in thinking that the natural education of children should be purely physical; the soul, too, has its nature, which it was intended to perfect in the spiritual life,—the dominating power of human existence throughout all time. Our methods take into consideration the spontaneous psychic development of the child, and help this in ways that observation and experience have shown us to be wise.

If physical care leads the child to take pleasure in bodily health, intellectual and moral care make possible for him the highest spiritual joy, and send him forward into a world where continual surprises and discoveries await him; not only in the external environment, but in the intimate recesses of his own soul.

It is through such pleasures as these that the ideal man grows, and only such pleasures are worthy of a place in the education of the infancy of humanity.

Our children are noticeably different from those others who have grown up within the grey walls of the common schools. Our little pupils have the serene and happy aspect and the frank and open friendliness of the person who feels himself to be master of his own actions. When they run to gather about our visitors, speaking to them with sweet frankness, extending their little hands with gentle gravity and well-bred cordiality, when they thank these visitors for the courtesy they have paid us in coming, the bright eyes and the happy voices make us feel that they are, indeed, unusual little men. When they display their work and their ability, in a confidential and simple way, it is almost as if they called for a maternal approbation from all those who watch them. Often, a little one will seat himself on the floor beside some visitor silently writing his name, and adding a gentle word of thanks. It is as if they wished to make the visitor feel the affectionate gratitude which is in their hearts.

When we see all these things and when, above all, we pass with these children from the busy activity of the schoolroom at work, into the absolute and profound silence which they have learned to enjoy so deeply, we are moved in spite of ourselves and feel that we have come in touch with the very souls of these little pupils.

The "Children's House" seems to exert a spiritual influence upon everyone. I have seen here, men of affairs, great politicians preoccupied with problems of trade and of state, cast off like an uncomfortable garment the burden of the world, and fall into a simple forgetfulness of self. They are affected by this vision of the human soul growing in its true nature, and I believe that this is what they mean when they call our little ones, wonderful children, happy children—the infancy of humanity in a higher stage of evolution than our own. I understand how the great English poet Wordsworth, enamoured as he was of nature, demanded the secret of all her peace and beauty. It was at last revealed to him—the secret of all nature lies in the soul of a little child. He holds there the true meaning of that life which exists throughout humanity. But this beauty which "lies about us in our infancy" becomes obscured; "shades of the prison house, begin to close about the growing boy ... at last the man perceives it die away, and fade into the light of common day."

Truly our social life is too often only the darkening and the death of the natural life that is in us. These methods tend to guard that spiritual fire within man, to keep his real nature unspoiled and to set it free from the oppressive and degrading yoke of society. It is a pedagogical method informed by the high concept of Immanuel Kant: "Perfect art returns to nature."